SHORT FILMS FROM A SMALL NATION

Traditions in World Cinema

SHORT FILMS FROM A SMALL NATION

Danish Informational Cinema 1935–1965

C. Claire Thomson

EDINBURGH
University Press

In memory of William and Helen Ritchie

Edinburgh University Press is one of the leading university presses in the UK. We publish academic books and journals in our selected subject areas across the humanities and social sciences, combining cutting-edge scholarship with high editorial and production values to produce academic works of lasting importance. For more information visit our website: edinburghuniversitypress.com

Edinburgh University Press Ltd
The Tun – Holyrood Road
12 (2f) Jackson's Entry
Edinburgh EH8 8PJ

Typeset in 10/12.5 pt Sabon by
Servis Filmsetting Ltd, Stockport, Cheshire
and printed and bound in Great Britain by
CPI Group (UK) Ltd, Croydon CR0 4YY

A CIP record for this book is available from the British Library

ISBN 978 1 4744 2413 4 (hardback)
ISBN 978 1 4744 2414 1 (webready PDF)
ISBN 978 1 4744 2415 8 (epub)

CONTENTS

FIGURES

ACKNOWLEDGEMENTS

This book was made possible by two institutions of the Danish state: Det Danske Filminstitut (DFI), and Danmarks Nationalbank. I would like to thank the staff of the DFI unreservedly for welcoming me so warmly to Copenhagen and for sharing their expertise and their passion for film. Many DFI colleagues contributed with invaluable suggestions for films, leads and anecdotes, but without advice and help from Thomas C. Christensen, Birgit Granhøj Dam, Lisbeth Richter Larsen and Lars-Martin Sørensen, this project quite simply would not have happened.

Danmarks Nationalbank facilitated the project by generously allocating me accommodation in its guest apartments for researchers at Nyhavn 18 in 2013–14. This was an inspiring place to live and to work, and I would like to thank the residents of 'Nyhavnia' for their warmth and support.

I would also like to thank the School of European Languages, Culture and Society and the Faculty of Arts and Humanities at UCL for granting me research leave to undertake the primary research for this project.

I am grateful to have had opportunities to test out ideas and case studies in various contexts, including the Danish Film Institute, the University of Copenhagen, the University of Lund, the University of Edinburgh, the Danish Cultural Institute in Edinburgh, the Embassy of Denmark in London and the Anglo-Danish Society, a UCL Lunch Hour Lecture and Bright Club London. I would like to thank colleagues and audiences for their useful comments and the various leads they provided on those occasions. Students of Nordic cinema, European cinema and the module 'Short Films, Big Ideas' at UCL have contributed more than they know with their enthusiasm and engagement. Gillian Leslie and Richard Strachan at Edinburgh University Press have been unfailingly efficient, encouraging and helpful. I would particularly like to thank Pei-Sze Chow, Tiago De Luca, Birgit Granhøj Dam, Mette Hjort, Gauti Sigthorsson, Jakob Stougaard-Nielsen, Essi Viitanen, an anonymous reviewer and the series editors for their constructive and encouraging comments on the proposal and manuscript, and Sue Dalgleish for efficient and friendly copy-editing. Marc David Jacobs at Edinburgh Film Guild gave very generously of his time and knowledge to help me understand the role of the Edinburgh International Film Festival in the development of Danish documentarism. Peter Schepelern was kind enough to gift me a copy of the hard-to-find but essential book *Kortfilmen og staten*. Other friends, colleagues and students have asked questions and made suggestions that helped me think through particular aspects of the project and have provided much-appreciated input and encouragement, especially Julie K. Allen, Anna Ulrikke Andersen, Hans-Christian Andersen, Sarah Bell, Stephanie Bird, Ib Bondebjerg, Mads Bunch, Elettra Carbone, Sarah Death, Richard Farmer, Marita Fraser, Janet Garton, Erin Goeres, Lee Grieveson, Jesper Hansen, Thomas Uwe Henderson, Andrew Higson, Mary Hilson, Dominic Hinde of Leith, John Hogan, Gaby Hogan-Brun, Birger and Peta Jensen, Mats Jönsson, Tobias Juel Høj, Henrik Kjeldsholm, Dilwyn Knox, Mart Kuldkepp, Ellen Kythor, Gavin Lang, Clare Lees, Helga Hlaðgerður Lúthersdóttir, Carol O'Sullivan, Will Sayers, Madeleine Schlawitz, Margit Staehr, Emil Stjernholm, Bodil Marie Stavning Thomsen, Kirsten Thorup and Casper Tybjerg. Titus Hjelm entrusted me with his home at a crucial moment, and Gauti Sigthorsson brewed more coffee than anyone could reasonably be expected to. Warm thanks go to Asbjørn Nybo for his friendship during my year in Copenhagen, and to my parents, Catherine and Robert Thomson, and my sister, Lizzi, for unstinting moral and practical support, and lots of laughs too.

Watch the films discussed at q-r.to/balKqd.

TRADITIONS IN WORLD CINEMA

General editors: **Linda Badley and R. Barton Palmer**
Founding editor: **Steven Jay Schneider**

Traditions in World Cinema is a series of textbooks and monographs devoted to the analysis of currently popular and previously underexamined or under-valued film movements from around the globe. Also intended for general inter-est readers, the textbooks in this series offer undergraduate- and graduate-level film students accessible and comprehensive introductions to diverse traditions in world cinema. The monographs open up for advanced academic study more specialised groups of films, including those that require theoretically oriented approaches. Both textbooks and monographs provide thorough examinations of the industrial, cultural, and socio-historical conditions of production and reception.

The flagship textbook for the series includes chapters by noted scholars on traditions of acknowledged importance (the French New Wave, German Expressionism), recent and emergent traditions (New Iranian, post-Cinema Novo), and those whose rightful claim to recognition has yet to be established (the Israeli persecution film, global found footage cinema). Other volumes concentrate on individual national, regional or global cinema traditions. As the introductory chapter to each volume makes clear, the films under discussion form a coherent group on the basis of substantive and relatively transparent, if not always obvious, commonalities. These commonalities may be formal, sty-listic or thematic, and the groupings may, although they need not, be popularly identified as genres, cycles or movements (Japanese horror, Chinese martial arts cinema, Italian Neorealism). Indeed, in cases in which a group of films is not already commonly identified as a tradition, one purpose of the volume is to establish its claim to importance and make it visible (East Central European Magical Realist cinema, Palestinian cinema).

Textbooks and monographs include:

- An introduction that clarifies the rationale for the grouping of films under examination
- A concise history of the regional, national, or transnational cinema in question
- A summary of previous published work on the tradition
- Contextual analysis of industrial, cultural and socio-historical conditions of production and reception
- Textual analysis of specific and notable films, with clear and judicious application of relevant film theoretical approaches
- Bibliograph(ies)/filmograph(ies)

Monographs may additionally include:

- Discussion of the dynamics of cross-cultural exchange in light of current research and thinking about cultural imperialism and globalisation, as well as issues of regional/national cinema or political/aesthetic movements (such as new waves, postmodernism, or identity politics)
- Interview(s) with key filmmakers working within the tradition

INTRODUCTION

Between the mid-1930s and the mid-1960s, hundreds of short films were commissioned and often funded by the Danish state, on subjects ranging from agriculture to physics, from urbanism to social welfare, and from aviation to sculpture. These films were generally known as *kulturfilm* – literally, culture-films – though they were also publicised and discussed using a range of terms as various as the uses to which they were put. The films were seen by millions of Danes and many more millions of people around the world. They were screened in youth clubs, art galleries, community halls, libraries, schools, trade fairs, museums, at least once on the balcony of a nightclub, in cinemas and, later, on television.[1] They persuaded people to recycle, to eat bacon, to visit museums and not to speed; they explained the finer points of social security, safety systems on the transatlantic aviation route and abstract painting. In short, *kulturfilm* reflected and shaped Danish culture – culture understood in the social and in the artistic senses – as it rapidly changed and developed in the middle of the last century, through the aftermath of the German occupation (1940–5), the early years of the welfare state, and increasing technological and socio-economic integration on an international scale. Strictly speaking, such films are not documentaries, though their stylistic and technological development owes much to the international documentary scene before and after the Second World War.

This book tries to explain how and why such films were made, by looking closely at the commissioning, production and distribution of around twenty examples. The case studies vary in emphasis, according to the richness of detail available from the production files and other sources, how complex the films themselves are as texts, and how they engage with the cultural context of their times. In general, the films are treated as events that expand in space and time, and as nodes in complex networks of people, regulations, technologies, documents, images and ideas. A guiding principle is that the relationship between a film's commissioning and the film text is not linear; the films construct ideas about aspects of Danish life in ways that are contingent on ambiguous remits, contested ideologies, imperfect communications, the vagaries of film-making technologies and the contexts of circulation and consumption. This list includes our contemporary archiving and viewing practices, including the ongoing process of digitising the nation's film heritage.

This book is not a history of the state-sponsored film in Denmark. Such a book already exists: a monumental work of institutional history, *Kortfilmen og staten* (*The Short Film and the State*) was published in Danish in 1987 by Christian Alsted, Carl Nørrested and their team of researchers. It covers the relationship between the state and the short film in Denmark from a variety of angles, and encompasses film history from its beginnings to the 1980s. My starting point is a different one: recent scholarship on the kind of filmmaking of which the *kulturfilm* in Denmark is just one example. In recent years, industrial, educational and public information films made by a variety of organisations have become more accessible to researchers due to the possibilities afforded by digitisation. Scholars have begun to explore a wide range of film corpora that sprang up outside mainstream cinema throughout the twentieth century for more or less defined purposes. Such films are often grouped under the heading 'useful cinema' (after Wasson and Acland 2011) to emphasise their utility over their entertainment value. With the ambition of contributing to this developing body of work, I have chosen to focus on one particular institution, Dansk Kulturfilm (1932–65 approximately), to serve as a case study in useful cinema. Dansk Kulturfilm was, in practice, not a single entity but the centre of a shifting set of institutions which commissioned, produced and distributed films for the purposes of 'enlightenment, education, and general propaganda' (Dansk Kulturfilm 1933).

The original working title of this project was *Short Films in a Small Nation*. The switch of prepositions from 'in' to 'from' is non-trivial and reflects an unexpected finding: that a good proportion, perhaps half, of the films made under the auspices of Dansk Kulturfilm were not made with Danish audiences in mind, but were commissioned for export in order to promote Danish culture and industry abroad. Some of these films were later re-purposed for use at home, and others made for a national audience had afterlives overseas. Tracing the movement of such films from committee room to screening room thus provides insights into how Danish authorities and stakeholders wished to present Denmark to the outside world, how their strategies were affected by assumptions and realities relating to the image of Denmark abroad, and how such images and discourses might translate for a domestic audience.

The first three chapters of the book situate the study within the scholarly contexts that it tries to encompass. Chapter 1 outlines recent research on useful cinema and explains how this study both builds on and deviates from emerging principles and methodologies in the field. Chapter 2 connects the project to recent work on Danish cinema as a national and creative industry that has enjoyed exceptional success since the 1990s. In particular, this is a question of the peculiarities of 'small-nation' cinema, but the chapter also discusses the connections between cinema and nation more generally, iden-tifying the medium-specific and formal properties of the short informational film, which serve as a basis for textual and material analysis of films as they travel inside and outside Denmark. Chapter 3 explains how the project has been influenced by the mode of thinking offered by Actor-Network Theory (ANT). This approach, it is argued, allows for the full complexity of the network of material and social factors influencing the commissioning, pro-duction and circulation of the films to emerge. As a bridge between theory and case studies, Chapter 4 provides an overview of key developments in Dansk Kulturfilm's institutional history from the 1930s onwards and surveys how occupation-era filmmaking underpins the post-war flourishing of the Danish *kulturfilm*.

Chapter 5 takes advantage of the more comprehensive archival materials available for post-1945 productions to examine an ambitious series of films about Danish social security innovations, made expressly for a British audi-ence with the help of the English documentarist Sir Arthur Elton. Chapter 6 draws on three later case studies from the late 1940s to the mid-1950s to show how the practice of making films for international audiences was adapted to a range of forms of international collaboration, co-production and economic integration: the United Nations Film Board, the Marshall Plan film programme and the Nordic Council. Chapter 7 returns to the domestic scene, discussing five productions which explore aspects of national infrastructure, institutions and practices as the welfare state took shape through the 1950s. By the end of that decade, the golden age of the *kulturfilm* was over; filmmakers, functionar-ies and audiences alike were becoming more critical of the genre and the films themselves are more focused on critiquing society. Chapter 8 explores that tendency with a focus on a particularly contested and complex sub-genre of the *kulturfilm*: the art film. Finally, Chapter 9 is entirely devoted to one film, arguably the high water mark of Dansk Kulturfilm's production: the Oscar-nominated *A City Called Copenhagen* (Jørgen Roos, 1960). The Conclusion connects the further development of state-sponsored informational filmmaking in Denmark to more recent developments and prospects, both institutional and technological.

A few practical notes are in order. Firstly, it is important to specify that the project draws on copious quantities of archival material, screenplays, films and secondary sources in Danish, and to save space, I have provided only the English translation when quoting directly. All translations are mine, unless otherwise indicated.

Secondly, readers who wish to view the films discussed for themselves will find links to the films, where copyright permits, as well as a selective filmography on the Danish Film Institute's website (q-r.to/balKqd).

Thirdly, some chapters in this book draw on my previously published research on the same topic. Chapters 1 and 3 contain re-worked material previously published in the essay '"Education, Enlightenment, and General Propaganda": Dansk Kulturfilm and Carl Th. Dreyer's short films', in M. Hjort and U. Lindqvist (eds), *A Companion to Nordic Cinema*, London: Wiley-Blackwell, 2016, pp. 78–97. The discussion of *Thorvaldsen* (Carl Th. Dreyer, 1949) in Chapter 8 draws on material also used in two essays: 'Body Culture and Film Culture in Thorvaldsen's Museum 1932–63', in S. Ayres and E. Carbone (eds), *Sculpture and the Nordic Region*, London: Routledge, 2016, pp. 130–45; and 'The Artist's Touch: Dreyer, Thorvaldsen, Venus', written for the Danish Film Institute, *Carl Th. Dreyer – The Man and his Work*, 2010, <http://english.carlthdreyer.dk/AboutDreyer/Visual-style/The-Artists-Touch-Dreyer-Thorvaldsen-Venus.aspx>.

NOTE

1. *Kulturfilm* made for screening in cinemas and in clubs began to be shown on television from the early 1950s, at which point Dansk Kulturfilm and Ministeriernes Filmudvalg's (MFU) annual report stated that it would not make sense to enter into any licensing agreement 'at a time when the economic prospects of television are entirely unclear' (Dansk Kulturfilm 1952: 10). It may also be useful at this juncture to distinguish between *kulturfilm* and a more recent media phenomenon invariably mentioned by Danes when I discuss this project with them: the national broadcaster DR's public information adverts, known as OBS. An acronym echoing the Danish equivalent of NB, as in *nota bene*, OBS stands for '*Oplysning til Borgerne om Samfundet*': literally, information for citizens about society. Around 1,300 OBS, predominantly less than a minute in length, have been broadcast since the format's inception in 1977, with topics encompassing 'laws, regulations, environment, traffic and other safety advice, social security, home insurance, tax self-assessment, disease prevention' (Hoffmann 2017) – in other words, a range of issues not dissimilar to the back catalogue of Dansk Kulturfilm.

1. ENLIGHTENMENT AND UTILITY: INFORMATIONAL FILM AS USEFUL CINEMA

The last decade has witnessed a wave of scholarly interest in a dimension of world film heritage so myriad in its forms and purposes as to defy taxonomy and terminology. This is a parallel cinema, the scale and achievements of which have been obscured by the obsession of Film Studies and audiences with auteurs, classics, artistry and movie theatres; it is a world of un-sung practitioners, archived 16mm prints, functionality and community halls. Recent books on the subject have tended to adopt utility as a defining principle: for example, Vinzenz Hediger and Patrick Vonderau adopt the book title *Films That Work* (2009). Charles R. Acland and Haidee Wasson (2011) coin the term *Useful Cinema*, a turn of phrase that deftly encompasses the many variations in contexts of production and consumption of films made for purposes other than pure entertainment. The term 'useful cinema' is the one I shall adopt for the time being.[1] This 'other' cinema has existed since the earliest days of film; it is predicated on international networks and yet springs up locally, to serve contexts and needs that are culturally, historically and technologically specific. It accounts for a significant proportion of moving image production in the twentieth century, whether measured in terms of 'numbers of films, size of audience, penetration of technologies, or amount of economic activity' (Wasson and Acland 2011: 2).

For these reasons alone, useful cinema deserves attention, but it also constitutes, when interrogated, a rich seam of information on the relations between state and non-state institutions and the arts, and on the struggles of various actors for 'aesthetic, social and polical capital' (Wasson and Acland

2011: 3). In this sense, useful cinema can be regarded as an actor in its own right:

> Cameras, films, and projectors have been taken up and deployed variously – beyond questions of art and entertainment – in order to satisfy organizational demands and objectives, that is, to *do* something in particular ... Culture, in this respect, shapes debates, moves populations, directs capital, furthers authority, and ordains the self. (Wasson and Acland 2011: 3, emphasis in original)

Similarly, in their introduction to *Films That Work*, Hediger and Vonderau (2009: 12) stake a claim for the importance of industrial film research in excavating 'the complex interrelationship of visuality, power, and organization, and specifically how film as a medium creates the preconditions for forms of knowledge and social practice'. On the face of it, then, to study useful cinema is to investigate how films mediate and enact the intentions of those institutions which commission or fund them.

A third influential anthology in the field, *Learning with the Lights Off*, focuses on the use of film in educational contexts in the USA, and its title playfully draws attention to the importance of exhibition contexts in delineating this 'other' cinema. The portability of the narrow-gauge film used for much educational and industrial film facilitated screening and learning in a potentially infinite range of spaces: 'classrooms, auditoriums, places of worship, museums, libraries, fraternal lodges, union halls, and living rooms; at workplaces, convention halls, fairs, meeting rooms, seminars – even in movie theaters' (Orgeron *et al.* 2012: 1). As this litany of exhibition sites suggests, 'non-theatrical film' is a viable alternative term for useful cinema, a term which privileges how, where and to whom the films are screened, rather than focusing on their purpose – though in practice these are often two sides of the same coin. Wasson and Acland (2011: 2) emphasise how such improvised screening spaces often brought together 'a convergence' of media; projection operated in tandem with other media such as newspapers, photographs and radio, producing 'hybrid technological forms'.

The locus of exhibition is only the most concrete manifestation of how this prolific, widespread and dynamic 'other cinema' (Wasson and Acland 2011: 2) runs parallel to, or in the shadow of, the commercial, entertainment-focused film sector. To describe films as 'non-theatrical' posits theatrical exhibition, that is, in purpose-built, commercial cinemas, as the default. Similarly, feature-length fiction films have dominated Film Studies as a discipline. This can be attributed to the field's historical struggle for recognition:

> The allure of fictional narratives, an influential wave of auteur-based criticism that emphasized aesthetic expression, and an international film

history canon allowed film studies to align itself with other disciplines. Though the justification was often hard-won, cinema became an academically justifiable object of study in part through a process of exclusion. (Orgeron *et al.* 2012: 3)

As the three anthologies mentioned here suggest, what has been excluded from Film Studies is defined by the very fact of being excluded from the canon of mainstream cinema, and thus by its variety. This has a tendency to elide the multifarious nature of the films being rediscovered: multifarious in terms of organisation, commissioning, aims, distribution, reception and technological instantiation. The terms used to define and taxonomise such cinema are also myriad. 'Educational' and 'industrial' film are relatively straightforward as indications of how, where and why such films were produced and screened, while 'useful' is more ambiguous as a descriptor. Terms proliferate in local and national contexts; the vocabulary is not always easily translatable, rooted as it is in local needs, traditions and practices, and does not easily map on to the English-language terms that have emerged in recent scholarship. The proliferation of terms for useful cinema in Danish is both a rich example of such terminological problematics and can also be seen to reflect the attention and funding lavished on the phenomenon in Denmark.

Useful Cinema in Mid-twentieth-century Denmark

While space does not allow for a thorough discussion of all the sub-genres that appear listed in Dansk Kulturfilm's catalogues, a snapshot of the categories listed in the annual report for 1948–9 is indicative. Films completed that year are arranged under the headings *spillefilm* (feature films), *kortfilm* (short films), *reportagefilm* (reportage films), *eksperimentalfilm* (experimental films), *kulturhistoriske optagelser* (footage of cultural-historical value), *undervisnings- og instruktionsfilm* (films for teaching and instruction), *personoptagelser* (footage of personalities) and *versioner* (alternative versions of existing *kulturfilm*; shorter or longer versions, or foreign-language versions) (Dansk Kulturfilm og Ministeriernes Filmudvalg 1949: 44).

This list also illustrates the refusal of any of these terms to map neatly across languages. Danish also has two words with very different connotations but which imply the same ends: *oplysningsfilm* (literally, film for enlightenment) and *brugsfilm* (literally, film for use). While the first expresses an ambition to contribute to the Danish tradition of folk high schools and popular enlightenment, the latter is semantically close to useful cinema. However, perhaps because it lacks glamour, *brugsfilm* was not adopted as the name of the agency on which this book centres, Dansk Kulturfilm. That nomenclature is taken from the German term for culture-film, current in the 1930s. This point is discussed in more detail in Chapter 4, but for the moment we can note that the output of Dansk Kulturfilm stretched the term *kulturfilm* beyond its literal meaning; it is not suitable for all the case studies in this book, though it does encompass films about culture conceived as society, and culture conceived as art.[2] I use the word *kulturfilm* untranslated throughout this book, both to refer to the genre and in the name of the organisation under discussion. However, searching for a relatively neutral and more all-encompassing term, I settled on 'informational film' as the go-to term for most of Dansk Kulturfilm's output. 'Informational film' was used in the English-language film festival programmes of the period on which this book centres, but is not freighted with particular theoretical or ideological weight today. In short, then, as a parameter for this project's investigations, considerations of genre (or sub-genre) have been subsidiary to originating agency.

That originating agency is Dansk Kulturfilm. Established in 1932 as a semi-governmental agency for the production of films for 'enlightenment, education and general propaganda' (Dansk Kulturfilm 1933), it survived in one form or another until the 1980s, though its operations technically ceased around 1965. In practice, Dansk Kulturfilm never functioned as an independent entity, but was the central node of a shifting network of government committees, professional and trades associations, citizens' organisations, film production companies, distributors and, of course, filmmakers, all of which had the aim of putting film to work in the service of informing and persuading audiences in Denmark and abroad.

For most of its history, Dansk Kulturfilm functioned in tandem with Ministeriernes Filmudvalg (The Danish Government Film Committee, hereafter MFU), a government committee originally constituted during the German occupation (1940–5) to steer the production of films promoting industrial productivity and employment. A third body closely linked to these two was Statens Filmcentral (the State Film Centre, hereafter SFC), established in 1938, which dealt with the domestic distribution of informational films. Other organisations were instrumental in the development of state-sponsored informational film in Denmark, and these will appear and sometimes disappear from the story of Dansk Kulturfilm as we follow its activities through the three decades from 1932. Dansk Kulturfilm was also part of a worldwide network of informational and documentary filmmaking that was intrinsic to the ambitions of policymakers in the post-war era.

Tellingly, Dansk Kulturfilm's own definition of *kulturfilm* drifts over time. In successive versions of its founding document, the range of types of film falling under its remit is specified; the shifts in vocabulary indicate not only the changes in the institution's role, but also the inherent slipperiness of a genre that is defined by its ideological imperative to intervene in the national culture. Concomitantly, the definition of *kulturfilm* changes precisely because of that same institution's intervention in national culture and, not least, by dint of its intervention in the map of film culture in Denmark. The institutional history of Dansk Kulturfilm is traced in more detail in Chapter 4. As the centre of a shifting conglomeration of agencies, committees, associations and film production companies dedicated to filmmaking in the service of the state, Dansk Kulturfilm offers a particularly rich and complex case study in useful cinema. Its organisation presents a puzzle for scholars trying to understand the relationship between state and filmmaker, commissioning organisation and audience, original brief and finished film. Its output problematises the parameters of a range of genre terms. What is more, precisely because the work of Dansk Kulturfilm and its sister organisations was funded and overseen by the Danish state, its written records and many of its films have survived and are accessible to scholars. In the remaining part of this chapter, I outline how this book brings the extant scholarship on useful cinema into conversation with Dansk Kulturfilm as a case study.

METHOD AND SCOPE

The edited anthologies discussed above have had a crucial role to play in mapping the multifarious forms of non-theatrical film across the globe. Such collective projects are an effective way to marshal expertise, to generate knowledge and to scope out methodologies through painstaking comparative study. Useful cinema is a field in which profoundly local cultural and institutional contexts are seen to intersect with global flows of technologies, communication channels and practitioners.

Aside from its scope and focus, this book both builds on and deviates from emerging approaches to the study of useful cinema. Firstly, and most obviously, it is a monograph focusing in some detail on a sub-set of useful cinema in one national context. This has the advantage of situating a substantial and representative selection of such films within the continuities and transformations of a defined socio-cultural and political context over a period of three decades. As a Danish speaker with a background in Danish cultural, film and literary studies, I have had privileged access to policy documents, screenplays, correspondence and media sources in that language; this position is far from unique in a field which has produced case studies of useful cinema from Norway to Brazil, but coupled with the sustained focus over three decades, it allows for the teasing out of various profoundly local factors and their connections to global tendencies. Along the way, some comparisons are drawn with British and North American contexts, where these become important for the Danish filmmakers, but the overriding concern is to understand how state-sponsored non-theatrical filmmaking in mid-twentieth-century Denmark was organised. Much of what is revealed will be specific to Denmark rather than generally applicable, but I also try to identify recurring questions, dilemmas, tensions and accommodations which have the potential to be abstracted to the broader international context of non-theatrical film.

In an important sense, though, this book is not intended as an exhaustive chronological overview of the state-sponsored film in Denmark. Rather, like a multi-author anthology, it also adopts the strategy of zooming in on case studies. The availability of information from a variety of sources informed my decision to focus in detail on a number of individual film case studies that highlight certain trends and practices, rather than attempting to provide a comprehensive but more superficial historical overview of the period. Overall, the aim is to drill down into how state-sponsored useful cinema was produced over a defined period by one set of institutions. This approach is broadly consistent with Hediger and Vonderau's call for researchers to look not just at 'the situation that produced the films' via their production histories, but also 'the situation or constellation that the film produces' (2009: 11). The sources for this kind of enquiry are construed as a '*dispositif* ... of media, technology, forms of knowledge, discourse, and social organization' (11, emphasis in original), of which the film is just one element.

This methodology and use of sources is explained in more detail in the next chapter, but staying for the moment with extant recommendations on the methodologies best suited to the study of useful cinema, I want to identify Elsaesser's notion of 'film as event' as the model that best fits how I have organised this project. In order to re-frame research and analysis to suit non-theatrical cinema in all its variety, Elsaesser recommends a focus on the 'commissioning client, concrete occasion, and target use or target audience'; this demands in turn a reconsideration of film as an event conceived as

> a process tied to a site ... not as a continuum like narrative, but as pulsed, intermittent, and shaped by intervals. Events as spaces tend to be centrifugal, multilayered, and heterogeneous in their consistency and materiality; and event implies the notion of programming and planning but also of accident and coincidence. All these associations are useful for re-thinking non-fiction films in terms of an event scenario, in which the actual film is only one piece of the evidence and residue to be examined and analyzed. To think of film as an event is furthermore to prefer a network model, in order to determine the relation of one film to another, and to understand its place within wider histories. (Elsaesser 2009: 32)

The film case studies in this book can usefully be understood as 'events' as Elsaesser expounds on the term above. As they unfold, they intersect with other kinds of events in Danish political and cultural history. Also interesting is Elsaesser's choice of the word 'network'. It is not clear whether he is alluding to Actor-Network Theory (ANT), but his instinctively relational and non-linear approach to the event and to the *dispositif* of films' paratexts and screening contexts has affinities with ANT. This is an approach that underlies my project and this discussion is taken up in more detail in Chapter 3.

As with any archival work, the present creates the past in the sense that the preservation of some documents and not others has shaped my choice of case studies and their limitations. While Dansk Kulturfilm's filmmaking work petered out in the mid-1960s, its institutional history, or afterlife (and the scope of my study), has been determined by the survival of the papery traces of its work through political strategies, institutional change, information management practices, preservation technologies, finance, archival architecture and the expert knowledge of archivists. Similarly, the scholarship of the last decade, as outlined above, has been facilitated and shaped by digital preservation, restoration and exhibition techniques. While access to archival collections of industrial or government-sponsored films, say, was possible before the advent of the digital age, accessing such films could be cumbersome, time-consuming and expensive. This can still be the case, but private and national collections of non-theatrical film are, increasingly, being digitised and made freely available online. There is extensive overlap between non-theatrical films and so-called orphan films, whose copyright holders are unknown or uncontactable, facilitating their free use online.[3] We should be cognisant of the ways in which such technological advances shape and even distort our research, even while they facilitate it. Chapter 3 includes a broader discussion of the archival holdings to which I have had access and how their availability (or lack of such) have shaped the project, but for the moment I want to make the point that the focus and approach of this book, and by extension the field it describes, has been determined by the state-of-the-art at the Danish Film Institute in the mid-2010s. In this respect, the study of useful cinema creates and re-creates the filmic past it excavates by dint of established and emerging post-filmic technologies. Such technologies – digitisation, restoration, access via a range of platforms and interfaces – are inflected by institutional, political and financial considerations that affect what gets preserved, what is made available, in what form or degree of completeness, how, where and to whom.

However, neither should we be too quick to reify the power of the state and non-state institutions and actors that commissioned, funded and/or supervised the production of useful cinema. Hediger and Vonderau describe industrial films as '*interfaces* between discourses and forms of social and industrial organization' (2009: 11, emphasis in original). This is a fruitful metaphor to conceptualise the function of the films in mediating between institutions, ideologies and audiences. However, Hediger and Vonderau's model is based on the genre of the industrial film. More so than my data set, the industrial film readily lends itself to what they call, borrowing from Elsaesser as above, the three As and the three Rs of analysis. These are the *Auftrag* (occasion), *Anlass* (purpose) and *Adressat* (addressee) built into industrial film texts, and their possible purposes: '*record* (institutional memory), *rhetoric* (governance) and *rationalization* (optimizing process)' (Hediger and Vonderau 2009: 10–11, emphasis in original). The three Rs do not easily map on to *kulturfilm* or informational film. Elsaesser's three As are more applicable. Nonetheless, though Danish state-sponsored films can and often do have an identifiable *Auftrag* (occasion), *Anlass* (purpose) and *Adressat* (addressee), often these are more nebulous than assumed by scholars, and certainly by audiences.

This point can be further illustrated by citing an early intervention in the history of Danish state-sponsored film by the scholar Christian Alsted, who later went on, with Carl Nørrested and their team of researchers, to produce the book *Kortfilmen og staten* (*The Short Film and the State*, 1987). In his MA dissertation, Alsted describes his object of investigation thus:

> The films as a body of work are understood as a medial expression of an intervention by the state – on the conscious level – whose content is constituted by the societal needs which the state is trying to satisfy in the context of its economic possibilities. (Alsted 1979: 10)

Alsted's MA dissertation has been a valuable source of information about the conduct and output of MFU. It wears its political heart on its sleeve as a Marxist reading of a particular episode in Danish film history, and was researched and written at a time when such an approach to film and history was common in Danish academe. With these caveats in mind, I nevertheless take the liberty of citing the above passage from Alsted's dissertation as an illustration of how easily the discussion of state-sponsored film can slip into a kind of determinism: the assumption that the finished films are a conscious and direct expression of the initial brief. On the face of it, this is a reasonable hypothesis and one which underlies the very concept of useful cinema in contemporary film studies. Instinctively, 'useful' or 'purposeful' films are assumed to exist for a reason and have a goal, however well defined or vague it might be.

When I began this project, I also shared the assumption that Dansk Kulturfilm's and MFU's productions functioned as a more or less direct conduit of information and ideas between government and public. However, it quickly became clear that neither the film texts themselves nor their production histories support this notion. As the case studies in this volume show, the original commission may indeed result in a film that dovetails in certain respects with the vision and aims expressed in the brief. The process of production, however, entails a myriad of constraints, compromises and interventions from human and non-human actors (among them the economic constraints mentioned by Alsted). So too do the conditions of distribution and reception – sometimes traversing many years and several cultures – confuse, nuance or consolidate the original 'message' of the film. And the original commissioning brief is itself fraught with contradictions, vaguenesses, competing interests, compromises and fast-changing financial and political parameters, not to mention a widespread lack of understanding of what film (as opposed to other media) can actually render visible or intelligible. A central tenet of this book, then, is that useful cinema cannot be regarded as 'a medial expression of an intervention by the state', or at least not straightforwardly so. In reassembling the histories of a number of *kulturfilm* and in reading the films *qua* film, one of my aims is to trace how ideas are re-shaped and renegotiated in non-linear ways as they move amongst media and spaces: between committees, manuscripts, studios, screening rooms and newspapers. None of this is to deny the potency of cinema as a medium of communication, nor the political, cultural or economic power held by those who commission and distribute the films. However, I do want to posit that to over-simplify the mechanics of the use of visual culture by political interests is to miss many of the effects of that power.

A corollary of the focus on institutions and power structures in useful cinema scholarship is that the content of the films – how they represent and mediate, and thus how they do their work – is sometimes neglected. Wasson and Acland (2011: 5) call for research that combines aesthetic and institutional analysis: 'All genres of cinema, including neglected ones such as the orphan or ephemeral film, are most fully revealed when subject to methods of analysis that consider institutional location and deployment, in addition to aesthetic and formal analysis.' Hediger and Vonderau (2009: 10), on the other hand, specifically discourage analysis of non-theatrical film 'through the auteurist lens'. Elsaesser (2009: 31) goes so far as to argue that questions such as 'who commissioned the film', 'what was the occasion for which it was made', and 'to what use was it put or to whom was it addressed' are the very questions that avant-garde and documentary filmmakers often do not want to answer, for fear of undermining their artistry. While it is undeniably an important task to carve out a critical praxis pertinent to the 'other' cinema of public, educational and industrial films, I want to claim that the 'auteurist lens' can, in fact, be crucial to our appreciation of how 'films that work' actually do their work. This book posits that the role of the auteur or artist can in fact be fundamental to the film's construction of its national audience, and to its multivalent project of enlightenment. The role of the director is unequivocally central to the history of Dansk Kulturfilm, in terms of the ambitions and functioning of the institution and the state it represented, the debates it engendered around artistic freedom and the relationship between the state and culture, and the circulation of the films in an international network of non-theatrical cinema. My approach to the films analysed in this book draws on the multiple functions of the filmmaker as practitioner and artist, but, crucially, as one amongst many agents who produce the films as texts and as objects. In most cases, then, my analyses incorporate readings of the films *qua* films, from a variety of critical-theoretical perspectives. This is not done merely to reiterate the value of humanistic studies for their own sake, but with the conviction that the films can only 'do their work' in their encounter with the viewer. On that note, in Chapter 2, we now turn to examine how film – both theatrical and non-theatrical – represents, images and shapes the national context from which it emerges.

NOTES

1. I am grateful to Andrew Higson for his thought-provoking comment in response to one of my papers that the term useful cinema is problematic in that it suggests that film for entertainment is not useful. Higson himself employs the term 'use' in his 1989 article 'The Concept of National Cinema', when he calls for more research into how audiences 'use' cinema for their own ends (Higson 1989: 45).
2. Many thanks to Birgit Granhøj Dam for crystallising this point as she passed my desk one day at the DFI.
3. For a discussion of the intersections between educational film research and orphan films, as well as issues of access and digitisation, see Orgeron *et al.* (2012: 11–13).

2. WE ARE A LITTLE LAND: INFORMATIONAL FILM AND SMALL-NATION CINEMA

'*Et lille land*' – a little land – is an epithet that recurs many times in the film treatments, scripts, voiceovers and press and popular discourse around much of the output of Dansk Kulturfilm, from the 1930s through to the 1960s. The expression is often used when commentators are reflecting on how the films and their ideas will be received abroad. One example is a film funded by Marshall Aid in the immediate post-war period, *Den strømlinede gris* (*The Streamlined Pig*, Jørgen Roos, 1951). This film exploits the trope of the 'little land' to underline the dominance and excellence of the country's agriculture. The first line of the voiceover text reads: 'Denmark is only a little land – a farming land. Four million people live here – one million of them work in agriculture' (Roos 1950: 1). A decade later, a newspaper review after the premiere of Jørgen Roos' *A City Called Copenhagen* (see Chapter 9) was jubilant that the outside world would realise that humour was something that was a top priority in 'the little land of Denmark' (V-r 1960). More examples of the use of this trope arise in several of our case studies.

The existence of the bodies described in Chapter 1 testifies to the importance attached to film as a communicative medium by the Danish government before and after the Second World War. The *kulturfilm* was a vehicle for national imagining: the films responded to collective anxieties, taught domestic audiences to be Danish citizens and informed foreign viewers about aspects of Danish culture. But whose notions of Danishness did the films mediate and how did the medium-specific properties of the short film shape those visions of the nation? This chapter considers how the relations between cinema and nation as theorised in scholarly work since the mid-1990s might inform our understanding of how Danish informational film reflects, shapes and renegotiates national imaginings. As my use of the term 'imagining' suggests, Benedict Anderson's *Imagined Communities* (1991) haunts the discussion, not least because Anderson's insistence that national narratives and images are constructed in medium-specific ways prompts us to tease out the spatial, temporal, affective and material specificities of the short film as a carrier of the national message. 'Imaging' and 'imagining' recur in this chapter as we survey the various scholarly contexts with which this book engages.

The Nationness of National Cinema

Film scholars have long been attentive to the role of cinema as a conduit for national imagining and to the ambiguities of the label 'national' in the context of a profoundly transnational medium. The nation as a cultural lodestone has outlived the socio-economic conditions of its emergence from the Enlightenment and the Industrial Revolution (Gellner 1983), the convulsions of post-1989 Europe and spiralling globalisation of late modernity; at the time of writing, the twin shocks of Brexit and the election of Donald Trump as US President are still being digested by cultural commentators as expressions of a nationalistic retrenchment on both sides of the Atlantic. In Film Studies, too, interest in the relationship between cinema and nation is enduring and unavoidable, even as terms such as 'transnational', 'intercultural' and 'postnational' cinema proliferate in order to keep pace with the impact of globalisation on cultural politics: 'national categories continue to be invoked with reference to sites of production, exhibition, acquiescence, resistance or some form of transformation' (Hjort and Petrie 2007: 11). Andrew Higson's agenda-setting article 'The Concept of National Cinema' of the late 1980s identified a tension between two different approaches to Film Studies generally and mapped them on to current and potential avenues for research into national cinemas: a focus on the political economy of cinema versus textual analysis of film's mediation of culture (Higson 1989: 46). Before the 'cultural turn' of the 1980s, an essentialistic approach often characterised interpretations of national cinema, with the work of auteurs read as expressions of the essence of the history from which they emerged. Such analyses

> looked to the cinema, its narratives, iconography or recurring motifs with the expectation that they could reveal something unique or specific about a country's values and beliefs, at once more authentic and more symptomatic than in other art forms or aspects of (popular) culture. (Elsaesser 2005: 63–4)

More recently, the 'institutional turn' in Film Studies, within which this book locates itself, has focused more attention on national film institutions as they intersect with local, regional and transnational entities (in the Nordic context, see Hjort and Petrie 2007; Hjort and Lindqvist 2016; Chow 2016).

In their overview of the development of scholarship on national cinemas through the 1990s, Hjort and MacKenzie note how film has often been conceptualised as a space in which national identity is thrashed out rather than settled:

> National cinema is more fruitfully understood in terms of conflict. Films, it is claimed, do not simply represent or express the stable features of a national culture, but are themselves one of the loci of debates about a nation's governing principles, goals, heritage and history. It follows that critics should be attuned not only to the expressive dimensions of a nation's films, but to what these films and their categorisation as elements of a national cinema may elide or strategically repress. (Hjort and Mackenzie 2000: 4)

Indeed, the emphasis on the contestedness of national identities in cinema is already present in Higson's 1989 article: 'Histories of national cinema can only therefore really be understood as histories of crisis and conflict, of resistance and negotiation' (Higson 1989: 37).

Clearly, the notion of films as textual sites of negotiation of collective identity is of great import for state-sponsored cinema. In the case studies in this book, the film texts themselves as well as the constellation of documents that accompany their genesis and circulation bear the traces of such negotiations. The very concept of a commissioned film evokes the idea that an ideology is imposed on the text (and thereby on the viewer) by dint of the legal and/or financial authority of the commissioning institution. In practice, the complexity of the filmmaking process undercuts the asymmetry between the commissioning institution's vision and that of the other actors involved. Nevertheless, I have found it useful in some cases to work with the idea of a national 'pedagogy' as one of the competing ideas in the films. This term draws on the work of Homi K. Bhabha, whose essay 'DissemiNation' [sic] engages with Anderson's *Imagined Communities*, but distinguishes between 'pedagogical' and 'performative' dimensions of the imaginative construction of the national narrative (Bhabha 1994). These dimensions of national imagining are defined thus:

> the people are the historical 'objects' of a nationalist pedagogy, giving the discourse an authority that is based on the pre-given or constituted historical origin in the past; the people are also the 'subjects' of a process of

signification that must erase any prior or originary presence of the nation-people to demonstrate the prodigious, living principles of the people as contemporaneity: as that sign of the present through which national life is redeemed and iterated as a reproductive process. (Bhabha 1994: 145)

Bhabha's work is used here to underscore the non-linearity of the semiotic traffic between commissioning body, funders, filmmakers and audiences. I want to stress that it is not always the case that the national 'pedagogy' is imposed by commissioners and functionaries on an unwilling filmmaker or viewer struggling to assert or perform an alternative national narrative, though the power differential is sometimes construed that way by filmmakers fighting for artistic freedom (see especially Chapter 8). In other words, we can reconstruct (at least to some extent) how the nation is imagined by those responsible for producing one form of national pedagogy, and we can also catch a glimpse of how that vision of the nation is reinterpreted, misunderstood, subverted or (sometimes) assimilated by filmmakers, reviewers and viewers. Occasionally, the commissioning process throws up evidence that national pedagogy is informed by the ongoing dynamics of everyday 'performance' of Danishness. If we really pay attention, as this book tries to do, we can also begin to understand how national pedagogy is shaped by happenstance, that is, by a myriad of constraints, accidents and opportunities that are often driven by technology and other material factors.

THE MEDIUM-SPECIFICITY OF NATIONAL IMAGININGS

The work of Benedict Anderson underpins much scholarship on national cinema, whether explicitly or implicitly. As Elsaesser (2005: 65) comments, Anderson's *Imagined Communities* 'came to the rescue' of the constructivist approach to the representation of national identity in cinema and other disciplines in the 1980s. First published in 1983, Anderson's book was revised and reissued in 1991 amidst the post-1989 re-mapping of Europe. The book's central insight is that nations are imagined, but not imaginary (Anderson 1991: 6). They are political constructions whose power over their citizens is not only judicial and military but also affective. Anderson is particularly interested in how various forms of media function to disseminate ideas of nationhood and belonging; his examples are restricted to eighteenth- and nineteenth-century media, however, as his focus (as indicated in the book's subtitle) is the age of the 'origin and spread' of nationalism.

Of particular interest for our purposes is Anderson's theory of how the literary genre of the novel enacts and disseminates a new framework of spacetime which is analogous to 'the kind of imagined community which is the nation' (1991: 25). The classic novel, explains Anderson, schools the reader in the idea of 'meanwhile', thanks to its cast of characters who are narrated as existing and acting within the novel's shared spacetime, though they may not know of each other's existence. The reader is implicated in an imagined community which Anderson defines as 'a sociological organism moving calendrically through homogeneous, empty time' (26), a turn of phrase borrowed from Walter Benjamin's 'Theses on the Philosophy of History' (Benjamin 1999). Put differently, the novel organises its time, space and characters into a shared, linear, measured history which projects itself back into the past and forward into the future, analogous to the grand narrative of national actualisation. Cairns Craig (1996: 121) has pointed out that this is as much a function of the material form of the book as it is an effect of literary narrative.

If we accept that the nation is constructed, and nationness imagined, in ways specific to the medium in question, film as a medium offers a number of complex and elegant tools for the task. Thomas Elsaesser's work is one example of a commitment to textual analysis as a means of deconstructing what he calls 'the historical imaginary' in film. While, as we saw above, he insists on an excavation of the what, who and why in research on the commissioned film, he also reminds us that the 'historical imaginary' on which a film draws and to which it contributes (thus, his adaptation of Anderson's 'imagined community') is dependent on the basic building blocks of film as art and as medium. These include

> composition and mise-en-scène, the architecture of the optical point of view, on- screen and off-screen space, depth of field, flatness and frontal shots as the key indices of a formal inscription that could be read historically. They formed the basis on which to elaborate the properties of a representational system that enabled an individual film, a genre or a body of work to address the spectator as a national or art cinema subject. (Elsaesser 2005: 21)

Mette Hjort explores how 'themes of nation' emerge from a film both in its encounter with the viewer and as an effect of national film policy. A theme of nation is 'a semantic construct that emerges during the process of engaging with a given work' (Hjort 2000: 105). She differentiates between 'perennial' themes, which highlight universal and eternal human interests (love, the meaning of life) and 'topical' themes, which are relevant and meaningful only within a specific cultural context. She concludes that contemporary Danish films – in spite of the Danish Film Institute's attempts to promote the making of films with a Danish 'theme' – tend to be 'about' Denmark only in a topical sense, since elevating nationness to the status of perennial theme would not produce interesting or commercially viable films. Furthermore, many Danish films may be said to be 'about' Denmark in that their setting makes use of 'banal' (Billig

1995) or everyday elements of national culture such as flags, weather reports or references to sports teams; but unless such elements are 'flagged' or focalised in some way, they cannot be said to constitute even a topical theme. Banal nationalism as 'background noise' is labelled 'banal aboutness' by Hjort.

Anderson states teasingly that fiction 'seeps quietly and continuously into reality' (1991: 36). This is a seductive way to describe the role of literature in shaping, negotiating and disseminating popular ideas about the nation, but there is something frustrating about the resort to metaphor ('seeps') in place of a more empirical explanation of how acts of the imagination encourage acts of will; at the extreme, how does the citizen move from imagining himself as such to being willing to fight and die for his country? The latter question can, perhaps, only be satisfyingly answered by psychology or neuroscience, but there is nevertheless scope for a more detailed examination of the medium-specific processes that underpin the transfer (or 'seepage') of ideas about the nation between 'fiction' and 'reality'.

One place to look for this is in the realm of affect. This is not to be found in Anderson, but has become a central concern of Film Studies over the last two decades. Vivien Sobchack (2000) has observed that reviews and popular discussion of film have always had a vocabulary of affect: '"What impresses most is the tactile force of the images. The salt air can almost be tasted, the wind's furious bite felt"; "An unremittingly sensuous experience of music and fabric, of mud and flesh".' However, critical theory has not been able to account for affect until relatively recently. Sobchack and others (e.g. Marks 2000; Marks 2002; Barker 2009) have developed a mode of reading film that emphasises the senses beyond sight and hearing, examining how audio-visual media can activate viewers' experience of touch, smell and taste. This dimension of the filmgoing experience is, I want to argue, an important strategy or accident in useful cinema, and it is discussed and developed in the case studies as and when it seems important for the formation of an affective community around the film. The viewers of Dansk Kulturfilm's productions probably grimaced at the slaughter and flaying of animals; remembered the scent of a wriggly baby or the soothing touch of a nurse's hands; gasped as they were transported over the drop of the rollercoaster; squirmed as they felt the pricking of the tattoo artist's needle through the proxy of the sailor's skin. If these films move or touch us, it is not – or at least not solely – for art's sake. These films want to move their viewers to do something: understand something, change their behaviour, act as a Danish citizen or visit Denmark. The films do things with affect, so that the viewer is moved to do things. The converse also applies: the films may leave the viewer cold or send her to sleep. Boredom is also an effect of affect, and one which reviewers also have a vocabulary for, as we shall see.

Inspired by Anderson, in this book I consider *kulturfilm* to be (semi-)fictional texts that play an important role in reflecting, shaping and renegotiating ideas about the imagined community they describe. They organise time and space in ways that are historically, culturally and medium-specific. Over and above the formal properties of the medium, the *kulturfilm* also enjoyed a degree of democratic accessibility, a quality shared with Anderson's 'classic' novel. During the thirty-year period covered by this book, cinema in Denmark can be seen to play a role analogous to the nineteenth-century popular novel in terms of its ability to disseminate ideas amongst the general public. As outlined in Chapter 4, cinema was popularly acknowledged from the 1930s in Denmark as the most influential medium of its time, though the press hysteria around its deleterious effects and market penetration probably underestimated the influence of radio. Granted, while a cheap novel can be bought and read at will, *kulturfilm* audiences were dependent on organised screenings in cinemas and clubs. However, the collective nature of the viewing experience would seem to offer more opportunity for absorption and consolidation of the encounter with the text than does the solitary activity of reading a novel.

Anderson's work on the national novel can also function as a jumping-off point for our understanding of the kind of viewer constructed by the *kulturfilm*. Jonathan Culler (1999) fleshes out certain aspects of Anderson's model as it pertains to the reader. Culler observes that the projected reader of Anderson's 'classic' novel knows some things but not others, and the tension between the known and the new moves the reader between insider and outsider status in relation to the textual community. In a similar way, as we shall see in our case studies, the films tend to rely for their didactic effect on an assumption of various kinds of knowledge on the part of the viewer. In other words, the films, like Anderson's novels, construct an assumed or model reader/viewer, all the better to inform or persuade him or her. In some cases, this process is actually visible from documentation in the archival files (for example, committee discussions with commissioning charities or filmmakers' notes). In other cases, the 'national' viewer construed by a particular film has to be read from the film text itself.

In contrast to Anderson's model and to the auteur-driven fiction film cases that underpin most work on national cinemas, the *kulturfilm* are not spontaneously produced artistic works of fiction, but commissioned and made for a purpose. Moreover, underlying the declared purpose specific to an individual film is the nationalising mission of Dansk Kulturfilm. This does not, however, make the Denmark that they construct on screen easier to read; quite the contrary. That the films are commissioned and sponsored under the aegis of the state, and expressly for audiences conceived as national or foreign, offers an opportunity to investigate the tensions and affinities between the two dynamics of national imagining identified by Bhabha: pedagogy and performance. An interesting layer of complication is that not all *kulturfilm* were primarily intended for a Danish audience. In these cases, the files often record explicit speculation about what level of knowledge of Danish culture can be assumed on the part of the foreign viewer. The picture is muddied still further by films made for the domestic audience which circulated abroad and vice versa. The double-coding of such films – by which I mean how they could function to inform Danes and foreigners about Danish national heritage – is examined in case studies in Chapters 5, 6, 8 and 9 in particular.

A key tenet of this book is, then, that the nation is constructed and imagined in ways that are genre-specific and medium-specific. In the case of the state-sponsored short film, these specificities lie in the conditions of its commissioning and production, the conditions of its distribution and reception, and material instantiation of the film. However, they also lie in another aspect of its medium-specificity: its shortness.

THE SHORTNESS OF SHORT FILMS

In terms of the medium-specificity of the short film as a vehicle for national imagining, we can observe that the genre exploits potentials of spatio-temporal representation that are intrinsic to the medium of cinema generally, while the shortness of the short film implies certain constraints and possibilities specific to film length.

The short film is one of those subjects on which everyone who writes anything bemoans the lack of writing on the subject. One tendency is to compare the short film to other genres and media. Myles Breen, for example, asserts that 'while short films have been made from long novels and long films from short stories, there is a natural link between *all* film and the short story' (1978: 4, emphasis in original). He goes on to attribute a similar observation to Alfred Hitchcock: that film resembles the short story in that it is meant to be consumed in one sitting. Interviewed shortly before the premiere of his much-anticipated film *A City Called Copenhagen* (1960, discussed in Chapter 9), Danish filmmaker Jørgen Roos was asked if he wanted to continue as a director of short films, the majority of his fifty-odd films in a twenty-year career having been shorts. Roos' answer evokes a similar parallel between short films and short stories: 'I have never regarded short films as a springboard to feature films. The short film ought to be held in equally high esteem to short stories and poems, which no-one would argue are less meaningful than novels' (Vest 1959). Roos was speaking at a time when the emphasis in short filmmaking in Denmark was about to shift from state-sponsored informational films to more style-driven fictional shorts, a transition expressed both by an increasing focus in film policy on stimulating creativity and by the emergence of the term *novellefilm* (novella film). This term, inspired by a literary form, entered into official parlance in the 1960s and especially from 1994, when a funding scheme by that name was launched under the Danish Film Institute to stimulate the genre

(Schepelern n.d.). Raskin (2002: 3) compares this genre, usually stretching to forty or fifty minutes, to the French *court métrage*.

While comparison across media tends to elide medium-specificity, these observations are a useful starting-point to unpack the synergy of length, form and narrative that particularly characterises the short film. The informational film with which we are concerned often owes as much, if not more, to fiction storytelling than it does to documentary form, a tenet which is frequently made explicit by Dansk Kulturfilm's staff and filmmakers. Richard Raskin has contributed a great deal to our understanding of how storytelling functions in the short film form, not least in his book *The Art of the Short Fiction Film* (2002) and in his public lectures and masterclasses. Raskin posits a range of tensions which must be resolved in a successful short. These include character focus versus interaction between characters; causality as a function of characters and their choices; consistency of character versus surprise; an interplay of sound and action; characters' faces versus interaction with objects (or their inner lives versus the environment); simplicity versus depth; shortness versus wholeness (Raskin n.d.). As we shall see, an awareness of the need for characterisation (of humans and non-humans) and for tension, often expressed in terms of 'drama', is a common concern for those involved in Dansk Kulturfilm's pre-production.

Johannes Riis (1998) makes the important point that the shortness of short films entails an emphasis on engaging the viewer, rather than telling him or her something. Although Riis is concerned with the use of short fiction filmmaking as a tool for understanding narrative form, his observation is relevant to the remit of informational films. As we shall see repeatedly, Dansk Kulturfilm as an institution was acutely aware that its films would have to engage the viewer in order to fulfil their function of informing, persuading and enlightening. This ambition was not always achieved. The challenge of sustaining viewer engagement is one of the factors which create tension between the priorities of commissioning and funding bodies and the filmmakers. As discussed in Chapter 9, Jørgen Roos' *A City Called Copenhagen* successfully exploits this tension for comedic effect, but other films were critiqued for sacrificing clarity of message on the altar of drama or rhythm, such as Theodor Christensen's *Enden på legen* (*The End of the Game*, 1961, discussed in Chapter 7). Also, engagement seems to be culturally and historically specific and based as much on audience expectation of pace as on content. While lauded in its day, Theodor Christensen's *Her er Banerne* (*Here are the Railways*, 1948, discussed in Chapter 7) tends to elicit sighs of boredom today, even from an audience of older Danes, I have been surprised to observe.

The narrative of a short cannot be understood in isolation from the material instantiation of the film. Traditionally, the length of a film referred to the length of the film strip itself rather than to its running time; metres are the patois in which plans for Dansk Kulturfilm's projects are couched, translated into feet when corresponding with British or American filmmakers or funders. There is often a distinction in the correspondence between exchanges with cinema programmers, who would understand the currency of metres, and organisers of film screenings and discussions in clubs and associations, who would be concerned with the time allotted to the film screening on their programme.

Crucially, the length of the film – whether understood in terms of metres or minutes – affected its potential placement, and vice versa. There are two Danish terms which I have retained in some contexts throughout the book, because they are hard to translate into English. However, they map fairly neatly onto the concepts of theatrical and non-theatrical exhibition. On the one hand, a *forfilm* – a film intended for theatrical screening, that is, in cinemas before the main feature – would ideally be five to ten minutes long. A *foreningsfilm* – a film commissioned for use as a stimulus to debate in clubs, associations and societies – would be longer, perhaps thirty or forty minutes. With the advent of television, we start to see discussion in the production files of calibrating film length to the rhythm of slots between commercial breaks on North American television, for example. A less important but not entirely negligible factor in how Dansk Kulturfilm's shorts circulated and were marketed was the maximum length stipulated for the short film competitions at various film festivals. Raskin (2002: 3, 4n7) summarises the diversity of criteria at a range of festivals: '35 minutes for international entries at Oberhausen; 40 minutes at Clermont-Ferrand, the BBC Short Film Festival and the Academy Awards; 60 minutes at Krakow, Brest, Uppsala and the San Francisco International Film Festival', 15 minutes at Cannes and 30 minutes at Venice. There is no evidence that such film festival rules affected decisions about film length within Dansk Kulturfilm, but a number of its films were screened, and indeed won prizes, at international film festivals; the vagaries of maximum length regulations thus affected the potential for publicity and honours of the longer films.

The interplay between film length, exhibition context and narrative content is often non-linear. There was a tendency for the planned lengths of films to expand if the film was considered to be particularly good or if the story was discovered to need extra time to unfold, often blowing the budget. Examples of films which expanded from an initial five- to ten-minute brief include *Her er Banerne* (*Here are the Railways*, Theodor Christensen, 1948, discussed in Chapter 7), and *Noget om Norden* (*Somethin' about Scandinavia*, Bent Barfod, 1956, discussed in Chapter 6). In other cases, two versions of the same film would be made, one shorter and one longer, to satisfy different exhibition contexts. An example of this is *They Guide You Across* (Ingolf Boisen, 1949, discussed in Chapter 6).

The vast majority of Dansk Kulturfilm's productions were short films of ten to twenty minutes in length. This is the format on which I have chosen to focus in this book. Inevitably, given the range and permeability of the parameters that have been taken into account when selecting my case studies – parameters which are discussed in more depth in the next chapter – the cut-off point is arbitrary and inflected by a number of considerations. For example, I have chosen to devote parts of chapters to the twenty-five-minute *Her er Banerne* (*Here are the Railways*, Theodor Christensen, 1948) and *They Guide You Across* (Ingolf Boisen, 1949), the long version of which is forty minutes in length. On the other hand, in the case of *Hvor bjergene sejler* (*Where Mountains Float*, Bjarne Henning-Jensen, 1955), I took my lead from the Academy Awards, which judged this film, at fifty-five minutes in length, to belong to the Documentary Feature category (Sculpting the Past n.d.), and decided not to include it in the discussion as a short film.

A final point about short films as such is that they have tended to be regarded, and sometimes dismissed, as a training ground for inexperienced filmmakers (Riis 1998). Recent scholarship that emphasises the education of the filmmaker in the ecosystem of a national cinema (Hjort 2013) provides a less reductive assessment of the cultural importance of the short film form. Pei-Sze Chow, for example, sees funding and facilitation of short filmmaking by emerging filmmakers in contemporary Denmark and Sweden as a crucial expression of the risk-taking inherent in small-nation film policy (Chow 2016: 170–86). The same kind of discourse pervades the ongoing sparring between the administrative leaders of Dansk Kulturfilm and the filmmakers themselves; while different policy positions are taken by both sides at different times, there is a consistent commitment to the idea that short informational films serve as a petri-dish for the development of skills and styles amongst filmmakers, and were thus essential to the health of the national cinema industry more generally. It will be noted that this principle is not incompatible with the conviction of Jørgen Roos, Theodor Christensen and others that the short and documentary film forms were an art in their own right, not a springboard to feature filmmaking. However, intrinsic to the conception of state-sponsored short filmmaking as a sand-box for young directors is an undercurrent of tension regarding the relative degree of political and artistic freedom afforded to the filmmakers. We return to this debate periodically, and especially in Chapter 8.

As the title of this book suggests, its focus is on how *short films* mediate the culture of a *small nation*. Put differently, the shortness of short films is not incidental to their textuality, their production, their exhibition, their distribution, nor to their construction of nationness; the shortness of short films is a constituent element of the strategy and practice of informational film in mid-twentieth-century Denmark.

The Smallness of Small Nations

Denmark was not always a little land. From 1397 to the 1520s, she was the dominant state in the Kalmar Union, a medieval union of the crowns of Denmark, Norway and Sweden established under the reign of Regent Queen Margrethe I of Denmark. After Sweden broke away from this union, Denmark remained the metropole of a *helstat* (literally a 'whole state') incorporating Norway, Iceland, the Faroe Islands and colonies in Greenland. The nineteenth century, however, was a time of contraction of the Danish realm. This process began with the Napoleonic Wars, which saw Copenhagen bombarded by the British, Denmark bankrupt and the Danish fleet confiscated. In the settlement of 1814, Denmark lost Norway to a union of crowns with Sweden, an arrangement which lasted until Norway peacefully gained its independence in 1905. Denmark's southern border, where the neck of the Jutland peninsula meets the tangle of duchies of Schleswig, Holstein and Lauenburg, was the locus of two bloody wars with the German states in the mid-nineteenth century. The second, in 1864, ended with Bismarck's Prussia conquering the duchies and thereby a loss of some thirty per cent of Danish territory. Although the border was moved south again to roughly match the Danish-German language line following a plebiscite of the local population after the First World War, the collective self-understanding as a small nation has remained key to national identity. From the ground zero of the disaster of 1864, Danish national identity was re-imagined as homogeneous and centripetal. The landscape emerged as an allegory for the national character in the psalms and poems of the philosopher and priest N. F. S. Grundtvig (1783–1872), who promoted an egalitarian, self-sufficient society in which 'few have too much and fewer have too little' (Bjørn 2000: 128; Østergård 1996). The environmentalist and poet Enrico Dalgas was (erroneously) lauded as having coined the almost untranslatable mantra *'hvad udad tabes skal indad vindes'* (roughly, 'what is lost to the outside must be won on the inside'), a philosophy which underpinned the remarkable advances in agriculture and land engineering of the second half of the nineteenth century as well as linguistic and literary culture (Bjørn 2000: 123). The notion of 1864 as a watershed in Danish history has enjoyed a popular renaissance in recent years; in 2014, the 150th anniversary of the traumatic defeat at the Battle of Dybbøl inspired a welter of popular history books and a wave of national soul-searching, not least the controversy over filmmaker Ole Bornedal's anti-nationalist series *1864* for Danmarks Radio (DR), the national public service broadcaster (see Hedling 2015 for an extensive analysis of the press and popular debate).

This book is concerned with three decades of the twentieth century which saw a number of twists and turns in the national narrative. The occupation of Denmark by Nazi Germany from 9 April 1940 to 4 May 1945 was a trauma comparable to 1864, but less economically and socially catastrophic than in other occupied countries, due to the government's decision to capitulate to the invaders rather than fight an unwinnable battle. The tasks of sustaining socio-cultural cohesion and economic viability were important drivers in the development of state-sponsored and independent filmmaking during the occupation years, and for this reason alone the war is a key plot twist in the story of Dansk Kulturfilm and its associated agencies. The trope of the 'little land' resisting or emerging from occupation as a progressive, democratic and productive country is central to films made for domestic and foreign consumption during and after the war. A variant on the theme, as we move into the 1950s, is Denmark as one of a close-knit group of small Nordic nations collaborating to punch above their weight. Increasingly, the discourse of the 'little land' gets entangled with narratives and visions of modernity and futurity, as the foundations of the welfare state are laid down and mediated to the nation via informational film.

The expression 'a little land' is, on the face of it, more or less synonymous with the term 'small nation'. While the former, with its pleasing alliteration and assonance in Danish as well as English, resounds through the country's popular discourse, the latter has emerged in the last decade as a crucial concept in the critical analysis of the Danish cinema industry. Pioneering in this respect was Mette Hjort's *Small Nation, Global Cinema: The New Danish Cinema* (2005). With Duncan Petrie, Hjort also edited an anthology of essays entitled *The Cinema of Small Nations* (2007) which uses a range of case studies within Europe and further afield to map out the industrial and institutional specifics of small-nation cinema. The impetus to explore the cinema of small nations stems from an ambition to nuance the persistence of the nation state as an entity in the organisation and study of cinema, in an era where terms such as 'transnational', 'intercultural' and 'world cinema' have proliferated (Hjort and Petrie 2007: 1). The definition of 'small nation' varies across disciplines, emphasising territory or population size, gross national product and history as colonised or coloniser, all of which criteria are complicated by their application to the study of cinema (3–7). The smallness of small nations is necessarily a relative and therefore relational concept; as such, it opens up questions about the advantages and disadvantages of such a status in terms of relative power, visibility, state policy and strategy, the mobility of labour, international relations, language, finance and a wealth of other issues (7–18). Overall, Hjort and Petrie assert that cinema in small nations does not simply function as a scaled-down version of cinema in larger state contexts. Rather, a range of peculiarities pertaining to organisation, practice, strategy and policy can be observed in terms of production and distribution.

In the case of Denmark, Hjort identifies the origins of the New Danish Cinema in a confluence of events in the late 1980s and, particularly, the mid-1990s. These include the Academy awards for Best Foreign Film two years running in 1988 and 1989, for Gabriel Axel's *Babettes gæstebud* (*Babette's Feast*, 1987) and *Pelle Erobreren* (*Pelle the Conqueror*, Bille August, 1987); these awards constituted 'the kind of statistically unimaginable and thus quasi-prophetic event that could truly galvanize an entire milieu and make it an irresistible magnet for film talent' (Hjort 2005: 5). This was the inspirational springboard for a dynamic decade during which key figures including Lars von Trier achieved and exploited global fame to foster a new generation of film expertise at home. Institutions and projects flourished in the mid-1990s, such as von Trier's production company (Zentropa) and Filmbyen (Film Town), launched with Peter Aalbæk-Jensen, the renaissance of screenwriting at the Danish Film School under Mogens Rukov, Lars von Trier and Thomas Vinterberg's collaboration on the internationally lauded Dogme 95 Manifesto and Vow of Chastity, and a revamped and re-organised Danish Film Institute from 1997, with an agenda encouraging high production values, innovation and an inclusive cinephilia (Hjort 2005: 6–12). These factors and many others combined to suggest a blueprint for the cinema of a small nation to survive and indeed thrive in an era of globalisation, technological change and the concomitant 'death of cinema' (Mulvey 2006; Usai 2001). In the Danish case, the role of the state in supporting cinema was transformed over the same period. Two of the strategies which Hjort sees as crucial to the flourishing of the New Danish Cinema in recent years have interesting parallels with the environment in which Dansk Kulturfilm operated. A new Film Act of 1989 effectively decoupled Danishness from the language of the screenplay and the domicile of the cast and crew, opening up new possibilities for creativity and international collaboration. At the same time, the role of the consultants in charge of disbursing state support to film projects was revised: a system of match-funding (50/50 and later 60/40) was introduced, to allow filmmakers to pursue private finance for commercially viable projects, rather than, as had been the tendency, artistically worthy films driven by academic consultants' assumptions about art and heritage (Hjort 2005: 12–13).

While the case studies explored in Hjort (2005) and Hjort and Petrie (2007) focus for the most part on contemporary small-nation cinema – albeit with historical contextualisation as necessary – this book applies aspects of the concept to an earlier period, the 1930s to the 1960s. This move immediately makes apparent a number of differences, as well as continuities, in the realm of film technology – production, distribution and exhibition – as well as in the realm of film policy and the broader socio-political context. These will become apparent in the case studies throughout the book, but they boil down to a set of questions about the relationship between the state and its cinema which haunted film policy and practice in the period 1932 to 1965, just as they have been germane to the more recent 'second golden age' of Danish cinema. These questions include: what makes a film Danish? How should Danish film engage with the outside world? How can it be made attractive to domestic audiences? What should the role of the state be in influencing content and form? Past and present can thus inform each other; just as contemporary small-nation policy and practice in Denmark and elsewhere can help to inform our understanding of the dilemmas and successes of mid-century informational film, so too can looking for continuities and breaches in the historical relationship between cinema and the state enrich our perspective on the recent astonishing success of this small-nation cinema.

A related field in which the behaviour of small Nordic nations has recently been re-assessed is nation branding and public diplomacy. In an introduction to their edited volume on the topic, Clerc and Glover (2015: 4) assert that small nations have a particularly acute and 'intuitive urge to see one's nation through the eyes of others'. This tendency is not narcissistic but driven, at different times, by the need to gain and sustain recognition through national propaganda, to survive and thrive through public diplomacy, and to market the nation and its products in a more commercial sense (Browning 2015: 288). While the means and ends of such activities have changed over time, in the Nordic region the use of some form of public diplomacy to 'curate and promote' the national image abroad has persisted since at least the early twentieth century (Clerc and Glover 2015: 7). This dynamic has not been exclusively government-led; the interest of press and public discourse in the image of the nation abroad has 'spilled over into politics and administration, and has been seen as a major policy challenge worthy of engagement and resources' (8). More precisely, the 'self-perception of being a "small state"' has imbued this cycle with 'a specific dynamic' (9). Small states can be observed to use what Clerc and Glover call a 'toolkit' of cultural diplomacy. Strategies have included the use of networks and diasporas abroad, often single actors with local knowledge who can be construed as 'foreign relations entrepreneurs' (9); we will encounter several of these in this book's case studies. A smaller and more homogeneous population facilitates the crystallisation of '"total", consensual national images' (10), which must be constantly crafted, renegotiated and contested with the public. In the outside world, small Nordic states have often taken advantage of their 'blank canvas' status, whereby they are 'already perceived as innocuous and benign international actors. Small states can be easily imagined as being more dependable, less duplicitous and less imperialistic than their larger counterparts' (11). On the one hand, such images can be difficult to control; on the other, the exploitation of prevailing ideas about a nation abroad can be exploited as leverage and can be used to 'nudge' domestic populations towards new or intensified self-perception (11–12). All of these observations about the perils and opportunities of small-state intervention in the construction of their image at home and abroad are germane to the textual and political strategies adopted by Dansk Kulturfilm. The idea of the 'little land' is an important example of a recurring trope that functions domestically and internationally in many of the ways just described. We now turn to look more closely at how such images have been theorised to travel.

THE MOBILITY OF IMAGES

Anderson's play with Gellner's distinction between 'imagined' and 'imaginary' nations is echoed by Clerc and Glover (2015: 3), who identify a recent turn in politics and international relations from the study of 'imagining' to 'imaging' national communities. They situate this trend in the broader context of the USA's use of '"soft power", "new public diplomacy" and "nation-branding"' in the wake of 9/11. Focusing on Nordic and Baltic case studies, their anthology argues that 'closer historical examination is needed to understand the connections between contemporary practices of external national imaging and the broader cultural and political processes of imagining national community' (Clerc and Glover 2015: 3). They further point out that nation branding has always entailed 'different organisational patterns, varied interplay between external images and self-conceptions, and idiosyncrasies of domestic and foreign policy' (4).

This interest in imaging and its use in public diplomacy is just one example of a tendency within the field of Scandinavian Studies, where interest in the image of the Nordic countries, individually and as a region, has been gathering steam since around the millennium. On the whole, such research has been the genuinely interdisciplinary work that often emerges from language-focused area studies, with anthologies and theme issues drawing on the expertise of human geographers (Jones and Olwig 2008), historians (Andersson and Hilson 2009) and media scholars (Harvard and Stadius 2016). Most scholarly attention has concentrated on Sweden, the largest of the Nordic nations, but research has ranged widely over time and space from, for instance, the role of telegraph networks in the development of mid-nineteenth century pan-Scandinavism to images of blonde bikini-clad Nordic women in South America (Harvard and Stadius 2016).

A key set of concepts in much of this body of work has been the distinction between autostereotypes and xenostereotypes, the discussion of which has been most comprehensively developed in the Nordic context by Kazimierz Musiał in his book *Roots of the Nordic Model* (2002). These are, respectively, images and discourses of a nation or group generated and circulated within that group, and those images that crystallise outside the nation or group they represent. The term 'imagology' has been used in the same context to denote the analysis of 'national and regional stereotype production and reproduction' (Harvard and Stadius 2016); it is images of social formations rather than the social formations themselves that are the focus (whether such social formations exist independently of images of them is a moot point). Auto- and xenostereotypes are, of course, not watertight categories and have a symbiotic or non-linear relationship; as Harvard and Stadius (2016) put it, 'instead of picturing intellectual novelties as rays from one node, researchers are increasingly identifying multi-polarity and reciprocity in the exchange of intellectual influences'. The productive tension between the interrelated dynamics of auto- and xenostereotypes is of particular interest in the study of Dansk Kulturfilm because many of its films were commissioned for either domestic or foreign audiences, but ended up serving both. Such films are interesting examples of the flow and interpenetration of national images and imaginings between domestic and foreign audiences. It is sometimes, but not always, clear from the production files of Dansk Kulturfilm's output that (some) functionaries and filmmakers were aware of the distinctions between the various auto- and xenostereotypes on which they were drawing. Some films were edited when different language versions were made, but this, as we shall see, was the exception rather than the rule. The films are thus a node where 'the ostensible distinction between the depoliticised and strategic imaging of the nation abroad and the political process of imagining and forging the nation at home' (Clerc and Glover 2015: 8) emerges as, precisely, ostensible.

Also relevant to the current study is the role of the state and other stakeholders in using media to harness existing xenostereotypes and kick-start new ones for the purpose of nation branding. This concept has piqued scholarly and popular interest in Denmark in recent years (Mordhorst 2015; Ren and Gyimóthy 2013). Nation branding tends to be assumed to be a 'late modern' manifestation of an older set of phenomena constituting the soft power 'toolkit' of small nations, 'a way to inject a dose of legitimate, modern corporate ethos into a basically state-coordinated process' (Clerc and Glover 2015: 18). Many of the case studies in this book are suggestive of continuities between contemporary nation branding and older practices referred to in their time as 'cultural diplomacy' or even 'propaganda', despite the different media landscapes which the strategies have to navigate. What I want to suggest here, as do Clerc and Glover (2015: 20), is that by historicising cognate practices of soft power, cultural diplomacy, propaganda and nation branding, we nuance our understanding of how nations are imaged and imagined in ways that are specific to, but also transcend, shifting political environments and media cultures.

A particular concern for Harvard and Stadius is the materiality of what they call 'imagological discourses' and, in particular, the material conditions of their movement:

> The idea of nationalism would not have come into being without the
> Romantic philosophers, nor would it have had the enormous impact it

had without steamships, railways, telegraphs and printing presses. The same applies to images, which, as ideas and perceptions, need to be documented and thus materialized in the form of 'goods' that can be passed on through the channels of communication. (Harvard and Stadius 2016)

As will be explained in more depth in Chapter 3, but is perhaps already clear from the foregoing discussion of medium-specificity, I share this concern with the material instantiation of images and narratives. For the most part, this is a matter of the physical properties of the films themselves, but it also extends to the means by which they are produced, stored, transported, exhibited, preserved and restored. My thinking in this respect has been influenced by Stephen Greenblatt's 'Mobility Studies Manifesto'. Greenblatt argues that 'the glacial weight of what appears bounded and static' in culture is always a tale of movement (Greenblatt 2010: 252). This mobility must be taken literally:

Only when conditions directly related to literal movement are firmly grasped will it be possible fully to understand the metaphorical movements: between center and periphery; faith and skepticism; order and chaos; exteriority and interiority. Almost every one of these metaphorical movements will be understood, on analysis, to involve some kinds of physical movement as well. (Greenblatt 2010: 250)

Greenblatt urges scholars of culture to investigate '*hidden as well as conspicuous movements* of peoples, objects, images, texts and ideas' (250); to look for culturally and historically specific zones of contact and the 'mobilizers' who facilitate cultural exchanges; and to pay attention to the tension between '*individual agency and structural constraint*' (251, emphases in original). The films of Dansk Kulturfilm, then, are mobile as images, concepts and material objects, and their movement is caught up in a more complex field of mobility of filmmakers, functionaries, practices, styles, reviews, documents, soundtracks and filmmaking technologies. We now move on to consider a set of concepts which can help to tame this dynamic complexity without simplifying it.

3. MAPPING MESSINESS:
THE INFORMATIONAL FILM ARCHIVE
AND ACTOR-NETWORK THEORY

In the introduction to his book *After Method*, John Law provocatively asks 'what happens when social science tries to describe things that are complex, diffuse and messy'? His equally provocative answer is that 'it tends to make a mess of it' (Law 2004: 2). Law is one of the founders of Actor-Network Theory, an approach to the sociology of science and other complex systems. As another founder, Bruno Latour, has famously joked, Actor-Network Theory is 'a name that is so awkward, so confusing, so meaningless that it deserves to be kept' (Latour 2005: 9).

As a means of giving voice to all the elements and agents involved in the production of *kulturfilm* in Denmark, in this chapter I draw on Actor-Network Theory (ANT) to help tame and structure the relations between them. This book is, to my knowledge, the first sustained, in-depth analysis of a national case study in useful cinema; as such, the density of information involved requires a more thoroughgoing organisational principle than do the individual chapter-length case studies that have thus far defined the field. In adopting ANT as an approach to the material, I also want to contribute to developing the tool kit currently available to scholars of useful cinema. However, this book does not adopt ANT wholesale; it is used here as a way of thinking rather than a theory. For Latour, inclusion in a notional corpus of ANT research is not determined by terminology, methodology or even explicit allegiance. Rather, there are three litmus tests: the extension of the notion of 'actor' to encompass a role for non-humans that is more than causal or symbolic; secondly, an unsettling of the stable notion of the social; and thirdly, a commitment to re-assembling the social (Latour 2005: 10–11).

My intention is not to burden the story of Dansk Kulturfilm with the dead-weight of theory, but to adopt a mode of thinking that pays adequate attention to the role of things as well as people in conjuring up films from the decisions of a committee. Accordingly, in this book, the author, the archives and their documents, the offices and committees associated with Dansk Kulturfilm, the commissioning bodies, the filmmakers, the distributors, the viewers, the tech-nologies of film, the film texts and a myriad of material phenomena caught up in the process – all are woven into a narrative which tries, nonetheless, to remain a very human story. The story is all the more human, I venture, because of the non-human things, the gear heavy and light, that accompany us on the way.

This chapter first gives an overview of the tenets of ANT and their appli-cability to the study of film and media in general and the informational film in particular – including the limits of that applicability. I then introduce the network of actors around Dansk Kulturfilm: the institutions, the technologies, and finally, the archive and the papers, films and humans it houses.

ANT AND THE INFORMATIONAL FILM

ANT is an increasingly popular but still controversial tool in Science and Technology Studies, Business Studies, Tourism Studies and other branches of Sociology and Human Geography which need to account for complex rela-tional fields. The approach was developed from the mid-1980s by Latour and Law, amongst others, as a descriptive practice that sees the world relationally and non-hierarchically, and refuses dualisms such as material versus semiotic, nature versus culture, human versus non-human. Importantly, ANT is also concerned with how 'facts' and 'truth-values' are constructed and travel. These tenets grow out of the original purpose of ANT, which was to explain how scientists produce scientific facts (Gershon 2010: 161).

Bruno Latour provides an introduction to ANT as it developed over the previous two to three decades in his book *Reassembling the Social* (2005). The first part of the book is structured around a series of 'sources of uncertainty', all of which have the aim of breaking down the concept of the 'social' as under-stood in sociology. The first of these is the precept that the many social groups that are taken for granted as building blocks of 'society' should be jettisoned in favour of tracing group formation; 'social aggregates are constantly evoked, erased, distributed, and reallocated' in often contradictory ways (Latour 2005: 41). As outlined in Chapters 1 and 2, the case studies in this book try to trace the shifting and contested formations of 'Danishness' that are renegotiated in the pre-production processes and in the viewers' encounter with Dansk Kulturfilm's informational films.

The second 'source of uncertainty' is concerned with agency, warning against essentialising the social as a force or adopting a meta-language of social explanation to explain who or what is acting in a given situation (Latour 2005: 52–5). Nick Couldry argues that ANT's value for Media Studies lies in its hostility to monolithic notions of the social. It offers the potential to challenge a dangerous tendency in Media Studies: to equate media with the social and thus to render it invisible or mystical, effacing 'the vast linkage of networks that make up the media process' (Couldry 2008: 97–8). This is one reason why, argues Couldry, ANT has not achieved the sustained link with Media Studies that would constitute a stable network, the kind of stable network that acquires the 'force of nature' that ANT describes as a 'black box' (93).

The question of who or what is acting and has agency in any process is where the term 'actant' comes into play, and this term is central to the next uncertainty, which declares that it is not only humans who act: 'objects too have agency' (Latour 2005: 63). This principle is both sufficiently outlandish and sufficiently important for this book to dwell on at relative length here.

Making Objects Talk

A controversial but fundamental tenet of ANT is its refusal to adhere to dualisms such as human/non-human, culture/nature, technology/society or material/ semiotic. For Latour, human society must be understood to be held together not just by 'social ties' but also by tools, artefacts and other material things appropriated by humans to consolidate and develop social structures. This aspect of ANT has been controversial and often misrepresented as attributing agency to the non-sentient world. Broadening the category of 'participants' in any action or situation does not, as Latour jokes, 'designate little goblins with red hats acting at atomic levels' (Latour 2005: 72); rather, it suggests that

> there might exist many metaphysical shades between full causality and sheer inexistence. In addition to 'determining' and 'serving as a backdrop for human action', things might authorize, allow, afford, encourage, permit, suggest, influence, block, render possible, forbid, and so on. (72)

Thus for ANT, agency in any network is distributed as widely as possible, amongst non-human actors as well as human agents. This is a counter-intuitive approach to agency, for it breaks its association with consciousness. Latour coins the term 'actant' for this purpose, expanding participation (described using verbs such as those in the passage above) to matter and forces from microbes to machines. For our purposes, this means that factors as wide-ranging as weather, laws, film stock and mechanical breakdown emerge as influential in the ongoing process of filmmaking.

Latour uses the metaphor of 'talking' to describe what happens when we pay attention to the non-human actors in a network. Objects are silent and unaccountable unless a trace of their intervention is recorded:

> Objects, by the very nature of their connections with humans, quickly shift from being mediators to being intermediaries, counting for one or nothing, no matter how internally complicated they might be. This is why specific tricks have to be invented to make them talk, that is, to offer descriptions of themselves, to produce scripts of what they are making others – humans or non-humans – do. (Latour 2005: 79)

He suggests a series of tricks that can be employed to make objects talk, some of which are very relevant to the matters, and the matter, we will be dealing with in this book. The first trick is to pick out innovations to analyse, because these leave traces through meetings, plans, sketches and trials (Latour 2005: 80). The second is to look for distance from the analyst in terms of time, culture or skills. When we look for distance, he argues, we come face to face with 'the irruption into the normal course of action of strange, exotic, archaic, or mysterious implements. In these encounters, objects become mediators, at least for a while, before soon disappearing again through know-how, habituation, or disuse' (80). A third and similar move is to pay attention to accidents, breakdowns, strikes and risks. Here, he offers the compelling example of an accident on a building site, and the chaos which ensues, in which 'even objects, which a minute before appeared fully automatic, autonomous, and devoid of human agents, are now made of crowds of frantically moving humans with heavy equipment' (81). A more challenging way to defamiliarise objects is to use archives, museums and historical documents in order to 'artificially produce, through historians' accounts, the state of crisis in which machines, devices, and implements were born' (81). A final trick is to resort to mining fiction, but only as a last resort. Literary, filmic and other imaginative texts characterised by 'counterfactual history, thought experiments, and "scientification"' (82) can render taken-for-granted objects and their relations with humans fluid and strange once more.

Latour's box of tricks provides ample scope for thinking through the significance of artefacts of various kinds in this study. As a general rule, I have allowed objects to 'irrupt' into the narrative where they emerge in the archives as exemplars of Latour's first category, the innovation, or his third, the breakdown or strike. The project as a whole is based on the second trick, distance from our contemporary film culture in terms of historical time, culture and skills. The reliance of the project on archival production files and similar documents repeatedly allows for a sense of distance and even bemusement at 'the state of crisis in which machines, devices and implements were born'.

Latour's final trick is particularly interesting in that our central object of study is *kulturfilm*. Whether a given case study explores a documentary, a 'film of fact' or a fictionalised informational film, the very purpose of most of these films (the reason for their commissioning) is to explore and mediate some kind of innovation or breakdown, or to defamiliarise and present anew to the population some kind of collective practice. This means that the film texts themselves, in different ways in our contemporary context and in their own time, perform Latour's fifth trick and render loquacious the objects and systems they explore.

The operation of non-human objects in documentary films is a key concern for film scholars Ilana Gershon and Joshua Malitsky (2010). They offer the example of misbehaving microphones in two documentaries about Fidel Castro to illustrate how objects intervene in and impact on historical events. They conclude that 'thinking about actants means thinking about the pro-filmic space of representation differently' (Gershon and Malitsky 2010: 73). I push this point further, beyond the pro-filmic space, to encompass attention to how non-human matter is caught up in the networks that generate films.

Latour also insists that we pay attention to the differences between actants, or their historical contingency. These differences are effects of historical and social forces, but also a function of their materiality. While matter shapes and limits how a thing can act, conversely, matter also 'condenses social assumptions', as Gershon (2010: 165) puts it. Things are formed as they are because of historical and social relations. A hat 'condenses' historical relationships of manufacture, exchange and use (163). ANT would ask where the fabric and other materials used to make the hat came from, which tools and skills were used in its fabrication, how it was moved from factory to consumer, in what circumstances it is worn and how it will age. Building on the hat as an example, Gershon goes on to summarise how these investigations identify the constituent elements of the ANT acronym:

> Hats, people, trains, everything in the world condenses a specific set of heterogeneous relationships, and then interacts with other condensations of different sets of heterogeneous relationships. Actors are condensed bits of a network; networks are fashioned through the interactions of actors. (Gershon 2010: 164)

Turning to the informational film, we can say that the film is a 'condensed bit of a network'. The network might include, but not be limited to, the individual or institution that commissions the film project, the document in which the remit is recorded, the whisky sipped by the filmmaker in her summer house as she drafts the screenplay by hand, the telegram confirming funding, the aeroplane wheel that hits a camera primed to film its take-off, the portable 16mm projector borrowed from the local library, the sports club that organises the screening, the Eastman colour film stock that renders the master copy unusable due to magenta shift. All these actors crop up in the case studies in this book, though not all in the same one. That 16mm copy of the ten-minute film, in turn, 'condenses' a set of technological practices and material properties, as well as a range of assumptions and constraints having to do with audience attention span, available funding, costs of transport and projection facilities.

Not all actants are equal. This can be a question of how many other networks an actant is connected with; tracing these asymmetries can serve as a means of analysing power relations and privilege in a network. How actants affect networks and vice versa is also a concern of ANT. For Latour, all actants are to some extent mediators of a network, though some have more impact on the network than others: 'networks are chains of mediators, in which knowledge and networks alter a little through every node through which they flow' (Gershon 2010: 168). Theoretically, actants could exist that do not affect a network at all, and these are termed 'intermediaries'. In his preface to a recent anthology of critical essays and case studies surveying the territory, Markus Spöhrer muses that ANT was 'predestined' as a hermeneutic in Media Studies because the idea of mediation is built into the model: the negotiation and communication between actors and a network is conceptualised as occurring via 'mediators'. So too do several of the classic early studies in the field rely heavily on forms of media such as scientific referencing systems and other forms of inscription (Spöhrer 2016: xiv).

Latour has developed concepts to describe the effects of network relations on actants themselves. 'Immutable mobiles' circulate through a network without themselves being changed by it (maps, graphs), while 'black boxes' coalesce as immutable but conceal the relations that have served to form them. These concepts are particularly useful in thinking about how films circulate as actants in the networks described in this book. Finished films can be regarded as black boxes in the sense that they conceal the multifarious relations involved in their production to circulate as discrete works. Nevertheless, they still have the capacity to interact with the network in that they may be versionised in additional languages or inspire new productions.

MATTERS OF FACT

Latour's fourth source of uncertainty deals with 'matters of fact'. ANT originated amongst sociologists who embedded themselves within science labs and other such institutions to observe how facts were constructed by processes and procedures. The notion that facts could be constructed was not received kindly by the scientists and other colleagues, explains Latour, because 'constructed' was conflated with 'fabricated' (2005: 90), a false dichotomy reminiscent of the confusion between 'imagined' and 'imaginary' nations discussed in Chapter 2.

Precisely because of this concern with matters of fact, it has been argued that ANT is of particular use for understanding the operation of documentary film. Gershon and Malitsky (2010) apply a range of key ANT concepts to documentary as practice, process and product. The documentary itself can be regarded as one actant in a much more complex network encompassing its production, distribution and reception and all the actants and interactions involved along the way. Gershon and Malitsky draw a parallel between the labour of documentary – how the film performs the sleight of hand of rendering the world as it is – to the establishment of a network in ANT. Both are predicated on recreating or performing apparently stable, cohesive and sustained relationships (Gershon and Malitsky 2010: 68). Accordingly, they conclude that the ANT perspective on documentaries would involve 'refusing sharp distinctions between documentary production, distribution and reception, and instead seeing all aspects as central to how documentaries themselves function as actants and representations' (75).

While this principle could potentially be applied to any film or other media object, it is particularly fertile in the case of documentary because of the truth claims of the genre. A documentary's 'truth-value' and authority is constructed not only by the text itself but from the network conditions in which it is made and circulates (Gershon and Malitsky 2010: 75). The 'facts' with which documentaries are concerned are outcomes of the networks which produce the films and in which they circulate. The idea that social relationships are condensed by matter poses a particularly acute set of problematics for documentary scholars. The truth-value of a documentary cannot be divorced from its circulation and exhibition: 'to understand how information comes to be interpreted as facts entails understanding the processes of circulation underpinning how facts are made' (69).

The Danish *kulturfilm* (and its cognate genres) is closely related to documentary but defined by the presence of a commissioning body. The construction of 'fact' in the *kulturfilm* is thus a function of the tension between the interests of the commissioning body, the strategies of the filmmaker and the contexts of encounter with its various audiences. Crucially, this requires engaging with the film texts themselves as one element of meaning-making in a complex network of what ANT calls 'actants': actors in the process, not all of which have consciousness or volition. Accordingly, this book tries to pay attention to some of the many non-human actants that influence the process of filmmaking and the film texts themselves.

ANT and Film Studies

On the other hand, a significant weakness of ANT in relation to Media and Cultural Studies is that it cannot easily account for one of the concerns of humanistic, textual analysis: what happens after a network has been established or, more precisely, 'the acts of interpretation and attachment' that arise out of the encounter of a viewer, reader or listener with the film or novel or piece of music that has emerged from a network (Couldry 2008: 103). Nick Couldry thus concludes that ANT is a useful part of the media analyst's toolkit, but not in isolation from other critical theory that can better account for asymmetries of power and interpretive or affective response. I am also drawn to this middle ground.

Moreover, ANT has been criticised for not paying sufficient attention to differentials of power in society, such as gender and race. Couldry diagnoses the apparent blindness to asymmetries of power in ANT as linked to its insistence that humans do not have the monopoly on agency:

> Power differentials between human actors matter in a way that power differentials (if that is the right term) between non-humans do not: they have social consequences that are linked to how these differences are interpreted and how they affect the various agents' ability to have their interpretations of the world stick. ANT has much to contribute to understanding the 'how' of such asymmetries, but it is strangely silent when it comes to assessing whether, and why, they matter. (Couldry 2008: 102)

Latour specifies that 'it is just because we wish to *explain* those asymmetries that we don't want to simply *repeat* them – and even less to *transport* them further unmodified' (Latour 2005: 63, emphasis in original). This echoes my point in Chapter 1 about taking seriously the operation of institutional power by accepting and working with its messiness. The institutions explored in this book can be seen to exemplify the usefulness of not assuming that 'power' obtains as a pre-existing entity, lurking somewhere behind the scenes. The institutional and procedural messiness demonstrated in many of this book's case studies support Latour's assertion that 'power, like society, is the final result of a process and not a reservoir, a stock, or a capital that will automatically provide an explanation. Power and domination have to be produced, made up, composed' (64).

Dansk Kulturfilm: Institutions and Actors

From Chapter 4 onwards, the establishment and development of the institutions central to informational film in Denmark will be related in broadly chronological terms, as they become relevant to the films and sub-genres under discussion, each of which functions as a distinct prism in the broader institutional landscape. Here, however, I try to map out the institutional actants in the network of Danish informational film in a fairly atemporal way. The map is necessarily partial and selective, but is intended as an introduction to what is at times a bewildering network of nodes or stakeholders.

Dansk Kulturfilm functioned from 1932 until the mid-1960s as a semi-governmental agency responsible for facilitating the production of films commissioned by government ministries and popular associations. It did not undertake the film production process; this was farmed out to a wide variety of film production companies. However, Dansk Kulturfilm generally did appoint filmmakers to write, shoot and edit the films.

As we shall see in Chapter 4, Dansk Kulturfilm was occasionally referred to as 'the cooperative store of the film world' because its Board consisted of a plethora of representatives of *foreninger*, the local and national associations representing interest groups of every shape and size from gymnastics to tourism in Denmark. *Foreninger* were, and remain, a fundamental building block of Danish civic society. Their role in the constitution of Dansk Kulturfilm reflects the status of their members as a primary audience for the films and in turn is indicative of the function of the informational film as continuing education in mid-twentieth-century Denmark, a role consonant with the strong tradition of self-improvement via the folk high school movement founded a century earlier (see Borish 2004). An important sub-genre of the Danish informational film was the so-called *foreningsfilm*, film commissioned by and/or made specifically with club screenings and discussions in mind.

Ministeriernes Filmudvalg, known as the Danish Government Film Committee in international contexts and referred to as MFU in this book, was a government committee established during the German occupation of Denmark, initially to commission films required by various ministries to promote employment, rational use of raw materials and the war effort generally. After the war it was retained as a sister institution to Dansk Kulturfilm; the two functioned more or less in parallel and at times shared an administration, despite Dansk Kulturfilm's semi-governmental status. A range of government ministries were represented on the MFU committee; for most of its existence, its budget was controlled by the Justice Ministry (Justitsministeriet).

The work of Dansk Kulturfilm and MFU was supported and sometimes disrupted by a network of consultants and advisors with subject-specific expertise. Many of these were civil servants, but others came from *foreninger*, professional associations or academia. At points where their intellectual and sometimes more material labour in shaping the films encounters the expertise of filmmakers, we witness the productive friction generated by the translation of ideas into images.

Statens Filmcentral, the Danish Film Centre, usually referred to as SFC in this book, was the distribution agency operating in close – though not always smooth – coordination with Dansk Kulturfilm and MFU. SFC also acquired and distributed informational and educational films from other countries for its film library. SFC hired out films to a wide range of associations and clubs, schools, libraries and other screening venues across Denmark, and was able to hire out projectors, projectionists and related equipment. Some local libraries had projectors on permanent loan and rotating stocks of films. Libraries, union halls, museums, schools and a practically infinite range of other venues and organisations are thus also caught up in the network. The head of SFC, Ebbe Neergaard (1901–57), also undertook educational work on cinema, holding lectures and workshops at a range of venues around Denmark, often at folk high schools.

The Press Bureau of the Foreign Ministry (Udenrigsministeriets Pressebureau) was primarily responsible for the distribution of Danish films overseas, for collating information about their reception, and for liaising with embassies and consulates. Beyond the diplomatic service itself, film festivals, international cultural organisations, exhibition curators, businesspeople, the diplomatic entrepreneurs mentioned in Chapter 2 and many others were thus also involved in the circulation of some films overseas.

Informational films were not exclusively screened in non-theatrical spaces. Many had a theatrical run in Denmark and/or abroad, usually before they were released for hire via SFC. Thus the agency of Danish cinema managers, distribution companies at home and overseas, and cinema audiences can be witnessed in our case studies to influence several films even at the pre-production stage. Dansk Kulturfilm operated its own cinema, Toftegaard Bio, for some years as a source of income.

Coming back full circle to film production, we encounter the filmmakers themselves, as well as production companies. Several filmmakers owned or worked for their own companies; most were polymaths, in the sense that they would be skilled screenwriters, camera operators and editors, amongst other areas of expertise. Different constellations of filmmakers and writers are seen to collaborate in different ways across our case studies. They were also organised into a union, Dansk Filmforbund, from 1947.

It should start to be apparent, then, how this complex network of actants produced informational films in all senses of the word: produced them as texts, as reels and as a concept. Informational films become informational films as and when the network crystallises – differently in different places at different times. This is as much a matter of matter as it is of travelling concepts. The physical instantiation of the informational films facilitates and indeed materialises their informational function; it is possible because of the portability and duplicability of 16mm film stock and projectors, but the same format condenses a host of institutional knowledge, practices and assumptions about audience attention span, interlingual translation, the public value of culture and much else. All aspects of the films' production, distribution, reception and circulation are 'central to how documentaries themselves function as actants and representations' (Gershon and Malitsky 2010: 75). Two crucial actants in the network remain to be discussed, however, and these stretch the network into the present day: the archive and the researcher.

ARCHIVE FEVER: THE RESEARCHER IN THE NETWORK

ANT insists that the researcher must locate herself within the tapestry of actants in any network under investigation, 'reflexively accounting for how [her] own analytical labour contributes to the ways the network operates' (Gershon and Malitsky 2010: 75). Elsaesser makes the more playful point that the 'why', 'how', and 'by whom' of industrial films can be so seductive and consequential for scholars that they will undertake 'ruinously expensive' and potentially endless tours into the hinterlands of such films in an often fruitless attempt to answer such research questions (Elsaesser 2009: 23–4). For example, of his work at the British Film Institute, Patrick Russell (2013: 417) offers the disclaimer: 'a project such as this is born of twin sensibilities: one archival, analytic, evidence-based; the other curatorial, excitedly animated and, no doubt, a little romantic and sentimental. Both sensibilities are valid and no apologies are offered for either.' Attached to the Danish Film Institute while I researched this book, I was soon transformed into what my Danish colleagues playfully called an *arkivrotte* (archive rat), nesting behind piles of seventy-year-old committee minutes and scampering from cupboard to cupboard in search of the latest morsel of newsprint. As I dived deeper and deeper into the archive, the volume of carefully typed and filed information was as overwhelming as the knowledge of the gaps in between, of everything not preserved: the decisive conversations over coffee, the last-minute production decisions on set. Some film reels had been well preserved or even digitised, but no documentation had survived; more often, I had access to a wealth of background information but not to the film itself.

Jacques Derrida (1996) wrote of the *mal d'archive* – *mal* as in both fever and evil. As Carolyn Steedman has pointed out, from the English translation of the title of Derrida's little book, *Archive Fever*, we get only the insatiable, feverish searching of the historian in the archive and none of the sin or evil of the infinitely larger archive that is the history of state power. In both senses, this *mal* is about a compulsion to search for origins. In her discussion of Derrida's text, Steedman offers a poignant account of how 'archive fever' is brought on by the tension between the everyday minutiae on one's desk and the more abstract answers for which one is searching:

> Your anxiety is that you will not finish, that there will be something left unread, unnoted, untranscribed. You are not anxious about the Great Unfinished, knowledge of which is the very condition of your being there in the first place, and of the grubby trade you set out in, years ago. You know perfectly well that despite the infinite heaps of things they recorded, the notes and traces that these people left behind, it is in fact, practically nothing at all. There is the great, brown, slow-moving strandless river of Everything, and then there is its tiny flotsam that has ended up in the record office you are working in. (Steedman 2001: 1165)

For Steedman, the metaphorical fever turned out to be a real illness, and she goes on to examine the dangers, real and imagined, of breathing in the dust and bacteria that lurk in the archival files. In Denmark, the folders, like the storage rooms, are reassuringly clean. Similarly, it must be said that if the Dansk Kulturfilm archive is the repository of state power, it reveals that power to be a most innocuous (and perhaps therefore insidious) kind of bumbling, messy power that neither articulates clear strategies for its films nor makes serious attempts to evaluate their impacts.

Because they worked in the service of the state, the entities and agents central to this study left a trail for the researcher to follow in the National Archives (Rigsarkivet) and in the archives of the Danish Film Institute. From around the end of the Second World War, films trail behind them files of material, some fat, some thin, revealing much detail about their production. These originated in the joint administrative office of Dansk Kulturfilm and MFU, and were transferred to SFC when that institution outlived the productive life of the other two from the mid-1960s. Physically, the records are distributed between Rigsarkivet (the national archives) and the DFI. They contain various combinations of correspondence between the agencies, the commissioning bodies and the filmmakers, treatments and screenplay drafts, relevant newspaper clippings, press releases, screening invitations, details of the film's circulation and reception, and various other treasures. There are also catalogues, annual reports, boxes and scrapbooks of clippings, stills, photographs and posters. It is in these files that the film can be seen to emerge out of the tension between the interests of different actors. It is also in these files that the work of non-human actants often makes itself felt: weather, car breakdowns, misbehaving film stock, typographical errors.

Thus far, I have described the archive as resolutely papery. And yet this is a book about films – at least ostensibly. In a sense, it is a book about the archive that is its condition of possibility – both the records archive and the film archive. Had it been researched and written a few years earlier or later, it would have been a very different book, for it is a product of a transitional period, somewhere on the analogue/digital cusp. When I began my research,

I was labouring under the assumption that my eventual selection of film case studies would be driven by the relative richness of the production histories, and that any archived shorts not currently digitised could be viewed in the film archive. This would have been possible, given enough time and funding, but I eventually shaped my 'short list' according to the availability of films via digital platforms. In part, this was for pragmatic reasons: to maximise the chances of the films being available to the future reader. The digitised files were available to me through four interfaces: the DFI's internal database, Psilander; its public-facing platform, Filmdatabasen at dfi.dk; a new website for schools and libraries with a Danish IP address, Filmcentralen.dk (to which we will return in the Conclusion); and digital movie files.

But the decision to 'go digital' also seemed consistent with my critical-theoretical approach to the material. In *From Grain to Pixel: The Archival Life of Film in Transition* (2011), Giovanna Fossati brings the turn-of-the-millennium philosophical anxieties about the ontological difference between analogue and digital film into conversation with archival and restoration practice. One of her concerns is how different film archives and other institutions undertaking film restoration conceive of the status of the digital objects produced as the output or by-product of restoration. One possible framework for digitised films offered by Fossati is to re-work the idea of the *dispositif*, as in the apparatus theory developed by Baudry (1986) and later adapted by Kessler (2006).[1] Fossati observes that while some *cinemathèques* prefer to privilege and even reconstruct the original screening conditions of films, an alternative approach is to accept that films continue dynamically to find new modes of circulation and exhibition, new encounters with the viewer on new kinds of screens, when digitally instantiated. For example, 'a silent film viewed on an iPod should not be seen as a historical falsification but rather as one of the many possible *dispositifs* that can take shape' (Fossati 2011: 127). Allowing the films covered in this project to enter into new *dispositifs* with me as researcher and with other viewers, whether or not in conjunction with this book is, I want to suggest, entirely in line with their original remit. Most circulated in a number of different formats, in multiple languages, and for audiences that were as unpredictable as the spaces in which they were screened; many of them were transferred to VHS for ongoing hire to schools, before being scrapped in the 1980s. To say that the films lent themselves to a kaleidoscope of *dispositifs* is another way of saying that they entered into networks where some of the actants were a wide range of different kinds of viewers, screens and ancillary equipment. Again, the archive is also caught up in this dynamic pattern of circulation:

> The institutional framing of the archive would also be one to look at carefully, not only for the ways it should or could re-present films in terms of dispositifs, but also for all the dispositifs that it has produced throughout

the years while carrying out its tasks of preserving, restoring and showing film heritage. (Fossati 2011: 127)

When I looked up from the screen or the production files, I was surrounded by another dimension of the archive: the flesh-and-blood archive, the institutional knowledge personified in the people around me, the DFI's archivists and researchers, who were always willing to share what they knew over a cup of coffee. Like the aroma of coffee (or the occasional fifty-year-old coffee stain on a document), affects are also to be found in the archive and thus in the network. For example, annoyance leaves its traces in the carefully controlled wording of the letters. In one case, an irate letter from Sweden seemed to have been typed with such vehemence that the umlauts on the Swedish letters had bored through the paper. Another file contained a jokey drawing in red crayon of two Danish flags side by side, one at half mast, the other fluttering high. From time to time, an unexpected find would provoke a giggle, a wave of fascinated joy, or a lurch in the stomach at a sudden connection made. Before I left Copenhagen at the end of my stay, I had a keen desire to visit the graves of some of the people whose letters and films I had spent so much time with. Affects such as these have also left their traces on the book produced by this network.

NOTE

1. Fossati adopts the approach called SCOT or Social Construction of Technology for her analysis of how archives and archivists work. She explains that she has chosen not to adopt ANT because of its attribution of a form of agency to non-human actors (Fossati 2011: 273 n131).

4. THE FILM WORLD'S COOPERATIVE STORE: INSTITUTIONS AND FILMS OF THE 1930S AND 1940S

The title of this chapter comes from a remark by Dansk Kulturfilm's first director, Thomas P. Hejle, that Dansk Kulturfilm's constitution as the film-making agency for a sprawling union of societies and governmental and non-governmental interest groups was reminiscent of the very Danish tradition of cooperative organisation of farming and other industries. A profoundly pragmatic means of organising labour, production and insurance, the coopera-tive movement is also a compelling metaphor for Hejle and for our discussion, predicated as it is on the notion of a network in which all actants are co-dependent. Indeed, the cooperative movement was the focus of a 1952 *kultur-film* for the anglophone market directed by Theodor Christensen, *The Pattern of Cooperation.*[1] However, before we can consider the fully fledged output of this institutional network as it crystallises in the mid-1940s, we need to under-stand the tentative and exploratory beginnings of the institutions themselves, the films they produced and their archival traces (or lack of the same).

Taking a broadly chronological approach to how Dansk Kulturfilm crystal-lised as one of a set of institutions in the decade from 1932, this chapter makes excursions to consider a selection of the filmic output of its early years. These case studies illustrate the 'messiness', as discussed in Chapter 3, of working with archival informational films, not least in our encounter with two of Dansk Kulturfilm's earliest productions, films for which no production records are available. These are contextualised by a short detour to consider a canoni-cal Danish *kulturfilm* of the same period, not made under Dansk Kulturfilm's auspices: Poul Henningsen's *Danmark* (1935). An important institutional and artistic turning point for state-sponsored filmmaking in Denmark comes during the German occupation of the country: the establishment of Ministeriernes Filmudvalg (the Danish Government Film Committee) under Mogens Skot-Hansen, which harnessed a new generation of Danish filmmakers deeply influenced by the international, and especially British, documentary movement. Two of their occupation-era films are examined as examples of the early output of the now twin agencies, Dansk Kulturfilm and MFU. The entanglement of this generation of filmmakers with the Danish Resistance, and thereby with contacts on the other side of the North Sea, sets the scene for the post-war flourishing of informational film with which the rest of this book is concerned.

THE INSTITUTIONAL DEVELOPMENT OF DANSK KULTURFILM

Dansk Kulturfilm was incorporated as a company in 1932 by a small knot of entrepreneurs. Its remit was laid down as follows:

> § 1: 'Dansk Kulturfilm,' which is located in Copenhagen, is established August 30th 1932 with the purpose of working for the promotion of films which serve the advancement of teaching and enlightenment or of general propaganda for Denmark or Danish business. (Dansk Kulturfilm, 1933)

The institution's proposed work in procuring educational films, distributing them to schools and training teachers in their use is subsequently detailed in § 2. Only then does the text specify that 'the institution works for the promotion of cultural film [*kulturfilm*], including through the exhibition of films in associations and institutions'. In § 3, it is specified that films should focus on 'Danish nature, literature, history and other areas of culture'.

It seems likely that *kulturfilm* already existed as a concept in Denmark in the early 1930s, because the business name had to be bought from a pre-existing small company (Nørrested and Alsted 1987: 113). While the term has no obvious equivalent in English, it comes direct from an established German genre. The year or so between the establishment of Dansk Kulturfilm as a company in 1932 and its being co-opted by the state to fulfil the recognised need for *oplysningsfilm* in 1933 coincided with Adolf Hitler's elevation to the office of German Chancellor. However, the embarrassing conceptual origins of Dansk Kulturfilm in the Italian and German iterations of the tradition were quickly absorbed into an organisation whose structure was based on the voluntarist and collectivist Danish pattern of national organisations and institutions and other interested parties: 'from flirting with fascist-inspired models of cultural mediation, Dansk Kulturfilm was now established as a typically Danish and in many ways Social Democratic film institution' (Nørrested and Alsted 1987: 119). First and foremost, this is a function of the obvious differences between political regimes of the 1930s in the countries concerned: the *kulturfilm* in Denmark served to propagate and even shape the values of the nascent welfare state, rather than National Socialism. Crucial to this enterprise is the transformation of the agency into a very democratic *sammenslutning* (union) (Dansk Kulturfilm 1966: 1), and therefore referred to in jest by its first director, actor and educationalist Thomas P. Hejle (1891–1952), as 'the film world's co-operative store' (Nørrested and Alsted 1987: 117).

Of crucial importance for this transformation was the engagement of Prime Minister Thorvald Stauning (1873–1942) in the issue of the constitution of Dansk Kulturfilm. Stauning encouraged the nascent agency to appoint to its Board representatives of the Social Democratic Women's Association and of the various Ministries that already availed themselves of film (Nørrested and Alsted 1987: 116–17). By March 1934 an expanded Board of Representatives welcomed members from organisations such as the Association of Folk High Schools and Agricultural Colleges, the Danish Women's Society, and the Danish Tourism Association (Nørrested and Alsted 1987: 117–18).

The overall effect was to transform both the composition and the focus of Dansk Kulturfilm. It was now under the direct influence of ministries and the myriad associations whose members would be the end-users of its films: 'an independent institution with a broad popular basis' (Koch-Olsen 1957c: 9). While awaiting confirmation of government funding in summer 1936, founding member H. Andersen embarked on the production of a small number of educational films, armed only with a minimal budget and a newly purchased camera.

EARLY PROCESS FILMS

Both dating from 1936 and shot by educationalist and amateur filmmaker H. Andersen himself, Dansk Kulturfilm's earliest productions, *Kødbyen* (*The Meat District*) and *Hvorledes en Mursten bliver til* (*How a Brick is Made*) are examples of process films, a genre with a pedigree stretching back to the earliest days of the moving image. Using simple visual techniques and explanatory intertitles and animations, each film painstakingly tracks the stages of, respectively, the slaughter and processing of livestock for meat, and the production of a building brick. If the stories told by these films are linear and comprehensive, the narrative of their production and distribution is anything but.

One of Dansk Kulturfilm's founders, H. Andersen had been a prolific filmmaker in the 1910s, documenting Denmark's industry and crafts (Nørrested and Alsted 1987: 125). He himself wrote and directed *Kødbyen* (*The Meat District*, 1936), an eighteen-minute film that demonstrates the importance of the Copenhagen meat trade to the nation and shows the modernity and efficiency of slaughterhouse practices in often quite gruesome detail. No records detailing this film's production survive and it is absent from published catalogues of films available to schools, perhaps because of its visceral imagery. *Kødbyen* simply disappears from the records, seeming never to have been used for the educational purpose for which it was made. Perhaps it was for that very reason that the film survived in the DFI film archive to be digitised.

In contrast to *Kødbyen*, the film *Hvorledes en Mursten bliver til* emerged after the Second World War as one of the most frequently hired films on Statens Filmcentral's roster. The respective availability of the two films is representative of the occasional disparities between contemporary circulation, digitisation today and the survival of production information. The brick film was borrowed by schools and clubs 164 times in 1952–3, and 33 times as late as 1959–60 (SFC 1953; SFC 1960a). For that reason, I requested that the film be digitised, expecting a finely wrought account of the process of making a brick. But it consists of poor-quality images panning over rows of construction workers in carts, lingering close-ups of machinery excavating and shaping clay for brick production, and explanatory intertitles. Aside from an ongoing need for bricklayer apprentices, it is a mystery why this film should have been so appealing to schoolteachers and clubs, given the wide choice of films available to them via Statens Filmcentral through the 1960s. These two films, then, are most interesting for what we *cannot* know about them: the whys and whos of audience appeal.

Andersen continued to make films inspired by his personal interest in industry, but by 1937, Dansk Kulturfilm's production of *oplysningsfilm* (enlightening films) commissioned by its many associated organisations was underway. Bodil Begtrup[2] of the Danish National Women's Council pressed for a film about the nutrition of infants that could be used by her organisation in a planned nationwide health campaign. Begtrup herself wrote the screenplay for *Barnets Sundhed – Slægtens Fremtid* (*The Child's Health – The People's Future*, 1936). This project was also the first to be filmed by the documentary specialists Minerva Film, establishing a pattern of collaboration between Dansk Kulturfilm in the role of producer and commissioner, and independent film companies. This forty-five-minute silent film, distributed on 16mm film, was seen by an estimated 15,000 people in local community venues around the country (Nørrested and Alsted 1987: 127). A more ambitious and costly project was next: *Ungdom og Bøger* (*Youth and Books*, 1939), a sound film on 35mm commissioned by a campaign group against trashy literature.

Around the same time as Dansk Kulturfilm was taking its first steps in film production, though, one of the most important films in Danish cinema history hit the cinemas. This film is discussed here to underscore how unrepresentative *Kødbyen* and *Hvorledes en Mursten bliver til* were in the broader Danish film milieu and also to introduce the socio-political context into which Dansk Kulturfilm was born.

Poul Henningsen's *Danmark*

It is impossible to discuss the national film scene in 1930s Denmark without mentioning what Peter Schepelern (2006) has described as both the most interesting and the most scandalous reception case study in Danish film history: the 1935 production *Danmark* (*Denmark*), directed by the architect, designer and cultural critic Poul Henningsen. The film is often known as *Danmarksfilmen*, literally 'the Denmark film', an epithet which also signifies a genre with a long history. New *Danmarksfilm* have been commissioned and made at regular intervals throughout cinematic history to depict the nation's landscape, cities, people and aspects of heritage and modernity. The 1935 film by Poul Henningsen (1894–1967) – invariably known to his compatriots as PH – remains a canonical text of Danish cinema, not least due to its chequered production and reception history. Though the film was commissioned a little too early to be made under the auspices of Dansk Kulturfilm, the controversy surrounding PH's *Danmark* had an impact on the early development of the agency and coloured the cultural scene into which it was born.

The commissioning process for PH's *Danmark* began in 1930, with the aim of replacing a 1925 *Danmarksfilm* that was outmoded, not least because it was a relic of the silent era. The Foreign Ministry established a committee to oversee the process, whose members encompassed a broad range of industrial interest groups, including the national councils for agriculture, wholesalers, shipping, tourism, the Ministry for Public Works and large charitable foundations such as the Tuborg Fund (Hertel 2012: 133). This committee approved successive drafts produced by PH through autumn 1932 and into 1933; the concept took shape for a film that would be fresh, lively, modern and cheerful (Hertel 2012: 134). Henningsen's biographer Hans Hertel presents a selection of provincial newspaper clippings that show how communities across the nation eagerly tracked the progress of PH and his cameraman Poul Eibye in the architect's car and speculated about whether their local area would be included in the finished film (135).

Jørgen Sørensen (2006) argues, on the basis of extensive research into the film's reception history, that the hostile reaction stemmed from the tension between the film's status as a state-commissioned film and the radically modern vision of the nation it constructed. PH's biographer, too, stresses that the reception of the film was not really about the film itself, but about what it and Henningsen stood for (Hertel 2012: 133; see also Linde-Laursen 1999). Henningsen was not only a lamp designer but also a cultural-radical critic, who argued vehemently against nationalistic education and for government intervention in education as a buttress against totalitarianism, for example in his 1933 book *Hvad med kulturen?* (*What about Culture?*, Henningsen 1968). In particular, the soundtrack seems to have been the trigger for much of the hostility with which the film was met in the Danish press. The steering committee had appointed a young musician, Bernhard Christensen, to write the score, and he composed and conducted a soundtrack that was heavily influenced by contemporary jazz and followed the visual rhythms and cycles of the film. PH insisted that an international score using international instruments – albeit with Danish song lyrics – was necessary if the film was to speak to the international audience which it was meant to attract to Denmark (Hertel 2012: 136–7).

PH's *Danmark* thus acted as a lightning-rod for contemporary anxieties around the relationship between film and state, the potential for film to represent and inform national populations, and the financial implications of both. Wrangles over funding foreign language versions of the re-cut version of *Danmark* extended into 1936, dominating the Danish state's engagement with film-related issues, and thus also cutting off government funding to Dansk Kulturfilm (Nørrested and Alsted 1987: 123). This jeopardised projects such as the Theatre Association of Southern Jutland's request for films focusing on Danish culture, nature and business to function as a Danish counterweight to the German 'agitation films' circulating in the contested border region (122–3).

The *kulturfilm*: International Contexts and Parallels

If we look more closely at contemporary developments in non-theatrical film in neighbouring countries, the category *kulturfilm* seems also to have been a flexible term in 1930s Germany. William Uricchio regards the German term as encompassing film genres such as educational and industrial films, popular science films, documentaries and propaganda films. He contends that it is 'structural conditions' such as those imposed by film historians and archives that have tended to muddy the meanings of the term *kulturfilm* (Uricchio 1995: 266–7). The point here is not to suggest that the Danish *kulturfilm* can be neatly mapped – conceptually or in praxis – onto the German tradition, but to acknowledge the vagaries of translation of a term that, in the early 1930s, was not yet freighted with the associations with German National Socialism with which it soon would be burdened.

Indeed, Dansk Kulturfilm's founders cited National Socialist approaches to *kulturfilm* in Germany and Italy as aspirational more than once. There seem to have been two reasons for this admiration: a vague sympathy for the ability of such regimes to resist ideological and economic infiltration by American cinema (Nørrested and Alsted 1987: 144) and, more concretely, Germany's and Italy's demonstrably superior organisation in the sphere of films for schools. In the mid-1930s, Dansk Kulturfilm's director Hejle was dealing with the legacy of two pre-existing institutions that were incorporated into his organisation in 1934, fulfilling the emphasis on educational film in the agency's remit: Lærernes Lysbilledforening (the Teachers' Projected Image Association) and Skolernes Filmcentral (the Schools' Film Centre) (Nørrested and Alsted 1987: 119). A complex of challenges related to educational film provision had thus come under Hejle's remit: conversion of existing 35mm stocks to 16mm, now the standard medium for educational use; purchase of foreign educational films, quickly derided by teachers as irrelevant to Danish natural sciences (Nørrested and Alsted 1987: 128); and the urgency of new film production (125). Also apparent was a distinct imbalance in interest between urban school districts, where uptake was high, and more rural areas, which showed little interest in incorporating film into teaching (124). Distribution of educational film was one area in which the relatively didactic German approach to *kulturfilm* seemed to have the edge on the Danish context. Hejle noted enviously that every German school was required by law to have a 16mm projector and that the distribution centre for educational films (Reichsstelle für den Unterrichtsfilm) held a stock of thousands of copies of some 141 films in 1936 (Nørrested and Alsted 1987: 127; Uricchio 1995: 270).

Another inspiration for Dansk Kulturfilm as an institution was the Italian Istituto LUCE (L' Unione Cinematografica Educativa). This organisation, inaugurated in 1925, benefited from a legal edict that its newsreels should be shown at all feature film screenings (Nørrested and Alsted 1987: 113). Its newsreel production was as prolific as it was propagandistic, with some 900 newsreels made between June 1927 and the advent of sound in 1931 (Brunetta 2009: 74). However, the Italian example also held out to the founders of Dansk Kulturfilm the tantalising hope of state investment in cinema in general and educational film in particular. Italian Law 918, passed in 1931, was the very first time that 'a European state invested non-recoverable capital in the entertainment industry' (Brunetta 2009: 68). The rebirth of Italian cinema was thus cushioned and facilitated by state support, and unencumbered by pressure to propagandise; cinema (feature film and documentary alike) was seen by the regime as an art crucial to a modern and modernising nation, but not as a direct instrument of power (Brunetta 2009: 68–70).

A more attainable model for state support of *kulturfilm* was represented by Great Britain, whose developing film culture in the 1920s piqued the interest of Danish film pioneers. As early as 1926, a Captain Højer, appointed as advisor on film in education to the then Justice Minister in the liberal (Venstre) government of Madsen-Mygdal, declared his admiration for developments in Britain (Nørrested and Alsted 1987: 138–9). Later, in summer 1934, Hejle singled out the British Film Institute's 'composition and functioning' as a model for the further development of the Danish body in a memo to the Ministry of Education (Nørrested and Alsted 1987: 120). This admiration was probably based on the recent British report *Film in National Life* (1932), produced by the Independent Commission on Educational and Cultural Films (its nomenclature thus echoing Dansk Kulturfilm's remit). It recommended that a national film institute be founded by Royal Charter and publicly funded. Similarly, the proposal submitted by the newly constituted private company Dansk Kulturfilm to the Danish Government in December 1932 (in connection with a public consultation on the development of a Film Law) conceived of the agency as the lynchpin in a complex of national cultural institutions; it would oversee a film fund, it would have a monopoly on distribution of the some 300 foreign films imported annually to Denmark, and its activities would subsidise Det kongelige Teater (The Royal Theatre). This initial proposal was rejected by the Government, as it was unthinkable that a private institution could exercise such a degree of influence over the nation's cultural life (Nørrested and Alsted 1987: 115).

While the paths of British and Danish documentary and informational filmmakers cross most productively in the late 1940s (see Chapter 5), there was already some contact in the 1930s between filmmakers at grassroots level. Ingolf Boisen, whose film *They Guide You Across* (1949) is examined in Chapter 6, relates in his autobiography that he had meetings in London with John Grierson and other leading lights in the British documentary movement in the mid-1930s. Boisen realised that Denmark was in need of an equivalent institution to the GPO Film Unit, and was pleased to discover that Thomas Hejle was in the process of establishing Dansk Kulturfilm (Boisen 1977: 56–62). Boisen's film production company Minerva was contracted by Dansk Kulturfilm to make one of its first commissions, Begtrup's project *Barnets Sundhed – Slægtens Fremtid* (*The Child's Health – The Nation's Future*, Boisen with Axel Lerche and Jørgen Uhlig, 1936). Theodor Christensen, whose films loom large throughout this book, also visited London in 1939 to show Grierson and others his newly completed film *Iran – Det nye Persien* (*Iran – The New Persia*, 1939) (Roos 1968). Co-directed with Boisen, Axel Lerche and Tove Hebo, the film was commissioned by the engineering company Kampsax to showcase the railway it had built in Iran and features a closing montage of speeding trains very reminiscent of the British classic *Night Mail* (Harry Watt and Basil Wright, 1936). Influenced by his contacts in London, Boisen regarded this film as 'the first real Danish documentary' (Boisen 1977: 86).

FUNDING FOR DANSK KULTURFILM

Throughout its history, Dansk Kulturfilm was primarily supported by the Danish state, but used a variety of entrepreneurial schemes to secure funding for specific projects. Its original source of income was the surplus of the national Film Censor's office, established as early as 1913 to mitigate the corrupting effects of the entertainment industry and to channel some part of its profits towards more worthy productions. In order to avoid total dominance of the informational film in Denmark by Dansk Kulturfilm, the funding settle-ment from 1936 reserved around twenty-five per cent of the censorship budget surplus for projects proposed by government ministries, associations or indi-vidual projects (Nørrested and Alsted 1987: 136 n22; Koch-Olsen 1957c: 7).

Another source of funding was built into the early proposals for Dansk Kulturfilm: its work was supported by profits from a specially built 880-seat cinema, Toftegaard Bio, in the Valby area of Copenhagen, finished in December 1937 (Nørrested and Alsted 1987: 121, 126). In 1950, Toftegaard cinema was attracting some 400,000 paying customers per year, that is, an average of well over 1000 tickets a day; the management innovated throughout the 1950s to counteract a fall in cinema-going, experimenting with children's film clubs and documentary seasons (Dansk Kulturfilm 1952: 12–13), securing national premieres of feature films, pioneering facilities for the hard-of-hearing in 1952 (Dansk Kulturfilm 1953: 10) and installing Cinemascope equipment in 1958 (Andersen 2010). Popularly known as Toften, the cinema operated until 1976 (Andersen 2010).

Distribution via Statens Filmcentral

In April 1938, further legislation crystallised the relationship between state and film industry in Denmark. Nørrested and Alsted (1987: 138) identify this legislative framework as a key factor in the remarkable development of the state-sponsored short film in Denmark over the next two decades. Filmsrådet (the Film Council) was established as an advisory body for the industry. Filmsfonden (the Film Fund) expanded financial support for educational and enlightening films; the funds for this work would no longer be based only on censorship income, but also on taxes on the entertainment industry (Dam n.d.b). More importantly for our narrative and network, Statens Filmcentral (the State Film Centre; SFC) took over Dansk Kulturfilm's distribution work, including its film distribution to schools. Under its auspices, projectors were provided to libraries, training and projectionists were available to associa-tions and communities, and a wide variety of short films were imported and exported. Short films were distributed to cinemas with popular feature films, expanding the audience for some shorts to a fifth of the national population (Dam n.d.a).

With Statens Filmcentral in place as specialist distribution body, one further institutional development was to complete the triumvirate of institutions at the heart of this book. With the Nazi occupation of Denmark from April 1940, the need for targeted propaganda films informing the nation about matters such as food shortages and new laws became acute. This kind of film was to be separately funded and controlled via a new Government Film Committee, bolted on to Dansk Kulturfilm, so as to ring-fence the Film Fund's allocation for 'culturally worthy enlightening films' (Larsen n.d.), a move indicative of the state's commitment to the *kulturfilm* concept. In the first instance, this committee was constituted as Beskæftigelsesfilmudvalget (the Committee for Employment Films), indicating its instrumentalist remit. From 1944, a permanent version of this committee was established as Ministeriernes Filmudvalg (The Ministries' Film Committee, hereafter MFU). This effectively functioned until the 1960s as a twin institution with Dansk Kulturfilm, ensuring that propaganda and public information films were kept financially and conceptually separate from the *kulturfilm*, while in practice amalgamating their oversight, production and distribution. As the war came to an end, MFU focused particularly on films that could propagandise abroad for Danish industry, farming, social organisation and values (Larsen n.d.), as we shall see in Chapter 5.

OCCUPATION, MFU AND A NEW GENERATION OF DANISH DOCUMENTARISTS

In the late 1940s, there was a school of thought among British documentarists that their art was stagnating because the existential challenge of the Second World War had passed; 'documentary had been at its most vivid and energetic when mobilised around themes of progressive social reform in the interwar years and social unity in the face of national danger during the war' (MacDonald 2013: 455). In Denmark, there was a less circumstantial connection between wartime conditions and a quantum leap for documentary. If one compares, say, H. Andersen's brick film with an informational short made just six years later, Theodor Christensen's *Gammelt Metal – Nye Varer!* (*Old Metal – New Wares!*), the contrast is nothing short of astounding in terms of style, technique and exposition. But the progress is only astonishing if we restrict our story to institutional continuity. As we have seen in the case of Henningsen's *Danmark*, individual filmmakers in late 1930s Denmark were well informed about international styles and practices, even if the Danish cultural establishment was nonplussed by the results. A new generation of documentarists was emerging in Denmark, influenced by, and well connected to, the British scene.

The same year that H. Andersen was finishing his process films about the meat-packing district and brick-making, two young intellectuals and filmmakers published Denmark's first book about cinema, simply called *FILM*. Theodor Christensen (1914–67) and Karl Roos (1914–51) collaborated on what has been described as 'the first serious analysis published here at home of film as an art form, of the principles of montage and of the interconnections between film aesthetics and technology' (Boisen 1977: 137–8). Both Christensen and Roos would go on to make films for Dansk Kulturfilm and both took on leadership roles within the Danish filmmakers' association, Dansk Filmforbund, established 1947 (the same year as the international association World Union of

Documentary). Christensen's name and his films feature heavily in this book, as do the productions of the wider Roos clan; Karl Roos' younger brother Jørgen Roos (1922–98) and son Ole Roos (1937–) went on to be successful filmmakers in their own right (see especially Chapter 9).

Christensen was heavily influenced by the Scottish documentarist John Grierson (1898–1972) and the British documentary movement more broadly. This can be seen in *FILM* and his other writings from the 1930s onwards. A piece on documentary from 1938, for example, calls for 'a realism that dramatises modern life ... manipulated reality in images, words, sounds and music, which together create a narrative, a drama' (cited in Bondebjerg 2012: 41). We will discuss several examples of his films in this book.

Two key factors brought this pool of talent into the sphere of government-sponsored film: the rationalisation of the state's intervention in culture necessitated by the German occupation of Denmark from April 1940, and the appointment of a civil servant to run the government's filmmaking initiatives who happened to be both highly talented as an administrator and deeply committed to documentary film as an art in its own right, Mogens Skot-Hansen (1908–84). With the German occupation of Denmark on 9 April 1940 there followed a cultural offensive, the aim of which was to convert the Danes to National Socialism:

> Danish cinemas were now screening the dynamic editing of German documentaries and newsreels, in which the Third Reich was prevailing with its firepower on all fronts, productivity and employment were in high gear, and German excitement swelled about its superiority amongst European democracies, which were toppling before the German troops. The invasion of Denmark was not just military. (Sørensen 2013)

Ib Bondebjerg has argued that during the occupation, documentarism was able to fulfil the function of a collectively understood national image of reality, especially as a result of its presence in cinemas and the popularity of its light-hearted approach (Bondebjerg 2012: 44). The political and material conditions, then, affected not just the rate of film production, but also the films' style. Writing in 1948, the English documentarist Arthur Elton employed a military metaphor to compare how documentary was deployed in the two countries. In Britain, 'the documentary became a weapon of offence'; warmth, humanity and humour disappeared and quantity of films produced, not their quality, was all. The films' message was conveyed through the commentary and not the visuals, resulting in uninspiring and even uncommunicative films. In Denmark, on the other hand, style and 'frills' tended to win out over substance, because 'the documentary film became a weapon of defence. Its makers could not present the economic, political and social position as they experienced it. Had they done so, the Gestapo would have been after them' (Elton 1948: 8).

A different take on state-sponsored wartime filmmaking is provided by the man who coordinated such activity on behalf of the government: Mogens Skot-Hansen. Interviewed in 1944 on 'Danish Film's Chances after the War', Skot-Hansen identified the greatest dangers for informational filmmakers as the scepticism and boredom threshold of the public: 'If the films don't speak the truth, the Danish public will react against them – and then propaganda will have signed its own death warrant' (cited in Bondebjerg 2012: 49). Accordingly, the films made on his watch do not merely praise Danish achievements. They also emphasise what still has to be completed or improved. And they adopt a detached, ironic tone fundamental to national discourse.

Skot-Hansen was a civil servant in the Ministry of Education with a sideline in cinephilia when he was asked to chair a committee that would oversee the production of government-sponsored film commissioned by different ministries with the aim of promoting employment and productivity. The committee was initially named Beskæftigelsesfilmudvalget (literally, the Employment Film Committee). For Skot-Hansen, the function of the films produced under the auspices of this committee and its later iteration from 1944 onwards, Ministeriernes Filmudvalg (the Danish Government Film Committee), was threefold: a democratic task of enlightening the population, a cultural-historical documentary function and to educate the populace about film itself, renewing and developing filmic language (Bondebjerg 2012: 49). Elton lists Skot-Hansen's many qualities and skills:

> Skot-Hansen brought to the films a knowledge of civil service procedure and sense of public purpose. To these qualities he soon added first-rate technical skill, for he quickly became not only an ingenious script-writer, but also a capable director and film editor and developed a lively appreciation of the importance of non-theatrical distribution. Today he is one of the best documentary producers, and his special qualities have enabled him to find a compromise between the rigid civil service procedure and the creative freedom without which artists cannot flourish. Early in 1947 he joined the film department of UNESCO in Paris. (Elton 1948: 7)

Bondebjerg (2012: 48) points out how impressive it is that Skot-Hansen was able to attract and retain the services of around twenty key Danish directors of the period, while coordinating complex network of ministries, stakeholders and special interests – and on a war footing to boot. The thirty-six films produced by MFU during the occupation reached an estimated twenty million viewers, mostly via theatrical distribution (Nørrested and Alsted 1987: 202), and on topics ranging from recycling of raw materials for the war effort to charitable support for single mothers. We now take a quick excursion to look more closely at two quite disparate examples of such films: *Gammelt Metal – Nye Varer!* (*Old Metal – New Wares!*, Theodor Christensen, 1942) and *Kartofler* (*Potatoes*, Ole Palsbo, 1944–6). These are examples of, respectively, a public information film aiming to change citizens' behaviour around recycling raw materials for the war effort and a *kulturfilm* proper, detailing the history and contemporary use of that staple of Danish cuisine, the potato.

RECYCLING FOR THE WAR EFFORT

Gammelt Metal – Nye Varer! (*Old Metal – New Wares!*, Theodor Christensen, 1942) was commissioned in March 1942 by Danske Erhvervs Jern- og Metalindsamling (Danish Industry's Iron and Metal Appeal). The film is offered here as a first encounter with many of the qualities of Theodor Christensen's style and many of the tricks used to grab and hold audience attention in later films – here compressed into a few minutes.

Gammelt Metal uses the conceit of a dialogue voiceover between a business-like narrator and a country bumpkin who seems a little slow on the uptake. The former eventually persuades the latter that it will make a difference to Danish industry if he and all other citizens, especially farmers, would donate their spare metal to the war effort. The cinema-goer is thus spared the embarrassment of being the only person in the room who does not understand what is at stake; a voice within the diegesis asks the stupid questions. This is a strategy we will witness again. More compelling is the jaunty musical accompaniment, which makes lavish use of brass fanfares to announce the opening of the film and then to change pace around the same musical motifs as different metals are shown being processed. Towards the end of the film, a number of shots show heavy weights being used to break up larger metal objects, and the soundtrack produces suitably comedic crashes and bangs.

The film's visuals are more serious, apart from some amusing asides showing the fireside and slippers of, presumably, the kind of Danes assumed to have the kind of metal that industry needed: decorative metal plates on the wall, Aunt Thora's old broken candlesticks, a young boy's tin soldiers, and a forgotten copper fireguard in the attic. Processes for sorting and stripping different metals are shown, in one memorable shot with milk bottle tops being blown in enormous clouds towards the camera. Elsewhere, Christensen is in his element as he films showers of sparks from molten metals, mysterious poles and probes, and the interesting physiognomies of serious and jolly factory workers. The focus on individual workers is transformed at the end of the film into a crane shot of a large factory floor, as many voices in unison are heard to chant the mantra that raw materials mean employment for 400,000 Danish workers (Figure 4.1.). A clearer expression of the national principle *e*

Figure 4.1   The shop floor as metonym for the 400,000 Danish workers supported by recycling of raw materials (*Gammelt Metal – Nye Varer!*, Theodor Christensen, 1942).

pluribus unum is hard to imagine, especially on the back of several minutes of detailed illustrations of how the metal collected all over the nation is sorted and re-used by fellow citizens. The candlesticks, buckets and milk bottle tops in the film meld the people together in the face of occupation, literally and metaphorically.

The film was one element in a much wider media campaign encompassing a poster competition, radio addresses by government ministers and circulars. The urgency with which raw materials were needed for industry is hammered home by a letter from Theodor Christensen explaining a delay on the film's production: ironically, the factory where he was shooting the film in late April that year was at a standstill due to lack of supplies (Christensen 1942). No fewer than thirty copies of the film were to be produced, so that it could be distributed as widely and as quickly as possible to cinemas (Danske Erhvervs Jern- og Metalindsamling 1942) in order to address this very material need.

Gammelt Metal – Nye Varer! is thus a compelling example of a film which depicts the nation as a network of citizens and workers of various stripes, knitted together by the circulation of metals from home to recycling plant to industry. At the same time, the correspondence on the film's production and

Figure 4.2   The title sequence of *Kartofler* (Ole Palsbo, 1944–6) invites the viewer in with a modernist font.

distribution emphasise the intervention of material factors in these systems: the film was delayed by the same shortages it sought to address.

THE POTATO AS NATIONAL GOOD

Like many analogous films on subjects such as cattle, horses and turnips, Ole Palsbo's film about the history of the potato was commissioned by a committee established to facilitate and oversee export of Danish produce. In this case, the committee in question was Kartoffeleksport-Udvalget, the Potato Committee, a section of Landbrugsraadet, the Agriculture Council. Despite the technocratic nomenclature, the film has a lightness of touch bestowed by its liberal use of song. Rather than leaving the work of imparting information about the uses of the potato to a 'voice of god' narrator, the director Ole Palsbo persuaded his wife Susanne to write lyrics which were set to music by Kai Rosenberg, a regular collaborator with MFU and Dansk Kulturfilm, and sung by a male-voice trio. Another detail sustains this lightness: the use of a quirky, modern font against the process-film-style shots of potatoes being processed (see Figure 4.2).

The island of Samsø, epicentre of the Danish potato industry, emerges from the film as the centre of a national and indeed international network of ships, dock workers loading and unloading crates of the tuber, which end up on the lunch plates of Copenhagen gentlemen as well as in a dizzying variety of industrial and medicinal uses. The use of the potato in modern industry and national everyday cuisine is contrasted with a historical sequence depicting the first Europeans to taste the new food from across the ocean. In this way, though less obviously nationalistic than *Gammelt Metal*, Palsbo's potato film is a good example of the tendency of the *kulturfilm* to weave the nation together spatially and historically. The song on the soundtrack intensifies the sense of community and unison that such a humble material object as the potato weaves around itself as it travels.

Given that this film was predicated on the idea of promoting exports, an English-language version of the manuscript was produced. The translation on file was very obviously not prepared by a native speaker of English, but may have had the effect of promoting Danish potatoes by dint of its charming infelicities:

> We are at the isle of Samsø in the beginning of June. Samsø – the butter-hole of Denmark's porridge-dish – the small beautiful island with the delicious asparagus and the newest of the new potatoes. Now the potatoes are at stake, and the matter is urgent! To-morrow they must be served on the lunch tables all over the country. The first new potatoes of the year with dewy butter-sauce – uhm! (SFC 1944)

I have not been able to find any indication that it was possible to export the film to a British-speaking audience during the occupation. The translation bears witness to a long-standing ambition to share films with the Allies across the North Sea, an ambition which was coaxed towards fulfilment by the collaboration with the British documentary movement described in Chapter 5.

THE DANISH RESISTANCE AND FILMMAKING

In parallel with the state-sponsored informational film during the occupation, there was considerable filmmaking activity associated with the Danish Resistance movement. There was also considerable overlap between the roster of filmmakers recruited by Skot-Hansen to the cause of state-sponsored filmmaking and the band of Resistance filmmakers. A striking expression of this overlap comes in a set of MFU meeting minutes of 2 April 1945, when it was reported that two film manuscripts commissioned from Theodor Christensen have been delayed because, it is coolly reported, he has been arrested and detained by the Germans. The meeting resolved to ask the Foreign Ministry to secure his release (MFU 1941–).[3]

A key link in the chain between Danish government and Resistance filmmaking activities was Major Ole Lippmann (known by the pseudonym Lund in the

UK), of the SOE (Special Operations Executive, which coordinated parachute landings in occupied Denmark) and Frihedsrådet (the Freedom Council wing of the Danish Resistance). Lippmann had travelled to London in 1944 to be groomed for leadership of the SOE, and carried with him a batch of illegal footage provided by Theodor Christensen and Minerva Film; it was Lippmann who passed the material on to the Danish Ambassador in Washington, Henrik Kauffmann, who in turn gave it to the US Office of War Information. *Det kæmpende Danmark* (*Fighting Denmark*) was patched together in the US Office of War Information and circulated in Scandinavia in the last years of the war (Sørensen 2014: 387). The same US institution edited a ten-minute English-language film, *Denmark Fights for Freedom*, from footage provided by Theodor Christensen. Lippmann wrote and recorded the voiceover for that film (Sørensen 2014: 387–8). It premiered in London in October 1944 and was reported to have circulated via newsreels in 6000 copies in twenty-six countries (388–9). Though such figures may have been exaggerated for propaganda's sake, these two shorts amply demonstrated the potential of documentary film to disseminate the image of Denmark as a democratic land bravely fighting for its liberty.

Denmark was liberated by Allied troops on 5 May 1945. The next week, MFU seized the moment and advertised for footage of the occupation and liberation to be used in a film about the Danish Resistance for foreign distribution (Nørrested and Alsted 1987: 225). Despite the existence of extensive film material shot by Resistance groups, individuals and even the film company Palladium's subsidiary Dansk Film Co., production of a single state-sponsored Resistance film was rendered impossible by the competing interests of the various Resistance factions (226). Not until mid-1946 did a documentary retrospective of the work of the Resistance emerge: *Det gælder din Frihed* (*Your Freedom is at Stake*), directed by Theodor Christensen.

These Anglo-Danish links, however, constituted a useful basis for a project which MFU was already beginning to formulate: a post-war film project which would re-brand Denmark to the Allies as a democratic, progressive nation. This is the project to which we now turn.

Notes

1. For an extended discussion of *The Pattern of Cooperation*, its mediation of the cooperative movement to worldwide audiences, and its broader political and historical context, see Thomson and Hilson 2014.
2. Bodil Gertrud Begtrup (1903–87) was a leading figure in the Danish women's movement, as well as a film censor and Denmark's first female ambassador (to Iceland); see Olsen 2003 for biographical information. Her namesake appears in Chapter 5.
3. One of the films affected was reported to be a new Danmarksfilm, that is, in the tradition of Henningsen's *Danmark*. Christensen survived his encounter with the occupying forces to realise this project, which became *The Pattern of Cooperation* (1952).

5. A FILM-PROGRESSIVE NATION: THE *SOCIAL DENMARK* SERIES AND THE BRITISH DOCUMENTARY MOVEMENT

In the immediate post-war period, Danish film was all the rage amongst British film connoisseurs. By 1947, the Scottish film pioneer Forsyth Hardy could write that Denmark's documentary production 'would not shame a country six times its size' (Hardy 1947a), and the English documentarist Arthur Elton described the Danish post-war informational film scene as 'tough and lusty' (Elton 1948: 11). For Hardy, the body of films made during wartime to promote Danish industry and social cohesion – as discussed in Chapter 4 – had done for Denmark 'what the GPO Film Unit under John Grierson had done for Britain' (Hardy 1947b). Hardy's article appeared in *The Scotsman* during the Edinburgh International Film Festival (EIFF), which was organised for the first time in 1947 and featured half a dozen Danish films produced in the immediate post-war period. The selection included three of the five short films commissioned for the series *Social Denmark* (1947), an innovative exercise in cultural diplomacy conceived by MFU towards the end of the German occupation of Denmark, and developed under the guidance of Arthur Elton.

This chapter traces the commissioning, production and distribution of the *Social Denmark* films as a case study in the role of informational film in cultural diplomacy in the immediate post-war period. As subsequent chapters will show, Danish shorts travelled far and wide in the decade after the Second World War and, indeed, were produced in multiple language versions to facilitate their global reach. *Social Denmark*, too, was later distributed in French and German editions as well as English. However, this first post-war informational film project was fundamentally a British-Danish collaboration. This is so in three respects. Firstly, the kernel of the *Social Denmark* project as a concept can be traced back to MFU deliberations several months before the liberation of the country, as it became clear that Denmark's reputation amongst the Allies would need to be salvaged and that film would be an important tool to this end. Secondly, and consequently, the invitation to Arthur Elton to take on the role of consultant constituted an act of Anglo-Danish cultural diplomacy in its own right, as well as a bid to benefit from British expertise in state-supported documentary. Thirdly, *Social Denmark* kick-started a bustling traffic of filmmakers, consultants and films back and forth across the North Sea in the immediate post-war period, not least under the auspices of the EIFF and its founders. The story of *Social Denmark* is thus an example of the kind of bilateral cooperation that often underpins larger-scale international networks of informational film and filmmakers.

The *Social Denmark* films also constitute a rich case study in the construction of 'facts' on screen and from the commissioning, production and circulation of films, as discussed in Chapter 3. A brochure printed in 1948 for the English-speaking world (SFC 1948a) advertised a selection of one hundred Danish informational productions, including the *Social Denmark* films, as 'Films of Facts [sic] in War, Occupation, Liberation, Peace'. The branding of Denmark abroad was thus predicated on the purported truth-value of the films. As Gershon and Malitsky argue (2010: 68), 'information becomes facts by travelling through networks in patterned ways that imbue the piece of knowledge with authority and relevance'. Drawing on the surviving research material and manuscript drafts for the films allows us to trace how 'facts' came to be shaped not only by the influence of Elton, by domestic political and financial pressures, by the reputation of established directors such as Carl Th. Dreyer and the skills and creativity of other filmmakers, by their mobility and by technological constraints, but also by such vagaries as weather, shortages of petrol and film stock, and by interlingual translation – all of which can be seen to have helped to produce the 'facts' of national history and socio-political practices that emerge in the *Social Denmark* films.

THE LIBERATION AND THE ORIGINS OF *SOCIAL DENMARK*

A full year before Denmark was liberated from German occupation, the minutes of MFU meetings (MFU 1941–) begin to feature discussions about the role of film in post-war cultural diplomacy. The earliest example I have been able to find comes on 4 May 1944: a brief comment that the committee ought to start work on films that could be exported abroad to promote Denmark after the war. The subject comes up again at the meeting of 11 August, when shortages of film stock are also reported. On 10 October, the discussion turns to concrete suggestions for topics which might pique interest abroad. These include the training of Danish engineers; Danish schools and social housing; the new Serum Institute; the Royal Ballet; and the Free Harbour of Copenhagen as the 'Marketplace of the Baltic'. A few months later, on 12 December, a concrete title for such a film is suggested; *Et lille land bliver større* (*A Little Land Gets Bigger*) would tell the world about efforts to reclaim land on the island of Amager, on which the south-eastern part of the city of Copenhagen stands. It will be noted that the suggested title of this film echoes the refrain of Denmark as a 'little land', a prevailing trope as discussed in Chapter 2, pressed into service here at a critical time for the post-war reconstruction of the country's reputation. At the meeting of 19 December, more detailed consideration was given to the form such films might take. Four possible formats were identified: (1) 15–20 minute segments for use in newsreels; (2) *kulturfilm* on Danish arts and industry to be screened in movie theatres; (3) semi-lyrical *Danmarksfilm*, that is, portraits of Danish life and nature, an established genre discussed in Chapter 4; and (4) films for official use at trade exhibitions and by embassies.

The minutes of these meetings reveal, then, that MFU was anticipating its role in re-branding Denmark in the post-war world a good year before the end of the war. While the discussions about the use of film in the post-war world attest to the ambition and far-sightedness of the committee members, they are less surprising when considered in the context of the broader shift in Denmark towards optimism about the outcome of the war.

Though the subject of a possible film on the Resistance is, wisely, glossed over in the minutes, at least some of the members of the committee would also have been aware that film stock and filmed footage was already criss-crossing the Øresund Strait between occupied Copenhagen and neutral Sweden (Sørensen 2014: 387), and that smuggled clips of sabotage and similar activities were the basis of at least two propaganda films about the Danish Resistance, as discussed at the end of Chapter 4. But another topic was seen as equally crucial to the restoration of Denmark's standing as a democratic, progressive land: social security.

On 12 June 1945, just over a month after the liberation, it is reported in MFU minutes that Arbejds- og Socialministeriet (the Ministry of Employment and Social Affairs) had requested a film about social conditions in Denmark, for export to the UK, the USA and the USSR. The idea of the nascent welfare state as a topic in film and in cultural diplomacy was in fact not new. The Scandinavian countries had been promoting their social welfare innovations at world fairs and in English-language tourism and cultural diplomacy publications since the 1920s (Marklund and Petersen 2013: 248). A state-sponsored film on Danish social institutions had been approved in 1942 for circulation in Germany under the title *Das soziale Gesicht Dänemarks* (Denmark's Social Provision), and Swedish and Finnish versions were produced a year later. A Danish version of the film had been seen by some 70,000 people in cinemas and clubs by the end of the war (Arbejds- og Socialministeriet 1945). However, this film was regarded as too sentimental and insufficiently factual for post-war use (Nørrested and Alsted 1987: 227). In its German- and Danish-language voiceovers respectively, the same film had presented Denmark as a model protectorate not in need of remedial intervention from occupying forces, and as a more realistically sketched welfare-state-in-progress (Sørensen 2013). It is also clear from documents circulated in summer 1945 that both the Ministry and Mogens Skot-Hansen were convinced that the British and American audiences would have to be tackled separately, given the differences between the two nations with respect to mentality, social organisation and filmic language (Arbejds- og Socialministeriet 1945). At MFU's meeting on 12 June, however, the suggestion recorded is that a film about social security in Denmark should be produced in collaboration with British filmmakers specifically, and this was the starting point for Skot-Hansen to make enquiries of contacts in London.

The correspondence on file evokes the peculiarities of that historical moment, when key figures in the Danish Resistance and exiled Danes more generally were still influential in relations between Denmark and the western powers. As we know from his involvement in *Denmark Fights for Freedom* (see Chapter 4), Major Ole Lippmann (or Lund) was acquainted with the British documentary film scene, and put Skot-Hansen in touch with Jack Beddington of the Film Department at the British Ministry of Information (Skot-Hansen 1945a). Beddington was enthusiastic about the project and committed the Ministry of Information to the collaboration; this would allow for the resulting film to be distributed via British cinemas and, through the nation's established Film Library, to educational institutions (Skot-Hansen 1945a). Beddington recommended his 'old and trusted friend' Arthur Elton as a potential consultant (Beddington 1945).

Another Dane at the Ministry of Information was Terkel M. Terkelsen. He was London correspondent for the Danish newspaper *Berlingske Tidende*, and a member of the Political Intelligence Department of the British Foreign Ministry. Terkelsen was also acquainted with Elton and acted as middleman during the negotiations (Skot-Hansen 1945b). More generally, he enjoyed the idea of a bilateral Dano-British exchange of films and filmmakers. As he wrote to Skot-Hansen in mid-August 1945, documentary and informational film in Britain had undergone massive development during the war and had played an essential role in the war effort. It would therefore be of great value for Skot-Hansen himself to visit London, and Beddington was also in favour of this (Terkelsen 1945). Beddington and Tekelsen are examples of the diplomatic entrepreneurs described in Chapter 2.

By the end of July 1945, Elton had 'cleared a space in [his] life' from 9 to 30 August in order to travel to Denmark and start work on the planned film about Social Denmark (Elton 1945a).

A Good Friend of Danish Film

'Please allow me to say how honoured I am at your invitation and how happy I shall be if I can do something to contribute to Anglo-Danish and indeed, to international understanding in general, by means of film' (Elton 1945c). Thus wrote Elton to Skot-Hansen shortly before his departure for Copenhagen in mid-August 1945. Marked by the jovial politesse of the English nobility, his words nonetheless give expression to a certain internationalist idealism which pervaded the work of the British documentary movement, in which Elton was a key player from the 1930s until his death in 1973.[1]

The godfather of British documentary, John Grierson, has described the movement he founded as having a 'missionary zeal ... to explain its doctrine to countries outside Britain' (Grierson 1979b: 206). This compulsion was most notably directed at the remnants of the British Empire. Grierson moved to Canada in 1938 to develop its world-leading National Film Board, while the British Colonial Office established film units and training in Malaya, Ghana, India and elsewhere (Grierson 1979b: 207). Basil Wright and others insisted on the duty of documentarists to help the 'underdeveloped' world express itself in film until such time as local filmmaking capacity emerged, a calling which has been critiqued as paternalistic and blind to the possibility that local film-makers might have something to say other than a reiteration of internationalist values (MacDonald 2013: 463).

A kinder assessment would observe that the British documentary scene was the source of an international trickle-down effect whereby the skills and practices developed through more or less reciprocal knowledge transfer were bequeathed in turn to other national contexts. Grierson (1979b: 207) gives the example of the propagation of good practice via the National Film Board of Canada and by the role of some colonies in setting up non-theatrical distribution systems in others. Denmark very quickly took on a leading role in the international development of informational film, with Mogens Skot-Hansen resigning from MFU as early as 1947 to take up a post at the UN Film Board. By 1950, Denmark was a regular destination for international filmmakers and political functionaries from nations such as Turkey and Indonesia who wished to develop their knowledge and had received mobility grants from UNESCO (Dansk Kulturfilm og Ministeriernes Filmudvalg 1952: 11; Druick 2011). Arriving in mid-1945, Elton 'quickly felt' that 'even if English documentary could contribute something by pointing to technical and social paths which it might be profitable to explore, my colleagues and I in England had a great deal to learn from Denmark in return' (Elton 1948: 7).

Arthur Elton was in 1945 a Director of Film Centre Ltd on London's Soho Square, together with Edgar Anstey and Company Secretary Ernestine Roberts. Film Centre had been established in 1938 under the leadership of

John Grierson, as a 'consultative and policy-forming centre for the growing number of national corporations and public bodies using the documentary film for their purposes' (Hardy 1979a: 13). Film Centre's business model remains under-researched and thus 'somewhat enigmatic' (Russell 2013: 424); but like Dansk Kulturfilm, Film Centre liaised between documentarists and the organisations that commissioned and funded films, especially the pioneering Shell Film Unit (Canjels 2009: 245) and also the British gas, electrical and oil industries, Imperial Airways and the Films of Scotland Committee (Hardy 1979b: 89). In the case of the Shell Film Unit, it has been observed that the involvement of Film Centre resulted in an unrivalled body of corporate-sponsored films that functioned ostensibly as publicity and training films for Shell Oil, but, more importantly, as public relations for the company and as educational film generally worldwide (Burgess 2010: 218). This legacy was in no small part due to the influence of Elton, who was already described by Grierson in the early 1930s as the best industrial filmmaker in Britain (Grierson 1979a: 50). In his involvement with Shell, Elton consolidated his characteristic aesthetic based on 'sheer lucidity' and Shell gained a reputation for 'the production of films giving precise information and lucid explanation of complex scientific and technological subjects' (Burgess 2010: 217).

Thus it was as an experienced film producer and strategist and as a leading documentarist that Elton arrived in Copenhagen in mid-August 1945. He had been invited for his filmmaking skills, but it was his knowledge of the ethics, organisation and practice of semi-governmental filmmaking in the wider world that proved to be more relevant to the needs of Danish documentary. Elton's original understanding of the scope of his Danish assignment was as follows:

> When the preliminary reporting and investigating have been finished you will have in your hands a document laying out how – in my view – the film should be made, containing a 'treatment' indicating in some detail shape and content, and giving you notes on distribution in Britain, with further notes on distribution in the British Commonwealth and the United States. I will also give you any assistance I can in matters of equipment etc. (Elton 1945a)

Elton also states in this letter that he would be happy to act as producer of the film later on. Altogether, these early discussions provide a sense of the kind of help that MFU required in producing and distributing a film suitable for the British market. However, Elton's remit was revised – at his behest – not long after his arrival in Denmark. He and Skot-Hansen agreed that he should instead prepare 'a general report on how I consider that Denmark's contributions to social legislation can best be revealed to the world at large by means of film' (Elton 1945b: 1). This alteration of the remit did not reflect a previously unrealised need for remedial intervention in what he calls the 'Danish documentary school'. Rather, Elton had observed both strengths and weaknesses in current practice and extant output, which had potential to contribute to the burgeoning international documentary scene. The following detailed account of Elton's recommendations is offered here as a snapshot of the position and organisation of Danish, British and international informational film immediately after the end of the Second World War.

BECOMING A FILM-PROGRESSIVE NATION: ELTON'S REPORT ON
DANISH DOCUMENTARY

Elton's report, dated October 1945 and thus produced within a couple of months of his arrival in Copenhagen, consists of four parts: (1) a critical review of thirty-two films he had viewed (including several mentioned in Chapter 4); (2) the issue of distribution; (3) a plan for production and possible film topics; and (4) two proposed film outlines (Elton 1945b: 1). In revised form it constituted part of the comparative international survey Elton later produced for UNESCO (Elton and Brinson 1950).

Elton's initial assessment of the Danish films he viewed was very positive, praising both their quality and quantity. Denmark had

> developed a distinctive style of its own, which will provide a good foundation for the production of films for international use. The films are finely photographed, well directed and edited. Most of them can be sent overseas without any anxiety that they will appear inferior to the product of other countries. (Elton 1945b: 2)

He singles out five qualities in the films: 'fresh, lively and human direction'; 'a gay and imaginative touch in a number of propaganda films'; 'imaginative and clever editing'; 'fine and luminous photography'; and the 'musical accompaniments' (2). Elton also warns that the films might be *too* well made:

> The world will judge them by their ability to hold the attention of the audience for which they are designed, by the clarity of exposition, and by the way in which they interpret Danish life. Any preoccupation with film technique for its own sake will hinder their reception. (Elton 1945b: 2)

Elton's subsequent recommendations on the production process seem to be aimed at countering what he saw as the excessive interest in cinematic style and technique. He reminds his readers that documentarists are first and foremost public servants and that films should be made because the topic in question is important, not because it is inherently cinematic. Indeed, to prioritise aesthetic concerns is to betray the documentarist's vocation: 'it is part of the art of the film writer or film director to make filmic whatever subject they may be called upon to treat' (Elton 1945b: 3–4). In this respect and others, Elton's report echoes the tenets of the British documentary movement, calling for pragmatism and practicality in the production process, and for a clear-sighted view of the needs and desires of the commissioning body as well as the audience. Each film project, he writes, must begin with 'a clear statement of the reason for making it, its proposed length, the audience for which it is intended, and the purpose each must serve'. Equally, more attention should be paid to the preparatory, research and script stages of each film, and the role of the producer should be enhanced, to shield filmmakers from 'accepting instructions in defiance of good cinematic practice' and to help them gain perspective on their films (1945b: 5). Filmmakers should immerse themselves more fully in the worldwide documentary movement to which they belong and to which they could contribute, by borrowing film prints and studying advertising film techniques. Equally, as public servants, they should study sociology, education and psychology (5), and they should be encouraged to engage with the publics for which their films are intended by taking their films on tour around the country, discussing them with factory workers and farming communities (6).

Distribution of Danish films on the international stage was of particular concern, given that the country was emerging from the isolation of a five-year enemy occupation. Especially valuable was Elton's wide-ranging experience and his contacts via the British documentary scene and in the context of the growing international use of film in education and intercultural understanding (see Druick 2011). Elton's primary recommendation was to focus on the non-theatrical distribution system, except where it was desirable and possible to target cinemas. He advised that non-theatrical distribution on an international scale had developed considerably during the war, especially in Britain, Canada and the USA, and now reached both general audiences as well as very specialised ones, via libraries, clubs, trade unions and religious associations, reaching 'opinion-forming groups' that would not be influenced by theatrical film (Elton 1945b: 7):

> The non-theatrical system of distribution is world wide, deeply penetrating, and adjustable to any particular audience level. In the opinion of many people the non-theatrical system is superior to the theatrical as a method of disseminating information; in the opinion of all, it is a major factor in the world interchange of ideas. (8)

To enter this worldwide network of non-theatrical exhibition, Danish films could be lodged with local embassy attachés for further distribution, or donated or loaned to government-run or commercial film libraries (Elton 1945b: 8) or by the international library branches run by the British and Canadian governments (9). The Danish government should consolidate its own internal distribution system so it can offer reciprocal arrangements to British and other governments for the distribution, copying and lending of informational films (9). Denmark should also develop its domestic documentary distribution and lending arrangements beyond the 'skeleton' currently in place in the form of Statens Filmcentral, which was focused at that time on distribution of educational film to schools (10). Elton goes on (11–12) to outline the disadvantages and difficulties of theatrical distribution. Except in independent cinemas, primarily American short films and newsreels are distributed as packages with feature films; only established series such as March of Time and World in Action seem to penetrate the public consciousness. Approaches to these companies could be made early in 1946, and it should also be possible to explore a bilateral arrangement with the British Ministry of Information to subsidise the theatrical exhibition of one or more British and Danish documentary shorts in each country (13).

Of particular consequence for the project that became *Social Denmark* was Elton's recommendation that extant and future films for export be organised into series of short, focused films, rather than all-encompassing 'omnibus' films (14). Releasing sets of existing films, translated into English, in anticipation of the new social films would pique overseas interest. This emphasis on medium- to long-term planning reflects a principle more generally adopted by the British documentary movement: 'targeting particular interest groups for specific projects and following up on concrete results over the long term had been at the centre of Grierson's thinking about public information film for years' (Langlois 2016: 80). In turn – and this point is underlined in Elton's report – this would 'mean that Denmark would early establish itself *as a film-progressive country* in advance of the wave of films which will presently emanate from other countries' (Elton 1945b: 14, my emphasis).

There are two interesting implications here. On the one hand, if swift action is taken on the basis of the existing film production, Denmark could find herself in the post-war vanguard of film-producing nations. On the other hand, to make films about Danish social institutions constituted in and of itself an expression of Denmark's progressive nature. The enlightened use of film and the progressive institutions depicted in film were two sides of the same coin.

Lastly, Elton emphasised that the new social films should be honest, realistic and even humble about the strengths and weaknesses of the Danish social institutions exactly as they existed *anno* 1945:

> Let each film be accurate and objective; let each be reasonably detailed, yet lucid in presentation; let each be such that all who see it shall under-

stand in simple human terms its implications, yet let each command the interest of the sociologist, the reformer, the civic and government official; let the films exhibit the best in Denmark, but never let the best be shown as typical, for this kind of deception, practised at times by most nations of the world, can do great harm. Denmark has made notable contribution [sic] to the art and science of government. She has nothing to be ashamed of, and everything to gain in world esteem, by making frank statements of the economic and social problems she is facing and overcoming. (Elton 1945b: 15)

The content of the formal report is supplemented by a covering letter from Elton to Skot-Hansen (Elton 1945d), which reiterates Elton's perceived priorities. In this letter, Elton asks Skot-Hansen how he would like the formal report distributed, and also adds a few instructive and summative comments. A key point is that all film production and distribution overseen by the Danish government should be assessed holistically. A humble tourist film can have an influence over the best planned social film, warns Elton, if the former unexpectedly has an international breakthrough. In other words, he observes how films act on each other as part of a network. Secondly, Elton recommends that MFU pursues relationships with non-governmental organisations, especially large commercial concerns such as the shipbuilding firm Burmeister and Wain, and the cement and pharmaceutical industries, which could be persuaded to sponsor 'objective, scientific and other films', though care would need to be taken to avoid slippage between branding the films and their exploitation as product placement. Here, Elton is alluding to his own work with the Shell Film Unit. Further, he suggests that there would be great interest abroad in films on matters for which Denmark is renowned: agriculture, the cooperative movement and industry. He signs off by reminding Skot-Hansen of a range of other plans they had discussed: the bilateral exchange of film technicians and of films.

THE PRODUCTION OF SOCIAL DENMARK

Elton's own suggestion that a series of films be made eventually prevailed, but it was several months before the final constellation of topics was settled. On the whole, the planning process is an interesting instance of a broader phenomenon: many informational films were not conceived, shot and edited as monolithic wholes, but often emerged from interconnected projects and/ or were re-edited to serve new goals. The finalised Social Denmark series included three newly commissioned films, one portfolio film edited partly from extant footage and an English-language version of a wartime short directed by Carl Th. Dreyer. Respectively, these were People's Holiday (dir. Søren

Melson, script by Poul Henningsen, 1947), *Health for Denmark* (dir. Torben Anton Svendsen, script by Arthur Elton, 1947), *The Seventh Age* (dir. Torben Anton Svendsen, script by Carl Th. Dreyer and Torben Anton Svendsen, 1947), *Denmark Grows Up* (dirs Hagen Hasselbalch, Astrid Henning-Jensen and Søren Melson, 1947) and *Good Mothers* (*Mødrehjælpen*, dir. Carl Th. Dreyer, 1943).

In mid-June 1946, Elton returned to London, but planned to travel back to Denmark for a longer stay from July 1946 (Anonymous 1946). He was reported to be very excited about the proposed film on the Danish health system, because the subject was so topical in Britain at the time. His initial plans for the film included an outline of health provision in a typical Danish provincial town: sickness insurance, hospitals, and prevention of tuberculosis and other epidemics (Anonymous 1946).

By MFU's meeting of 6 November 1946 (MFU 1941–), the series had crystallised. *People's Holiday* and *The Seventh Age* were almost finished, and shooting of *Health for Denmark* was underway. Mogens Skot-Hansen was due to leave his post on 1 December 1946, and wanted to have the health film edited before then (Skot-Hansen 1946a). It was agreed that the fifth film in the series would be Dreyer's 1943 short *Mødrehjælpen*, re-named *Good Mothers* and with English subtitles. At the same meeting, it was advised that a film about Denmark's social institutions generally had been abandoned, and would be replaced by a more manageable project on services for children with the title *Denmark Grows Up*. To exemplify the aesthetic and narrative strategies of the *Social Denmark* films, we now turn to look more closely at *People's Holiday*.

PEOPLE'S HOLIDAY

Shot 4.15. Close up. A page in the Visitor's Book. A carefully drawn portrait of some wanderer with a subscription in Danish. The page is turned, and we read neatly written across the middle of a page in English WITH MUCH GRATITUDE FOR A SPLENDID HOLIDAY – ARTHUR ELTON.

(Anonymous n.d.: 11)

This textual cameo by Elton appears in an undated and anonymous shooting script for *People's Holiday*, which offers a progress report on the Danish law of 1938 on holiday allowance and pay. The film also presents the work of Folkeferie, a cooperative organisation founded in 1938 to make holidays accessible to the working class by running cheap hotels, holiday camps and a travel agency. *People's Holiday* was directed by Søren Melson and scripted by Poul Henningsen, who, a decade previously, had toured the country compiling his film *Danmark*, as discussed in Chapter 4.

Because the shooting script is in English and contains turns of phrase typical of Elton's writing as represented in correspondence around these films, it seems reasonable to assume that the film reached an advanced stage of planning under his guidance before being turned over to the director and scriptwriter; the shot list and voiceover text bear a close resemblance to the finished film. What is not articulated in Elton's outline is the intimacy with which Melson imbues the film, a quality which is essential to its persuasive power. While intimacy is intrinsic to the subject matter of the film – people captured off-duty – Melson directs the film to maximise the possibilities the scenario affords for suggesting access to 'facts' via a privileged, intimate view on the private life of the Danes.

On one level, this is about framing. The camera is often positioned in ways that are suggestive of privileged access and uses bodies as a framing device: youths checking in at a cramped hostel reception desk, a family eating around a table on a chalet veranda, or a farm bed-and-breakfast guest primping her hair in the mirror of a small attic room. A variant on this is bodies bustling around the camera, for example in the busy Folkeferie travel agency, and especially a stunning low shot of four young men in bathing trunks running towards and around the camera on their sprint towards the sea. A related strategy is the tendency of the shot to linger on the more contemplative moments of holidays: fishing (as in the opening scene), young couples entwined in each other's arms by the waterside, men playing cards in the shade of a tree. The liberal use of close-ups extends to expository shots of administrative items such as a youth hostel membership book and a page of holiday stamps, furnishing viewers with a screen-full of detail of the precious tokens of weeks worked and holidays earned. That particular shot is specified in Elton's own outline as 'a big close-up of the card full of stamps' (Anonymous n.d.: 2).

The focus on holidays on the Danish coast necessarily entails numerous sequences featuring holidaymakers in swimming costumes and other skimpy dress, often running, walking or cycling. In this sense, *People's Holiday* activates a set of visual tropes that had become associated with Northern Europeans in the first few decades of the twentieth century. Vitalism in Nordic art spanned the period 1900–40, decades during which 'the zest for life, health, beauty and strength' were central concepts in an 'intense cultivation of life, whether in philosophy, in art or in everyday life' (Hvidberg-Hansen and Oelsner 2011: 7; see also Thomson 2016b). A not unconnected point is that the culture of outdoor leisure in *People's Holiday* echoes one of the earliest themes of the *kulturfilm* genre in 1920s Germany. Films such as the popular *Wege zu Kraft und Schönheit* (*Ways to Health and Beauty*, Nicholas Kaufmann and Wilhelm Prager, 1924–5) juxtapose images of classical sculpture with demonstrations of gymnastics by scantily clad youth out in nature (Kracauer 1947: 142–4). Melson's film can thus hang the specific facts it has to convey about holiday pay on an existing framework of xenostereotypes associating the blonde body with athletic pursuits and nature (see Figure 5.1).

However, *People's Holiday* does not confine itself to displaying young, fit bodies. Towards the end of the film, a montage of holidaymakers enjoying the seaside includes shots of two plump ladies in bathing costumes paddling with a toddler. The bathing suits, while modest, reveal the women's folds of fat and the outline of their pubic area. This shot was felt to be inappropriate by a number of individuals involved in the approval process; they reacted so strongly (Skot-Hansen 1947) that Mogens Skot-Hansen was asked to edit the shot out without Melson's knowledge. Skot-Hansen also advised Melson to cut a shot of a housewife cooking. The reason for this request is not made explicit, but, judging by the extant film print, is likely to have been on the grounds that the contours of her nipples could be glimpsed through her bathing costume. Melson expressed his objection to these cuts to Theodor Christensen, then the leader of Dansk Filmforbund, the Danish filmmakers' newly established representative body. There appeared an article entitled 'Unofficial Censorship' in its organ *DF-Bulletin* in May 1947 which erroneously blamed film censor and women's campaigner Bodil Begtrup for the cut (Friis 1947). It was agreed that the offending shots would be left out of the film for the Danish premiere, and that the matter would be reconsidered before the *Social Denmark* series was sent to Britain. Melson was supported by Elton in his wish to reinstate the deleted shots (Melson n.d.), and the preserved version of the film includes the shots mentioned. It thus seems likely that the version that circulated overseas was Melson's cut, though I have not found any reviews that mention the offending details. This skirmish anticipates the long-running struggles over the extent to which directors should have a free hand in shaping their films creatively, a theme to which we return in Chapter 8.

The impact of landscape and weather on the film stock itself is particularly visible in *People's Holiday*. In at least two beach shots, the bright sun reflecting off the sea produces noticeably bleached-out images (possibly intensified by the transfer to the digital file on which I viewed the film). In a youth hostel campfire scene, the glow of the flames on the faces of young holidaymakers clustered around it results in a high contrast image, the documentary effect of which is intensified by the somewhat scratchy sound recording of their singing. The intensity of Nordic light thus emanates from the film as a kind of excess; it overwhelms the material on which the film is instantiated, insisting on the indexical trace left by the realness – or facticity – of the pro-filmic event.

Poul Henningsen's script corroborates the impression of factuality given by the visual exposition by framing the voiceover as a commentary about what is happening, or about to happen, in the images. The impression is given that life on screen is unfolding for the voiceover to comment on, as opposed to being selected by the 'voice of god'. For instance, as a housewife stands washing dishes in her bathing suit, the voiceover speculates that she has 'like as not' been left behind in the kitchen while the family goes to the beach. 'Yes, one might have guessed ...' says the narrator, his suspicions confirmed, as we see the father and children coming back from a swim. In this way, 'facts' emerge from the voiceover making observations about recognisably universal experiences unfolding on screen.

In a typescript entitled 'Notes and Terms of Reference for the Film on the Danish Holiday System' – undated but clearly pre-dating any screenplay drafts – the phrase 'near the beginning of the film we shall establish the law about holidays' has been corrected in Elton's handwriting to read 'establish some facts' (Elton n.d.). The list of facts to be included in *People's Holiday* is unusually well defined from the outset, and the presence of a range of correspondence from Arbejds- og Socialministeriet (the Ministry of Work and Society) attests to the involvement of the relevant government departments in identifying aspects of the law for inclusion. These include the principle that the worker not only has the entitlement but also the obligation to use two weeks' of paid holiday time between May and October; that a stamp system recording holiday time earned ensures that workers who move jobs have their leave honoured; and that Folkeferie functions as a cooperative. Also at this stage, the relevance of certain details for the British audience, understood to include the government, is laid down by Elton: 'The authorities in England will be interested in the stamp system and it should be given in some detail', while Folkeferie is compared to the British Workers' Travel Association (Elton n.d.). The presence in the production file of a range of brochures and annual reports from Folkeferie attest to the filmmakers' and policymakers' access to, and use of, documentation of legal and organisational developments in holiday provision, as well as statistical information. From such records, then, emerge three (overlapping) paths for 'facts' to follow into the film: they are specified as such by the ministry involved; they are projected to be understood as facts by the target audience insofar as they resemble known phenomena in the receiving culture; and/or they are interpreted and mediated by the filmmaker from published records.

People's Holiday closes with an appeal to the power of foreign travel to break down cultural boundaries between nations, a take on the subject matter which is outlined in Elton's draft treatment and which reminds us of *Social Denmark*'s roots in the internationalist British documentary movement. It also reflects Henningsen's humanist view of access to culture as necessary for enlightenment and peace (see Henningsen 1968). The film's voiceover concludes:

> The holiday problem cannot be solved inside one country. Angry frontiers and stubborn currency restrictions prevent the peoples of the world

Figure 5.1   The xenostereotype of the healthy Danish body in motion in *People's Holiday* (Søren Melson, 1947).

meeting and knowing each other. In spite of the aeroplane, manmade barriers sometimes make us seem as far away from each other as were the peoples of the middle ages ... Surely the great world powers can make it easy for everyone to see the countries and homes of their neighbours. If they fail to agree on such a simple thing, man may be set against man, and war may destroy the face of the earth.

The task of *People's Holiday* is to hold Denmark up as a country which has tried to democratise holidays for the sake of a healthy, happy population, but in doing so it also exhibits the landscape and coastline as potentially attractive holiday destinations. In a sense, this is the simplest of iterations of 'films of fact' – showing the country as pure spectacle. Elton himself acknowledged the potential of the film to draw tourists to Denmark precisely because of its lack of resemblance to the earlier generation of tourist films, which

seem to have been made for an audience that has been dead and buried these last twenty years ... I will bet a pound to a penny that Søren Melson's gay, intimate and good-humoured People's Holiday will do more to bring people to Denmark than all the spires and towers and landscapes and ruins and castles and historical monuments rolled into a ball and doubled. (Elton 1948: 10)

LEVERAGING THE AUTEUR: CARL TH. DREYER AND *SOCIAL DENMARK*

While *People's Holiday* was expressly commissioned to appeal to British curiosity about Danish social security and health, Carl Th. Dreyer was recruited to the project for more pragmatic, if not cynical, reasons. In his Introduction to the 1948 catalogue *Documentary in Denmark*, Elton writes:

> When I came to Denmark a little time after the liberation, almost the first film I saw was Carl Dreyer's masterly study of witchcraft, *Day of Wrath* (*Vredens Dag*) with its splendid acting and photographic quality and its moving formal stylised dialogue. (Elton 1948: 5)

Elton goes on to rank Dreyer's feature film alongside what he considers to be 'the world's most important contributions to the art of the cinema' (5–6), a list which, characteristically for Elton as documentarist, includes not only feature films by Eisenstein and John Ford, but also works by his colleagues Basil Wright and John Grierson. As Elton comments, at its Copenhagen premiere, *Vredens Dag* 'was almost unanimously condemned by the film critics' but was a 'sensational success' in London and Paris (6). Indeed, Dreyer was very popular in the UK at the time. In the wake of the rapturous reception of *Vredens Dag*, the British press was agog at his plans for a (never-realised) production on Mary, Queen of Scots (see Thomson 2015a).

Dreyer himself was curiously reluctant to get involved with the *Social Denmark* project. On the one hand, this was because he wished to focus on securing a feature-film deal in the USA. He went so far as to write to Skot-Hansen in October 1945, asking him not to introduce him to Elton during the Englishman's next visit to Copenhagen, as he did not want to be engaged to make a film in Britain (Dreyer 1945). Dreyer vacillated between prioritising either side of the Atlantic, though, failing to secure contracts during trips to New York in 1945 and 1948 (Drum and Drum 2000: 282), and after the London premiere of *Vredens Dag*, he entered into a contract with the British company Film Traders. The contract fell through, though not before Dreyer had submitted a manuscript that was 'perfect, but too expensive' (Drum and Drum 2000: 207). This was just one set-back in a fallow decade for Dreyer. He had not made a feature film since *Vampyr* in 1932. His reputation for blowing budgets and deadlines alike left him as 'a world-famous director without a job' (Roos n.d.). He had been granted the contract to make *Vredens Dag* with Palladium because Skot-Hansen had persuaded him to use an informational short film project, *Mødrehjælpen* (*Good Mothers*, 1942), to demonstrate his ability to work in a disciplined way (Kimergård n.d.a). This and subsequent short film productions for MFU and Dansk Kulturfilm helped Dreyer to patch together a living until he was appointed Director of the Dagmar Cinema in 1952. Dreyer was involved in about a dozen shorts in all, several of which are discussed in this book.

In the context of *Social Denmark*, Dreyer was engaged to write the script for *The Seventh Age*, but, perhaps more tellingly, his 1942 short *Mødrehjælpen* was also incorporated into the series. At the MFU meeting on 6 November 1946 where this decision was approved, the reasoning for its inclusion is left unarticulated, though voices were raised at the same meeting about the growing costs associated with the series. However, that the same committee was both aware of and ambivalent about Dreyer's kudos abroad is clear from its deliberations on another informational film by Dreyer: *Vandet paa Landet* (*Water from the Land*, 1946). This film was commissioned in 1944 by the National Health Board to publicise a programme of works improving water quality and hygiene in the Danish countryside. As Casper Tybjerg has noted (Tybjerg 2013), Dreyer's images of poor sanitation, rat-infested wells and muddy farmyards were simply *too* effective at evoking a sense of disgust in viewers, and the film was shelved by MFU before the editing process was complete. The Minister of Agriculture intervened on behalf of the farming organisations to stop the film before its premiere, realising that the impact of a film with Dreyer's name on it would be too great to risk releasing it, especially overseas (Nørrested and Alsted 1987: 271).

We can extrapolate from this episode that Dreyer's stamp on films for export was assumed to be helpful in the case of films which MFU and commissioning bodies actually did want to have widespread impact abroad. Perusal of reviews of his short films tends to corroborate this to some extent, but paints an ambivalent picture. On the whole, Dreyer seems to have functioned as a kind of 'carrier wave' for Danish informational film in the late 1940s; he could draw attention to the work of his compatriots, without necessarily being recognised himself as a great documentarist.

Arthur Elton's verdict on Dreyer's manuscript draft for *The Seventh Age* is interesting in that it reveals something about the tension between 'details', 'facts' and 'story' in the informational film, and the impact that a recognised director of fiction features might have on the narrative and circulation of shorts:

> I do not think he could have been trying very hard. I found it long, dull and too detailed. I also think it unpractical because, if you want to export the film, you should surely avoid synchronised dialogue. I am sorry to be so devastatingly negative, but I could find in it no trace of Dreyer's

artistry and no clarity of thought ... he gets around on page 5 to the life of the old pensioners themselves. For six pages he strings out architectural, human and administrative detail, in an un-articulated flood, and in the human detail there is no sign of the Dreyer touch ...Why do we want to use Dreyer? Because his handling of people, and of old people in particular, is superb. This is why we want him, this is the contribution he must make. If this very quality in him makes him incapable of seeing the general story of old age pensions and forces him to lose himself in detail, my answer is: Bring in another writer to supply the qualities which Dreyer lacks. (Elton 1946a)

The reception of *The Seventh Age* indicates the extent to which Dreyer's name on a film – even if 'only' as scriptwriter – attracted the attention of audiences and critics. For example, *Documentary Newsletter* published an enthusiastic response, which MFU extracted for use in a press release:

No words can adequately describe the way in which Torben Svendsen, the director, has translated Carl Dreyer's fine script to the screen. The problems of old age are brought vividly to our minds through the eyes of old people themselves; here by sheer film craft is caught the beauty and tragedy of old age. By turns serene or troubled, pathetic or gay, this film has a deep understanding of human nature. It is a film every detail of which remains in the memory. (MFU 1947)

Dreyer is also mentioned in *The Scotsman*'s review of the same film, from 11 May 1948:

The script is by Carl Dreyer, and it gives a modest and forthright exposition of the work done in Denmark for the care of the aged. In its facing of problems and existing inadequacies this is a valuable work for students of social service. (*The Scotsman* 1948)

The Seventh Age was shown at the EIFF in 1947 (*The Scotsman* 1948), and in London the next year it had a three-month screening round of cooperative societies. Arthur E. Jupp, Education Secretary of the London Cooperative Society Ltd was reported to have returned the print with the following words:

In expressing my Committee's gratitude for your kindness might I add that the film was most enthusiastically received by all of our organisations to which it was shown. There is no doubt that your films are doing much to create an understanding in this country of international problems. (Ebbesen 1948)

Two of Dreyer's later shorts for Dansk Kulturfilm were screened at the 1948 Edinburgh Film festival. *Landsbykirken* (*The Danish Village Church*, 1947) and *De nåede Færgen* (*They Caught the Ferry*, 1948)[2] were reviewed as examples of Dreyer's skilled craftsmanship' and as 'stamped with the quality of his visual imagination' (Hardy 1948: 16). On the whole, though, British reception of Dreyer's informational shorts was lukewarm. As Kimergård (1992: 49) has trenchantly observed, Dreyer's short films often have an air of tedium about them. In 1949, Dreyer's new short film *Thorvaldsen* (see Chapter 8) was shown at the Edinburgh International Film Festival, and dismissed as 'somewhat static' by Hardy (1949: 18). A year later, with *Storstrømsbroen* (*The Storstrom Bridge*, 1950), observed the *Daily Dispatch*, 'Dreyer [went] all lyrical', while *The Scotsman* grumbled: 'Nothing is explained. The director is content to look delightedly at his subject and praise it with his camera' (EIFF 1950: 4). Nevertheless, these short films kept Dreyer's name on the British film festival circuit in the decade between the UK premieres of his features *Vredens Dag* and *Ordet* (*The Word*, 1955).

SOCIAL DENMARK: DISTRIBUTION AND VERSIONS

The scheduled premiere of the *Social Denmark* series for a Danish audience was memorable for coinciding with the death of King Christian X, who had been on the throne since 1912, on 20 April 1947 (Melson n.d.). British distribution went ahead as planned. Statens Filmcentral's annual report for 1947–8 specifies that the rights to nine Danish documentaries had been given to the British Central Office of Information in return for eleven British Council films. This bundle included all the *Social Denmark* films, and up to twenty copies of each were distributed in the UK (SFC 1948b: 2).

Around the same time that Arthur Elton came to Copenhagen to work on a social film for the British market, Skot-Hansen was pushing for a different version of the same film project to be made for an American audience. Though this version never transpired, it is interesting to note that Skot-Hansen was convinced that the UK and US markets differed profoundly in their attitudes to Denmark, and that an American consultant would thus have to be engaged to make a suitable film. In an undated report adapted from his report to the Foreign Ministry of late July 1945, Skot-Hansen argues that the American people have no interest whatsoever in Denmark or its social security system (Skot-Hansen 1945c: 2). To make the film interesting, the country's social institutions would need to be narratively connected to the idea of a brave little land that had resisted Hitler's plans and emerged more democratic than before (3). Neither the Office of War Information nor the distributors March of Time could be persuaded to take on the project, and it seems to have been quietly dropped (Nørrested and Alsted 1987:

227) while the UK-focused *Social Denmark* series continued to develop into autumn 1945.

Danish versions of *The Seventh Age* and *Health for Denmark* were discussed in spring 1950 and were nearing completion by January 1951. The intention was to use the films in adult education, associations and schools (Koch-Olsen 1951a). The other two films were not to be made in Danish, though Ebbe Neergaard had pressed for a Danish version of *People's Holiday* (Arbejdsministeriet 1946). Decisions made by Arthur Elton to make the films more comprehensible for a British audience then had to be Danicised again. For example, references to weekly wage (then the norm in the UK) should be changed back to monthly, and the fictional town of Nordkøbing would be recognised by Danes as the medieval capital Roskilde. The National Health Service in the English voiceover was hard to translate (Rudfeld 1950).

The working Danish title of *Folkets Sundhed – The Health of the People* – was not acceptable to Sundhedsstyrelsen (the permanent secretariat of the Ministry of Health) because it covered a much broader scope than the film itself was concerned with. The alternative title *Sygeforsikret* (*Insured against Sickness*) was suggested instead (Hølaas 1950). As Sigvald Kristensen at the Foreign Ministry commented, the new title was quite correct, but not at all fun (Kristensen 1950). Kristensen's suggestions included: *Frihed for frygt – hvis sygdommen skulle ramme* (*Freedom from Fear – If Sickness Strikes*); *Far er medlem af sygekassen* (*Father has Sickness Insurance*); *Tryghed ved fællesskab* (*Security in Community*); *Ipsen bliver syg* (*Ipsen Gets Ill*). The last option was ringed in pencil and a note indicates that Rudfeld had agreed to this title (Kristensen 1950). The debate illustrates how seriously the ministries took the branding of their respective areas of responsibility in the nascent welfare state, but also the awareness that the films had to be entertaining.

As social provision was strengthened by successive governments and in light of the proliferation of specialist commissions in the 1950s (see Chapter 7), the versions for foreign markets of *Denmark Grows Up* were revised later in the decade to reflect developments in Danish healthcare. The initiative came from Socialministeriet (Ministry of Social Affairs) in March 1957 (Koch-Olsen 1957a). A small number of cuts to out-of-date sequences were requested. These included the wartime black market and rationing (Nielsen 1957), but it was felt that such details as prices and other figures could be left untouched, since foreign viewers were unlikely to have a sense of Danish norms (Koch-Olsen 1957a). In the first instance, it was investigated whether the relevant sequences could simply be edited out of the English and French versions (Nielsen 1957). This proved to be a workable strategy, ensuring that the films would be useable for a number of years (Friis 1958), though all existing copies had to be recalled to Denmark for editing. The films had a continued shelf life of about five years, whereupon the order went out to Danish embassies and consulates overseas to

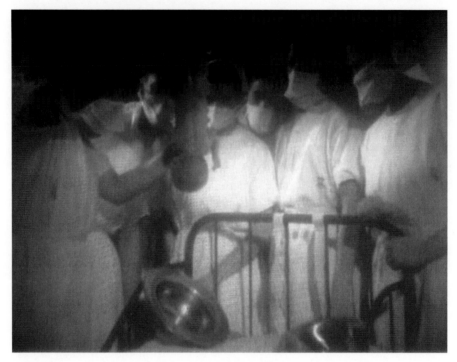

Figure 5.2   A nurse demonstrates resuscitation with a dummy in *Denmark Grows Up* (Hagen Hasselbalch, Astrid Henning-Jensen and Søren Melson, 1947).

destroy their copies (Rode 1963). The necessities of recalling and destroying the film reels remind us of the materiality of the films and of their travels.

BIRTHING FACTS: MODESTY, REALISM, PROGRESSIVENESS

There is a moment near the beginning of *Denmark Grows Up* which is emblematic of *Social Denmark*'s mediation of hard political facts into very human stories. Watched by a group of trainee midwives resplendent in starched white aprons and caps, a nurse demonstrates how to revive an unresponsive newborn by holding a doll aloft by the feet and squeezing its rib cage. After a few gentle compressions, a cut transforms the inert dummy into a wriggling, screaming baby. By reminding the viewer that film is, by its nature, an indexical medium that records and reproduces the exertions of living, breathing beings, *Denmark Grows Up* transcends for a moment the mixture of documentary and acted reconstruction that typifies the informational film in this period (see Figure 5.2).

British documentarist Basil Wright's review of the *Social Denmark* films reiterates the relationship between modesty, realism, progressiveness, and the facts that emerge from that mix in the films' reception in the UK:

Since the war ... we have been made increasingly aware of the highly organised documentary movement in Denmark, a movement which in its contribution to Danish life has had an influence more comparable to the documentary movement in Britain than any other country ... The three Danish films shown at the Edinburgh Festival are a good illustration of this fact. They are all of them part of a series dealing with the Danish Social Service, a series designed both for internal information and, perhaps more particularly, for overseas use. This is not to say that they are narrowly propagandist. For, while it is true that Denmark has much to teach the world in the social field and that such films are bound to be good propaganda for Denmark as a result, it will be found that each of them shows a healthy attitude of discontent with the status quo and an atmosphere of self-criticism which gives them a real validity for social students in all other countries. (Wright 1947: 24)

We now move on to consider how Danish informational films built on these achievements and tendencies in collaboration with other international networks around 1950, promoting aspects of Danish culture and politics as well as the notion of Scandinavia or Norden more broadly.

NOTES

1. On 26 February 1973, the newspaper *Politiken* ran an obituary of 'A Good Friend of Danish Film' (H. St. 1973): Sir Arthur Elton. Three decades earlier, Elton had embarked on what would prove to be an enduring relationship with Danish documentary. So enduring, in fact, that the obituary reports that the 'wise' and 'kind' Elton had planned to return to Denmark in late 1972 to co-write a film script with Mogens Skot-Hansen, but was forced to abandon the trip due to ill health.
2. See Thomson 2015b for an extended discussion of *They Caught the Ferry*.

6. SOMETHIN' ABOUT SCANDINAVIA: DANISH SHORTS ON THE POST-WAR INTERNATIONAL SCENE

The guest book of the 1948 Edinburgh International Film Festival contains the signatures of a seven-strong Danish contingent, among them Ebbe Neergaard, head of Statens Filmcentral, and leading documentarists Theodor Christensen and Søren Melson. Four younger Danish filmmakers had driven all the way from Copenhagen in a Ford Anglia emblazoned with a yellow pennant that read 'DANISH DOCUMENTARY'. Recalling their road trip, Ove Sevel relates:

> A big car it was not, but there was just about enough space for four, without too much luggage. And off we went, Nic Lichtenberg, Jørgen Roos, Erik Witte and me. Witte had been Skot-Hansen's right hand man in MFU and was now at Minerva Film. We drove across Holland and steered innocently into London and a level of traffic none of us had seen the likes of before. I'll never forget the first time I drove alongside one of those red London buses. Its wheel alone was taller than our little bucket of a car. We visited the Film Centre on Soho Square, we met Arthur Elton, we met another of the great names of British documentary's golden age, Alberto Cavalcanti, and all told we enjoyed a few very good days in the big city, before we set out for Edinburgh.
>
> We got to see a lot of films and met a lot of people. Amongst others, documentary's grand old man, Robert Flaherty (Louisiana Story). We established contacts that we were very glad of later in life. All in all it was a really good trip. (Sevel 2006: 46–7)

Sevel's memoir underscores the importance of Edinburgh and other such festivals for networking and professional development. The road trip is also an illustration of Greenblatt's point (2010, see Chapter 2) that cultural mobility must always be understood materially as well as metaphorically: ideas, films and filmmakers travel in a range of vehicles. This chapter focuses on the international mobility of Danish documentarists and informational films in the post-war period, an age when film was regarded as central to the work of intergovernmental cooperation and an internationalist ethos permeated an emerging worldwide network of informational film production.

The three film projects examined in this chapter exemplify three different (though interconnected) instances of international cooperation whose work was supported by informational film, though not necessarily by films the bodies themselves had commissioned directly. The first case study, *They Guide You Across* (Ingolf Boisen, 1949), is an example of a film commissioned at national level to showcase regional (Scandinavian) cooperation in the realm of aviation, which is 'adopted' by the United Nations Film Board to promote the idea of intergovernmental cooperation more generally. The second case study situates Theodor Christensen's *Alle mine skibe* (*All my Ships*, 1951) in context as a Danish contribution to the international corpus of Marshall Plan films. Funded and overseen by the European Recovery Program, colloquially known as Marshall Aid, hundreds of short films were made around 1950 with the intention of providing national perspectives on the international work essential to re-building post-war Europe. This chapter takes its title from the third case study, another film commissioned at national level to mediate an international project: the animated short *Noget om Norden* (*Somethin' about Scandinavia*, Bent Barfod, 1956).

The case studies thus span three different iterations of post-war internationalism. On the one hand, the UN Film Board and, later, the communications work of the UN's cultural arm UNESCO were focused on the promotion of a family of nations, an international cultural exchange that would 'circumvent the bipolarization of the world and the fraught relations between opposing camps' (Langlois 2016: 87). Sometimes this work was as concrete as securing international agreement on the mobility of films and filmmakers across national borders without the hindrance of import taxes (UNESCO 1950: 2). On the other hand, the cultural mission of the US-funded Marshall Plan films was to act as a bulwark against the influence of the USSR. More so than the output of the UN Film Board and UNESCO, the Marshall films were thus 'more marked by the Cold War, [and] focused on the colossal reconstruction efforts, the growing influence of an explicitly modern cultural model and an array of political weapons to fight the expansion of communism' (Langlois 2016: 87). Nordic cooperation, as it began to be formalised from the early 1950s, responded to this global polarisation by facilitating economic integration and cultural collaboration in the Nordic region.

While a robust network of screening facilities and interest groups at local level was the *sine qua non* of use of the informational film by post-war internationalist organisations, the role of the film festival was not negligible in shaping the direction and development of the genre on a worldwide scale. From its establishment in 1947 to the mid-1950s, the founders of the Edinburgh International Film Festival (EIFF) framed it as the premier gathering of specifically documentary filmmakers and policymakers, committed to advancing the medium through discussion and dissemination. This was a continuation of pre-war ambitions 'to forge international cooperation among the world's documentary workers' and to use film for humanitarian intervention, now 'on new ground, the developing world' (MacDonald 2013: 461). Festival programming emphasised documentary as an expression of national specificities which could fruitfully be compared and brought into conversation, a focus which 'reified culture as a form of national difference while simultaneously naturalizing the nation as a source of the traits of individuals' (Druick 2011: 84). While films were selected and presented as emanating from nation states, EIFF was also an important platform for films made under the auspices of bodies such as the United Nations Film Board and UNESCO (Langlois 2016: 75).

In all three case studies, as in the previous chapter, we see how fact-making and film-making are entangled with the mediation of aspects of national culture to other audiences. The production of the films themselves and the on-screen construction of the internationalist perspectives they convey emerges from the case studies as a process that is contingent on the movement of personnel, equipment and film stock across distances great and modest, of words in the form of transatlantic telegrams and pages of typescript across the Øresund, and of ideals from committee room to cartoonist's sketch.

The Viking Ships of the Air: Visualising Scandinavian Airline Systems

It was not just films and filmmakers that travelled from Denmark to Britain and back in the golden era of documentary. A Newman-Sinclair camera also made the trip, having been bought by Ingolf Boisen and his Minerva colleagues from their London-based documentarist friends at the end of the 1930s (Boisen 1977: 227). This particular camera had been used on *Night Mail* (Harry Watt and Basil Wright, 1936), and now it was to play a role in filming another informational short that would give audiences a behind-the-scenes glimpse into the workings of a vital piece of transport infrastructure: the new transatlantic flights from Scandinavia to New York. The inaugural commercial flight on this route had taken off from Stockholm Bromma on 17 September 1946, concretising the amalgamation of the Danish, Norwegian and Swedish national aviation companies into Scandinavian Airline Systems, or SAS (SAS 2009). On that maiden flight was Danish documentarist Ingolf Boisen (Boisen

1977: 228), tasked by MFU with capturing footage for a film about this new Nordic venture. The result was a forty-minute English-language film, *They Guide You Across* (1949), and various language variants thereof. This film is a salient example of how the model developed with Elton for *Social Denmark* could and did function in sometimes surprising ways to challenge and expand the work of Dansk Kulturfilm and MFU, in terms of inter-institutional and international cooperation, as well as technological know-how.

The Newman-Sinclair camera was popular among documentarists for its lightness and toughness. Stanley Kubrick described the brand as 'built like a battleship' and 'the most indestructible camera ever made'; he used a Newman-Sinclair in *A Clockwork Orange* (1972) to film the point-of-view shot of Alex's suicide attempt, throwing the camera off the roof of a building six times, and found that it still worked even after landing lens-down (Strick and Houston 1972). With his cameraman Nic Lichtenberg, in April 1948, Ingolf Boisen was planning to use his Newman-Sinclair to capture footage of the take-off of the DC4 aircraft 'Dan Viking' from Copenhagen Kastrup airport. They had positioned the camera a couple of hundred metres from the end of the runway, fastened down with steel wire and hooks hammered into the concrete. Additional film would be shot by Lichtenberg from the far end of the runway. Captain 'Yankee' Hedall-Hansen had been briefed to lift wheels as close to the position of the Newman-Sinclair as possible. In the event, he overshot the mark, hit the camera with the front wheel of the DC4, and got the plane airborne uncomfortably close to Lichtenberg at the end of the runway. Lichtenberg lived to make the road trip to Edinburgh with Ove Sevel a few months later. But the 'indestructible' Newman-Sinclair was smashed to smithereens; even the cassette holding the film had disintegrated and sixty metres of precious footage lay strewn across the runway. From Prestwick in Scotland, where the plane had to stop to refuel a few hours later, came a telegram: 'SORRY OLD BOY COULD NOT SEE THE BOX – HEDALL' (Boisen 1977: 227–8).

They Guide You Across is first mentioned in MFU meeting minutes in April 1946 (MFU 1941–) and premiered in September 1949 at the Edinburgh International Film Festival (Dansk Kulturfilm 1949a). In its September 1949 press release announcing the premiere at EIFF, the film is described as having been produced by Minerva Film with support from the United Nations Film Board and technical advice from the International Civil Aviation Organisation. SAS was credited as providing technical assistance and complimentary airline tickets (Dansk Kulturfilm 1949a). The relatively long production period was due to two factors: the range of technological challenges presented by the project, and an extended skirmish between Boisen, Dansk Kulturfilm and the new United Nations Film Board about the role the latter might have in the film's distribution. In both these contexts – technological and institutional – the production of *They Guide You Across* had unforeseen impacts.

TECHNOLOGICAL AND NARRATIVE DAREDEVILRY

The technological challenges of making *They Guide You Across* surpassed capturing the take-off shot that sealed the fate of the Newman-Sinclair. The focus of the film, as its title suggests, was the network of people and systems behind the scenes, ensuring the safety of passengers on the new transatlantic route. Telling that story therefore entailed capturing not just spectacular shots of aircraft in flight, but also detailed footage of a range of instruments, mechanisms and procedures on the ground, in the air and at sea in the Atlantic. Some of these were to be mediated via animation and models. Sound was a major challenge for the film: not just recording the deafening roar of the aircraft but also capturing noise on location inside the confined space of the cabin.

It is a truism that cinema and aviation were born and came of age more or less simultaneously. In the field of documentary and informational cinema, too, Boisen had a range of visual tropes and narrative strategies to choose from. Paul Rotha of the British documentary school had made a series of informational films in the late 1930s for Imperial Airlines (later British Airways), of which *The Future's in the Air* (1937) won particular acclaim for its script by Graham Greene and its portrayal of worldwide delivery of mail. Other informational films explained the workings of engines and airports. *Airport* (Roy Lockwood, 1935, Great Britain) was the first film made by the Shell Film Unit and explored the workings of Croydon, Britain's busiest airport at the time (Burgess 2010: 215). Arthur Elton's *Aero-Engine* (1933) was typical of Elton's interest in the precise details of machinery and was 'prized among a global network of engineering colleges by clearly communicating technological information' (Anthony 2011: 303). The Shell Film Unit's updated six-film educational series *How an Aeroplane Flies* (1945–7) was more or less contemporaneous with *They Guide You Across*, evincing popular interest in keeping pace with rapidly advancing aviation technology. *They Guide You Across* combines an interest in the details of mechanical and communication systems with a more humanistic engagement with the potential of air travel for international peace and cooperation.

Boisen was Denmark's leading expert in aviation film. He had been advancing the art of filming in the air since the time Dansk Kulturfilm was taking its first faltering steps with films about bricklaying and the meat industry. Boisen's resumé is a good example of how many directors came to Dansk Kulturfilm with varied and specialist experience gained working for their own production companies and for private businesses; once again, it is important to emphasise that state-sponsored film in Denmark did not operate in a vacuum, and that ground-breaking informational film production happened in other contexts. The first film Boisen made as director was of the parachutist John Tranum's March 1935 attempt to break the record for free-fall, an attempt which, sadly, ended in Tranum's death from oxygen deprivation at high altitude (Boisen 1977: 63–4, 75). Minerva Film, the production company Boisen helped to establish with Axel Lerche, made six films for Dansk Luftværnsforening (Danish Air Defence Society) in its first two years of operation, as well as for the army and private aviators (84). All in all, Minerva and Boisen in particular were the obvious choice for a film about the new transatlantic route, given their record of planning and executing specialist projects.

But another aviator on the Danish film scene was in New York to help with this. Aside from the ill-fated take-off shot at Kastrup, the film would have to show the DC4 in flight and its various mechanisms, such as landing gear, in operation. In order to capture footage depicting the plane's descent into La Guardia, SAS made 'Dan Viking' available for two hours one afternoon to fly over New York, while the city's Air Defence loaned a smaller Beechcraft plane so that Lichtenberg could film the DC4 against the sky. Serendipitously, an experienced filmmaker – none other than Carl Th. Dreyer – was on hand in New York to help Boisen with some of the footage in the flyover. Dreyer was in town on one of his research trips to try to develop and secure a contract for his never-realised film about the life of Jesus, and often ate dinner with Boisen and Lichtenberg during their stay in New York. Though nothing in his feature films would suggest it, Dreyer had been an aviator in his youth (Mygdal-Meyer n.d.). He was thus prevailed upon to operate (by wired remote control) a camera secured to the underbelly of the plane to film the wheels in operation against a backdrop of skyscrapers (see Figure 6.1), and Boisen became probably the only director in history to be able to boast that he had once had Dreyer as his cameraman (Boisen 1977: 234–6).

Persuading the flying public (or potential passengers) of the soundness of the safety mechanisms involved in transatlantic travel was paramount. On the one hand, this involved communicating details of the technologies and systems that were identified as crucial by SAS. Specialist expertise was provided by the constituent companies of SAS at an early stage of the screenplay drafting process. The manuscript as of February 1948 was generally approved, but a number of corrections were requested for precision. These ranged from the overly precise – for example, 13,500 litres of aviation fuel should be 13,246 – to the useful – that the 'no smoking' sign must be switched off before a character can light his cigarette (Det Danske Luftfartsselskab 1948). A range of technical data is allowed to penetrate the script, both in the plane's voiceover and in lines regarding weather, itinerary, flight plan and health checks for the crew, delivered calmly and briskly in Scandinavian, American, Scottish and English accents. The extended flight preparation sequence is tempered by an almost exuberant 'Ok boys, here we go!' from the Captain as he fires up Dan Viking's engines. Similarly, while the descent into Prestwick is tracked with a long, technophilic sequence of cross-cutting between cabin instruments and indicators

Figure 6.1   The wheel of a DC4 against the New York skyline, filmed by Carl Th. Dreyer for Ingolf Boisen's *They Guide You Across* (1949).

and long-shots of the aircraft from the ground, Hedall Hansen's homey declaration that he will 'get us on the ground in time for tea' is cosily reassuring. These two declarations by the Captain seem to have been prioritised for insertion into the script at a late stage; a note written in-flight by Boisen on his way west in mid-May 1949 confirms that Hedall Hansen had successfully delivered the lines earlier that day (Boisen 1949).

The safety systems covered in the film had to be transformed into a compelling story, if the audience was to grasp the human value of such systems. A text written by Boisen for use at film screenings indicates how he approached this aspect of filmmaking: for him, 'documentary' describes 'films that take their material from life today, but where there is an attempt to dramatise the subject, and the story is told in such a way as to emphasise a certain tension, a certain contrast' (Boisen n.d.: 1). Accordingly, he built three central characters into *They Guide You Across*: the charismatic pilot, Captain 'Yankee' Hedall Hansen; the plane itself, a DC4 Skymaster by the name of 'Dan Viking' (callname OBO FOX ITEM) which, awkwardly for visual continuity, was upgraded during the shoot to a DC6 Cloudmaster (Boisen 1977: 230); and a young passenger, Peter, who takes his first trip from Copenhagen to New

York. The original script called for the plane's engineer to be a recurring character throughout the film, but contacts at the International Civil Aviation Organization (ICAO) suggested that the film would be more compelling if Boisen's young son and wife could appear as passengers (230–3). Clearly, that the little boy's safety is at stake makes the narrative more compelling than it otherwise would be; the description of the unseen work of weather stations and itinerary planners is framed in terms of the toddler's obliviousness and his mother's occasional anxious glance out of the window. 'Dan Viking' emerges, though, as Peter's most staunch protector – the voice of the plane itself dominates the voiceover.

The emphasis on safety systems was also an opportunity to paint the world as diverse and interconnected, and to assert Scandinavia's place in it. SAS was formed a decade or more after other state-supported carriers such as Imperial Airways, Lufthansa, Sabena, KLM and Air France (Anthony 2011: 302), and heralded a decade of idealism in pan-Nordic cooperation. Auto- and xenostereotypes of Scandinavia's Viking heritage, redolent with notions of voyaging, tenacity and white ethnicity, permeated SAS's carefully curated image, from aircraft names ('Dan Viking') to in-flight stationery ('On Board the Viking Flying Ship!', Boisen 1949). The network of weather stations portrayed in *They Guide You Across* constructs a globality that is resolutely northern. In this respect, it is interesting to compare *They Guide You Across* with *Air Outpost* (Stuart Legg and John Taylor, 1937, Great Britain), which features a sequence explaining the role of weather balloons for Imperial Airways traffic in Sharja; *Air Outpost* cross-cuts between balloons released by meteorologists and Arab people releasing falcons, one of 'a series of striking visual equivalences' tying the Empire together (Anthony 2011: 304). A few years later, weather balloons also feature in a short film commissioned by Pan American Airlines to promote their new Jet Clipper service across the Atlantic, entitled $6^{1/2}$ *Magic Hours* (Kahlenberg, 1956). While the emphasis in that film is very much on the glamour of air travel – an effect enhanced by the rendering of passengers' brightly patterned suitcases, couture clothing and white-toothed smiles in Kodachrome – it also includes a montage of weather balloons released by technicians of every skin colour and reports being typed in a variety of alphabets. In all these films, weather balloons emerge as a surprisingly compelling visual trope, invariably shot with a vertical pan as they rise, tethered, into the sky, signifying both the elegance of flight and the concept of a global safety net(work) of invisible labour and communication technology.

In his study of 1930s informational films on Imperial Airways, the precursor to British Airways, Scott Anthony speculates that Paul Rotha and his fellow documentarists began to suffer from 'cabin fever', as their images and narratives of exotic destinations were increasingly affected by the disorienting effects of temporal and spatial disjunction, the result of many months embedded with the airline (Anthony 2011: 310). Similarly, Boisen estimates that he and his colleagues covered 120,000 kilometres, or three times around the world, at a time when the journey from Scandinavia to New York took the best part of twenty-four hours each time and involved layovers at Prestwick in Scotland and Gander in Newfoundland (Boisen 1977: 228, 238). Boisen also reminisces about the practical impact of his decision to focus on the same plane through-out the film. While 'Dan Viking' was undergoing maintenance, or the cabin crew were on vacation, or bad weather diverted the aircraft, he could be left stranded in Gander for a week (230). Emblematic of such travels and travails is, for example, a note about progress dated 14 May 1949 handwritten on SAS in-flight notepaper, which gives Boisen's location as '32 miles east of Gander' (Boisen 1949). Under such conditions, communication between Boisen and the authorities back in Denmark was not as smooth-sailing as it might have been – especially when the nascent United Nations Film Board expressed an interest in *They Guide You Across*.

United Nations Film Board Sponsorship

While the *Social Denmark* series exemplifies bilateral collaboration between the Danish and British documentary scenes, *They Guide You Across* – coming a little later and by dint of its subject matter – was instrumental in bringing Dansk Kulturfilm and MFU into contact with the nascent United Nations Film Board (UNFB). This episode is interesting as an example of the tensions that could arise between national and international players on the informational film scene, reminding us that the idealism of internationalist visions of film as educational tool was tempered by local politics.

Aviation safety was an obvious subject of interest for UNFB. As *They Guide You Across* hammers home early on in its voiceover and also in its closing shots, transatlantic air travel was not only a new phenomenon – only twenty-seven planes had crossed the Atlantic in the twenty years from 1919, against 100,000 crossings since 1939, we are told – but it was also a crucial element in post-war economic and cultural reconstruction. Indeed, Scott Anthony's observation about the factors driving 1930s aviation documentary was still applicable to post-war transatlantic flight: at stake was 'a new technology driven by nationalistic and territorial anxiety and yet the intrinsic internationalism of the technology also required the working out of considerable common legal, technical and organisational ground' (Anthony 2011: 301). UNFB had been established in 1946, shortly after the founding of the UN itself. Mogens Skot-Hansen, who had been head of MFU in Denmark, left at the end of 1946 to take up a post with UNESCO's film service in Paris, shortly thereafter taking up the leadership of UNFB's Paris office. His successor at MFU and Dansk Kulturfilm was Ib Koch-Olsen (1914–93). The commissioning and production period of *They Guide*

You Across, as with many other films, thus spanned the tenures of both Skot-Hansen and Koch-Olsen. But an additional player in the development of *They Guide You Across* was Jean Benoit-Lévy. A director of educational films and of a liberal bent, Benoit-Lévy and his family had fled from occupied France to the US in 1941. He was appointed director of the Films and Visual Information Division of the UN in mid-1946, later becoming Executive Director of the UNFB until July 1949 (Langlois 2016: 77–80), when he was succeeded by Jan Gunnar Lindstrøm. During one of their filming trips in May 1948, Boisen and Lichtenberg visited the then UN headquarters at Lake Success on Long Island, New York and met Benoit-Lévy. The filmmakers showed the shooting script to the Frenchman, who was immediately excited about the project and secured UN sponsorship for the film that same afternoon – conditional on a formal application from MFU back home. In practical terms, sponsorship would mean free supplies of film stock, free development and duplication of the finished film in a New York laboratory, the UN's name on the film credits as sponsor and distribution through the ICAO (Boisen 1977: 230–1).

However, Koch-Olsen was not as enthusiastic as the filmmakers had hoped, and indeed expected, given the apparent advantages of UN sponsorship. A flurry of letters and telegrams criss-crossed the Atlantic over the second half of May 1948 and into June. A significant sticking point was the UNFB's request that the film's length be increased to 1800 feet (about fifty minutes), which was around twice the length envisaged by MFU and therefore would considerably increase costs. Koch-Olsen insisted repeatedly, including in letters and cables to Benoit-Lévy himself, that Boisen should return to Copenhagen with the extant footage so that negotiations could take place in light of the film itself, that Boisen was not authorised to accept the UNFB's conditions, and that MFU needed (more) 'concrete information of [sic] the nature and extent of the intended support from UN' (Koch-Olsen 1948c). As Boisen summarises the skirmish in his memoirs (and as the production files confirm), it took thirteen telegrams, eighteen letters, three transatlantic telephone calls and the involvement of the Danish ambassador to the USA, the Foreign Ministry, the Ministry of Justice, SAS and the UNFB, to secure MFU's agreement to UN sponsorship of the film (Boisen 1977: 233).

But this is not merely a record of inter-personal and inter-institutional rivalries. Amongst this correspondence, a very detailed letter from Benoit-Lévy to Koch-Olsen provides a snapshot of the work and ambitions of the UNFB in mid-1949. UNFB was able to arrange both theatrical and non-theatrical distribution for the films it sponsored by facilitating contacts with distributors and arranging terms, in consultation with the producer. The producer was welcome to organise country-specific non-theatrical distribution, but coordination with the local UN Information Centre was advisable, and there should be a six-month firewall between theatrical and non-theatrical distribution in the same country. Koch-Olsen had also asked about economic returns for MFU; here, UNFB was unable to provide more than ballpark figures, as it took two years – longer than the agency had been in practical operation – to assess likely financial results and talks were ongoing to boost returns on US distribution. More concrete information was however available about audience size. Typical recorded audience size for existing UN films was given as 50 million. UNFB would be happy to distribute foreign-language versions of films, but could not subsidise the production of these. Finally, to compensate in kind for the expenses entailed in revising *They Guide You Across* to make it 'truly international', Benoit-Lévy offered to send 15,000 feet of film stock to Dansk Kulturfilm (Benoit-Lévy 1949).

Koch-Olsen's reluctance to throw Dansk Kulturfilm's lot in with UNFB is easier to understand if we take into account the untested nature of the UN Film Board and its lack of funds. Throughout 1945 and 1946, the groundwork for the nascent UN and UNESCO had envisaged a strong visual presence for both institutions, not least because it was estimated that half of the global population was still illiterate, but also because the immediate post-war years saw the peak of cinema-going as a pastime and of the use of film as an educational tool (Langlois 2016: 73). UNFB got off to a stronger and quicker start in filmmaking than UNESCO, which did not achieve its own film department until 1951 (74), though UNESCO's use of film has attracted more scholarly attention than that of UNFB (see for example, Druick 2011). In the late 1940s, UNFB was already filming UN-related meetings and events, coordinating film distribution and commissioning documentaries to support the work of the UN. However, UN filmmaking in general suffered from insufficient resources, which 'hindered concrete achievements and crushed some projects' (Langlois 2016: 87). There are hints of such troubles in the correspondence about *They Guide You Across*. In mid-1950, for example, UNFB requested five extra copies of the longer English version of the film from MFU to broaden its distribution in theatres. MFU, under financial pressures of its own, rejected the request on the basis that the original agreement had been to fund one copy only (Koch-Olsen 1950). Boisen found this frustrating, as the film was not screened in Denmark, and so SAS was the only body to use the film worldwide (Nielsen 1951). This refusal to fund extra copies is marked, as it flew in the face of declared interest from the International Civil Aviation Authority and the Civil Aeronautics Administration in distributing the film to their membership (Boisen 1950).

Nonetheless, the film did achieve wide distribution in Scandinavia and North America, though precise figures have not been preserved in the production files. The ICAO's Film Officer, for example, wrote to Boisen:

> I should like to say that the more your film is shown the more enthusiastic ICAO people are becoming about the picture. It will no doubt fill a

requirement for many years to illustrate a typical international aviation operation ... I shall do anything possible to promote your film – there is a definite requirement for such a picture. (Boisen 1950)

Boisen's memoirs confirm that he accompanied the film to various events of this kind around the Nordic region (Boisen 1977: 238). The production files contain a programme for an event which constituted the premiere of the longer Danish version of the film, *Sikkerhed i luften* (literally, *Safety in the Air*), and the film was introduced by Boisen. This gives us a glimpse into the kind of club social event at which informational films were sometimes screened, showing how adult education often combined with leisure:

28 February 1950: The Royal Danish Aeronautics Society invites members and their partners to a film evening and flying ball at Borgernes Hus, Rosenborggade 1. Programme:
Screening of three films generously supplied by Statens Filmcentral:
Hvor Vejene mødes (Meeting of the Ways, dir. Hagen Hasselbalch, 1948, a film about Copenhagen Kastrup airport)
Vejen mod Nord (The Pearyland Expedition, dir. Hagen Hasselbalch and Ib Dam, 1948)
They Guide You Across (world premiere of the unabridged Danish version of the film about safety on the transatlantic air route)
Before the films, Ingolf Boisen, director of Minerva Films will hold a short talk about the three films. Afterwards, there will be dancing to an orchestra performance conducted by Chapel Master Sc. Tognarelli. At 10 pm, those who wish to eat are offered two pieces of smørrebrød, two pieces of traybake, beer, schnapps, coffee, service included, for 9 kroner. Then dancing will continue until 1 am.
In the course of the evening, actors Ole Monty and Knud Pheiffer will offer entertainment.
Entry to the event is free; dress code casual. (Kongelig dansk Æroklub 1950)

SOUND AND LANGUAGE IN *THEY GUIDE YOU ACROSS*

They Guide You Across illustrates some of the practices around the making of different language versions and different length versions of informational films. Or rather, in both these respects, it is the exception that proves the rule. The original version of the film was in English, for worldwide distribution, and about twenty minutes in length. Upon its premiere, the press release promised a Danish version in due course for cinematic release in Denmark (Dansk Kulturfilm 1949a). However, a shorter Danish version does not seem to have been completed. Rather, several of the agencies involved in facilitating the original film – Dansk Kulturfilm, Statens Filmcentral, the UN Film Board and the International Civil Aviation Authority, as well as SAS – were keen for a longer version of thirty-five to forty minutes to be made, which would be used for non-theatrical distribution and in continuing education (Minerva Film 1949; Neergaard 1949). This longer version was made in both English and Danish, the latter produced by SFC (Koch-Olsen 1951b), and approved by the UN Film Board in summer 1949; this is the version discussed above. A German-language version of the film, *Sie sichern Deinen Flug*, was funded and produced by SAS to use for training airline staff (Hølaas 1955). The existence of multiple language versions and two different lengths caused some confusion and led on at least one occasion to cancellation of attempts to screen the film. For example, Foreningen Norden (the interest group which campaigned for Nordic cooperation, which crops up again later in this chapter) wished to show the film on 16mm during its annual meeting at Hindsgavl Castle on the island of Funen. SFC was asked to supply the relevant version, but was unaware of the existence of the English and Danish versions (Koch-Olsen 1951b).

Another unusual aspect of the sound in *They Guide You Across* is its use of dialogue, which, as we saw in Chapter 5, was already recognised during the development of *Social Denmark* as something to avoid in films likely to be made in multiple language versions. While, as discussed above, the voice of the pilot and safety workers contribute to a sense of their competence, it is particularly in terms of the voice that the sound quality in the Danish and English language versions of *They Guide You Across* strikes the contemporary viewer as poor. It transpires from correspondence in the mid-1950s with the German agency Institut für Film und Bild in Wissenschaft und Unterricht (Institute for Film and Images in Science and Education) that the sound recording equipment and mixing used in 1949 for *They Guide You Across* and *Thorvaldsen* (Carl Th. Dreyer, 1949; see Chapter 8) was soon superseded by use of tape and already regarded as unsatisfactory by the mid-1950s (Hølaas 1955). However, in the late 1940s, Boisen's production company Minerva Film had the distinction of being the first film company in the world to solve the problem of recording sound on-the-go, with a portable recorder which enabled instant access to the recording. The solution came via an engineer from the Danish company Bang & Olufsen, L. A. Duus Hansen, who pioneered wire recording on metal thread, adapting Valdemar Poulsen's electromagnetic recorder, *telegrafonen*, of 1898. Duus Hansen had developed the technology during the Second World War, when he was known by the codename Napkin, and organised radio communications between the Danish Resistance and the Special Operations Executive in London (Boisen 1977: 231–3). Duus Hansen acted as sound engineer on some of the flights during the production of *They Guide You Across*, facilitating sound recording in the cabin, the control towers and other small spaces. This film is therefore quite a rare example of the use of wire recording in informational film and cannot be said to have spawned a great number of imitators; the technology was swiftly surpassed by the use of magnetic tape. However, between 1945 and 1950 wire recording was used for a range of purposes, including in the field by researchers for recording oral testimonies and as a state-of-the-art domestic entertainment technology (Sayers 2011: 108, 126). Wire recording also features as a plot device in Arthur Miller's 1949 play *Death of a Salesman* (Sayers 2011: 126–7; Miller 1961), dating the play, like *They Guide You Across*, to the very short heyday of an ephemeral technology.

CRISIS AT HOME AND SUCCESS ABROAD AROUND 1950

Nørrested and Alsted (1987: 269–70) see 1949 as a watershed year for Dansk Kulturfilm, firstly because production hit a high water mark with sixty films. Secondly, various retirements and deaths transformed the membership of the Board. Thirdly, there was a financial crisis which shaped the following years: the Justice Ministry refused to underwrite a loss in the annual budget. *They Guide You Across* had overshot its projected costs and embroiled Dansk Kulturfilm in a transatlantic tug of war with the UN Film Board for artistic control. More serious were the losses sustained on two feature-length *kulturfilm* on the country's political history: *Kampen mod Uretten* (*The Fight Against Injustice*, Ole Palsbo, 1949) and *For Frihed og Ret* (*For Freedom and Justice*, Svend Methling, 1949), which each cost substantially more than the half-million kroner of an average feature film. The latter film in particular was castigated in the press, attracted poor box office figures and triggered calls for a review of the management of Dansk Kulturfilm and how it was using taxpayers' money (Nørrested and Alsted 1987: 274–5).

Ib Koch-Olsen, who had succeeded Mogens Skot-Hansen and Thomas P. Hejle as head of both MFU and Dansk Kulturfilm, also came under intense pressure from Dansk Filmforbund, the Danish Filmmakers' Association led by Theodor Christensen, which decided to boycott all cooperation with him, if not with MFU and Dansk Kulturfilm (Nørrested and Alsted 1987: 275). Dansk Kulturfilm's Board resolved not to bend in the face of what it regarded as chicanery on the part of Dansk Filmforbund, and the boycott lasted six months (277). Matters came to a head in December 1949, when Christensen published an article in the left-wing newspaper *Land og Folk* threatening a filmmakers' strike. Negotiations revealed that Koch-Olsen, in May the same year, had made verbal promises to Dansk Filmforbund about a heftier role in shaping the content of films, but had not brought the proposals to the Dansk Kulturfilm Board (279). Ultimately, the strike could not hold, given that Dansk Kulturfilm was the largest employer of documentary filmmakers in Denmark, and even Christensen began to work for the organisation again by 1950. However, Christensen's successor as Chair of Dansk Filmforbund, Karl Roos, declared Danish documentary 'non-existent' by February 1950; it had lost contact with developments on the documentary scene out in the wider world (cited in Nørrested and Alsted 1987: 281). This diagnosis seems overly lugubrious, given the warm reception of a range of Danish informational films abroad around 1950.

The same tension between gloomy prognosis at home and success abroad also obtained in the sphere of distribution. Koch-Olsen was worried about domestic distribution of Dansk Kulturfilm's productions, especially theatrical distribution. There was inadequate information about audience numbers, a weakness in the distribution chain that was never adequately resolved. On the other hand, international distribution – mostly undertaken under the auspices of the Press Bureau of the Foreign Ministry – was accelerating by mid-1949, not least due to liaison with agencies such as Films of the Nations in North America (Nørrested and Alsted 1987: 272; see also Chapter 8) and the Marshall Plan film programme, to which we now turn.

The Marshall Plan Films

What is the price of peace? In the early 1950s, Americans were informed that it was eighty dollars apiece – the estimated cost per US citizen of the European Recovery Program, better known as Marshall Aid. *Your Eighty Dollars* was the title of a television programme on ABC-TV of 1952, edited together from films made in Europe under the auspices of the Marshall Plan (Hemsing 1994: 274).

During the Truman administration, US Congress established the Economic Cooperation Administration (ECA) in April 1948 to administer and execute the Marshall Aid programme (or European Recovery Program), which grew to an 'unprecedented' 12.5 billion dollar fund (Hemsing 1994: 269). Headed by Averell Harriman, the Paris headquarters set up an information division, which benefited from the five per cent allocation to administration and communication of 'counterpart' funds, the match funds provided by the eighteen signatory countries (270). Film was an important dimension of the ECA's propaganda efforts and it is estimated that around 200 (Hemsing 1994: 271) to 300 (GCMF n.d.) such films were made across Europe. The proportion of films preserved in the US National Archives is incomplete; the former head of the ECA's film unit, Alfred Hemsing, rounded up some 117 films in the early 1990s (Hemsing 1994: 270) and just under 200 are listed in a more recent filmography (Christenson 2002). The film unit's first chief, Lothar Wolff, was seconded from the newsreel company The March of Time and 'understood how to address European audiences' (Hemsing 1994: 272); he was succeeded by Stuart Schulberg. The Paris-based staff encompassed specialists in non-theatrical distribution, writers, producers, cameramen and technicians from the European documentary film milieu, a team that could 'assist our country missions in developing a film proposal, researching a story, supervising a weak contract-producer, or livening up a limp narration' (272).

The faith of the Marshall Aid organisation in the efficacy of informational films as propaganda is perhaps expressed most clearly by the funding arrangements. The Mission of the ECA would fund the cost of producing the films in its entirety, in Denmark up to 100,000 kroner per film, to be paid in four instalments each due at key stages in the production process: agreement of subject matter, approval of script, completion of the film, submission of final account. A series of 'six to twelve' Danish films was initially envisaged (Marshall 1950). In Denmark, the production of Marshall films was overseen by a committee of three men: Ebbe Neergaard for MFU, section head Henrik Hjort-Nielsen for the Foreign Ministry and the Information Officer of the ECA, Thomas D. Durrance, later succeeded by Stuart Schulberg, representing the Marshall programme (MFU 1950a). This committee, invariably referred to in the archival files as 'Tremands udvalget' (the three-man committee), considered and approved the treatments of the films as forwarded from MFU and approved the choice of directors. Production of the films was then placed with film companies, including Nordisk Film, Minerva, Teknisk Film and Saga Studio. An unusual degree of freedom in production was accorded to the independent studios; this was because MFU considered it inappropriate to have oversight of a project that was effectively led by a foreign government. There was also the knotty issue of the ongoing feud between Koch-Olsen and the filmmakers, which was at its height around the time the Marshall remit was being thrashed out (Nørrested and Alsted 1987: 283).

From the first informal meetings in November 1949 between Ib Koch-Olsen and Lothar Wolff, the purpose of the films was conceived as two-fold: to disseminate knowledge of individual nations' contributions to the reconstruction of the European continent, and to exchange and promote practices leading to increased industrial productivity (Koch-Olsen 1949a). These principles were fleshed out in a memo from Durrance on 25 November 1949. Providing a list of tentative proposals for film topics specific to the Danish context, Durrance was also keen to emphasise the importance of an international perspective focused through local challenges:

> It is important to keep in mind that all these films should deal as much as possible with the international rather than the national aspect of each subject. The more this is done, the better chance there is for the picture to be used outside of Denmark and the more they will comply with the basic concepts of European economic cooperation. (Durrance 1949: 3)

By insisting that Marshall-funded films should constitute national iterations of international problems, the ECA introduces a productive tension into the texts. As Frank Mehring has astutely observed, on the one hand, this obviates 'a one-way process of cultural imperialism' and opens up the possibility of 'a creative process of appropriation and re-appropriation'. However, as a result, the films become 'the site of cultural misunderstandings and transcultural confrontations' (Mehring 2012: 3). This is certainly the case with Theodor Christensen's *Alle mine skibe*, our case study below.

Durrance's language when outlining the desired tone of the films also chimes with Hemsing's recollection of the ECA's reluctance to advertise its involvement in the films too explicitly. There would be a maximum of one reference to Marshall Aid in a one-reel film or three references in a two-reeler (Hemsing 1994: 273). Or, in Durrance's rather Hollywood-esque language in his late 1949 memo:

> It is understood that these films will, in no way, be propaganda films for the Marshall Plan or the USA. Rather, they will attempt to interpret Denmark's role in the over-all European scheme of things ... None of us wants these films to conclude with a girl and a boy walking hand-in-hand towards the sun. We want to inform and to stimulate, not to soft-soap or to brush over lightly the hard facts of economic life. (Durrance 1949: 1–2)

It was Lothar Wolff who established this softly-softly approach. With his experience of filmmaking in Europe and the USA, he was able to mediate between the conflicting expectations of audiences on each side of the Atlantic, explaining in 1951 to a New York audience that: 'If their pace seems somewhat slower than Americans are accustomed to, and if the propaganda content seems perhaps too subtle, it should be remembered that these techniques are considered most effective for transatlantic audiences' (quoted in Hemsing 1994: 273).

The Danish Marshall Films

The formal protocol for the production and distribution of the Danish Marshall films was laid down in a memorandum of understanding of February 1950, between the ECA's 'Mission' to Denmark and the Danish Foreign Ministry:

> it is contemplated that the subject matter of such films will deal with recovery in Denmark and the extent to which this was made possible by the European Recovery Program, as well as Denmark's place and responsibilities in an integrated European economy, and with technical aspects

of production in Denmark. Each film shall conform to the policies of the Danish Government as well as to those of the ECA. The films will be produced with a Danish commentary; they will be approximately 300 m long. (MFU 1950a)

The primary audience of the Marshall films can easily be surmised, given that they were to have Danish-language dialogue; the films were meant to promote the work of the European Recovery Program to Danish audiences. Nonetheless, SFC would be allowed to publicise the Marshall films in their catalogues and incorporate them into their domestic and overseas distribution procedures, in line with domestically funded films. The arrangements for distribution therefore open up the possibility of Marshall films circulating internationally, exemplifying national iterations of post-war recovery work and the contributions of particular nations to the international community (MFU 1950a). The wish-list of possible film topics encompassed both these potential audiences: the themes would serve to inform the Danes of the workings of the most successful industries nationwide, while also satisfying the curiosity of international audiences on recognisably Danish exports. However, it is noteworthy that Marshall-funded films were formally barred from circulation in the USA itself, due to a law forbidding US-funded informational materials to be used to 'propagandize' the American population (Hemsing 1994: 276).

In the list drafted in early 1950 (MFU 1950b), we can glimpse the priorities as negotiated between the ECA's Mission and MFU:

1. Report on the reconstruction of Denmark
The story of Danish produce:
2. The Danish Big Red Cow (butter and the cow)
3. The Streamlined Pig (bacon and the pig)
4. Little White Mama (eggs and the hen)
5a. The history of Danish beer

At this point, the list pauses to note that Mr Durrance of the ECA and another colleague were particularly keen on a film about Danish beer, as part of the reconstruction of Danish industry, but also because of the 'idealism' of the Carlsberg, Tuborg and Stjernen breweries. Specifically, the film could explore the long history of Carlsberg, its historic buildings, its modern laboratory and its charitable fund; Tuborg's pioneering rationalisation of its production, the first in Denmark; and the organisation of the cooperative brewery, Stjernen. In this last case, as with Theodor Christensen's contemporaneous project *The Pattern of Cooperation* (see Thomson and Hilson 2014), we witness the interest of American actors in the Danish phenomenon of cooperative organisation of industry, an interest which was being overtaken in the US by the increasing anti-communist sentiment.

The list of possible films continues with a plan B for the beer film, in case the topic met with puritan resistance:

5b. A film about the cultivation and care of the soil
6. The Ship (Burmeister & Wain)
7. The Farm (the rationalization of agriculture)
8. Efficiency (the particular practices of Danish industry)

The document includes an interesting note here that number eight was originally conceived as a film about the modern power station Kyndbyværket, but the film-makers said they would prefer a film about productivity, and the Marshall representatives acquiesced at this stage – the film about Kyndbyværket was eventually included in the final list of projects. This suggests that informal discussions have indeed been multilateral as the list of topics crystallised. The list ends with another two suggestions pertinent to Denmark's place in the world, followed by three extra topics which were conceived as very short 'didactic' films aimed at spreading good practice that would reduce the need for imports in certain areas:

9. The Vikings of the Road (the fish vans and fishing – the vans that bring Danish fish to Europe – Danish fish is always fresh!)
10. Denmark's contribution to the reconstruction of Europe
11. Work hygiene (increasing efficiency through ergonomics)
12. The problem of grass fields (the fields should yield more fodder)
13. The problem of animal fodder

The final list of six Danish Marshall films had been settled by the beginning of May 1950, and was announced in a press release by SFC. The press release is careful to emphasise that the films are not propaganda for Marshall Aid, but that their aim was to enlighten the Danes themselves, as well as European and American audiences, about the organisation of industrial and agricultural production in Denmark (SFC 1950). It has been observed by one Danish historian that this press release presents 'a very national presentation of a project whose premise is international and in which the Americans explicitly wished to underplay the national aspect' (Kobberrød Rasmussen 2013).

In fact, seven films embarked on production, but only four of the films were actually finished, all in 1951: *Fabrikken Caroline* (*Caroline the Factory*, Søren Melson), *Kyndbyværket* (*Kyndby Power Station*, Ove Sevel), *Den strømlinede gris* (*The Streamlined Pig*, Jørgen Roos) and *Alle mine skibe* (*All my Ships*, Theodor Christensen). The unfinished films were *Rapport om Danmarks genopbygning* (*Report on the Reconstruction of Denmark*), *Fiskebiler* (*Fish*

Export Vans) and *Bidrag til Europas genopbygning* (*Contributions to the Reconstruction of Europe*).

Of the unfinished films, the case of *Fiskebiler* is perhaps the most interesting. The concept for the film involved following three Danish fish delivery trucks around Europe, specifically to Vienna, Milan and Marseille. Visually and narratively, the film thus had enormous potential to fulfil the remit of tackling national subjects from international angles. However, the filmmakers experienced a run of bad luck: snowstorms in the Alps, a breakdown in Vienna and being arrested in Marseille. The film also exceeded its budget, due to the necessity of expensive travel, and its rushes were rejected by the ECA's Stuart Schulberg as being too foggy (Nørrested and Alsted 1987: 291). Here we see in action the kind of intervention Hemsing describes in his account of the ECA's relations with local filmmakers in order to guarantee quality (Hemsing 1994: 272).

A Post-war Fairytale: *Alle mine skibe*

The film project that was to become *Alle mine skibe* (*All my Ships*, 1951) had a number of working titles, including *Skibet* (*The Ship*) and a charming first English working title, *Mermaids and Horsepowers* [sic]. Director Theodor Christensen's comments on the May 1950 draft are interesting in that they reveal his thinking about priorities for content and how much footage certain incidents would require (Christensen 1950). Due to the restrictions of a 'one-reeler', he had had to leave out two events crucial to the history of Danish shipbuilding: the launch of the world's first diesel-engine ship 'Selandia' in 1912 and the bombing by the British Royal Air Force of the Burmeister & Wain shipbuilding plant in January 1943. On the other hand, 'the story of the people strike takes much footage' [sic] – by this he means the general strike of August 1943, a protest against occupation conditions, and that he could use some of the substantial wartime footage of the associated street protests (see Chapter 4). Christensen was also giving thought to the question of how to depict Denmark's international contribution to post-war reconstruction, a central plank of the Marshall Film remit. He suggested including a sequence showing the lowering of the Danish flag on the ship and the hoisting of the receiving country's flag, and perhaps also the film's main character – a shipbuilder by the anonymous name of Jensen – sailing on the ship he has helped to build to the port of arrival. Christensen seems to be 'thinking aloud' in English about how the film's narrative can communicate the interconnectedness of the Danish shipbuilding industry with the world:

> But the feeling of contributing something to European economy is certainly much stronger and more direct, if we deliver the ship on the spot – e.g. Havre or some other big port in Western Europe.

The point: it is through improvement in our technique and in the skills of our workers and techniques that we can contribute to an integrated economy – because the resources we have not got. On the contrary, we must import most of the raw material for a ship.

It should be felt, that this point was started when, during the war, we improved the methods of the shipyard, whilst Jensen improved his knowledge and skill. (Christensen 1950)

In Christensen's own archive at the Danish Film Institute, two English-language drafts of *Mermaid and Horsepower* have been preserved. They are undated, so it is hard to surmise in which order they were submitted. One adopts the conceit of presenting Helge Jensen's train of thought in 'stream-of-consciousness' style; the main elements of the finished film are in place, but the voiceover would have been more fragmented and impressionistic. Another fragment of a draft covers the early history of Danish shipbuilding, including the Selandia segment which Christensen later cut out.

A crucial change along the way is, indeed, the revision of the title to *Alle mine skibe*, or *All my Ships*. The possessive pronoun 'my' encompasses the perspective of the film's two main characters: Helge Jensen, the shipbuilder, and The Little Mermaid, the statue on Langelinie harbour which quickly became emblematic of Copenhagen after its installation in 1913. While the latter voice runs the risk of seeming hackneyed or too 'cute', Hans Christian Andersen's fairytale heroine was (and remains) an instantly and internationally recognised cipher for Denmark. Her position on the waterfront gazing out to sea – even if, in practice, her view is obstructed by the Burmeister & Wain shipbuilding plant, a spatial relationship which the film exploits – visually crystallises the ECA's insistence on a thematic internationalisation of the national (see Figure 6.2). And her presence in the narrative defuses the film's quite overtly ideological take on the web of connections between the workers of the world – for who could accuse a fairytale princess of fomenting communism? The 'my' in the film's title, then, can be construed as anti-nationalist, in the sense that the mermaid's naive possessiveness regarding ships she has had no hand in building both represents, and pokes fun at, Danish patriotism.

Helge Jensen the shipbuilder also has a claim to use the word 'my' about the ships. In contrast to the sedentary Little Mermaid, he helps to build them, an idea that is quite literally hammered home in the course of the film. One constant in successive drafts of *Alle mine skibe* is the inclusion of a shipbuilder whose thoughts are shared with the viewer, particularly his memories of his days in the Resistance. Christensen's own record of Resistance activity, speculates Kobberrød Rasmussen (2013), 'had built up a certain goodwill that would protect him from criticism'. That the former Resistance man in the film is also a shipyard navvy is a clever move that inextricably entangles his identi-

Figure 6.2   In Theodor Christensen's *Alle mine skibe* (1951), the Little Mermaid watches her ships across the harbour at Burmeister & Wain.

ties as wartime hero and working-class everyman. The figure of the worker as hero in the gorgeous ballet of the industrial shop floor is a recurring trope in Christensen's films. As Kobberrød Rasmussen notes (2013 n. 23), *Alle mine skibe* owes a debt to one of Christensen's earlier films about Danish shipbuilding, the industrial film *7 mill. HK – En film om Burmeister & Wain (7 Million Horsepower – A Film about Burmeister & Wain,* 1943). There are also echoes of *Gammelt Metal – Nye Varer!*, Christensen's promotional film for wartime recycling discussed in Chapter 4. Christensen was simply in his element when filming on the shop floor, amid the showers of sparks from welding torches, the glow of the smelting furnaces and enormous metal ship parts swinging through the air. As observed in connection with his wartime short, Christensen was also wont to study the faces of workers, often in close-up at canted angles.

THE RED SCARE

By the time that the Danish Marshall Films were finished and premiered, the ECA had withdrawn – at least officially – from the collaboration. The reasons for this outcome remain a little hazy. The episode has been described as a salutary lesson in Cold War film politics, and as an expression of McCarthy-era anti-communist hysteria (Nørrested and Alsted 1987: 281–2). The Danish relationship with the ECA foundered in July 1950, when it was agreed that the American agency would withdraw from the cooperation. Moreover, the planned film on the reconstruction of Denmark would be replaced with the early suggestion of a film on the Kyndbyværket power station, thus shifting the emphasis away from Marshall activities. It is not entirely clear why this breach between MFU and ECA occurred, but historians have interpreted it in the light of an ongoing debate in the Danish press about the communist sympathies of some of the filmmakers and of Ebbe Neergaard himself. One possibility is that the ECA's withdrawal was connected to an article in a conservative regional newspaper, *Sorø Amtstidende*, on Theodor Christensen's call for filmmakers to emulate activist documentarists such as Joris Ivens of the Netherlands (Nørrested and Alsted 1987: 286). Kobberrød Rasmussen (2013) gives an English-language overview of the press coverage. This centred on the apparent irony of critics of the Marshall Plan being appointed to make films about the programme, fulminating 'that Danish short films in general were controlled by a sort of communist league that was only lacking control of Ib Koch-Olsen's directorship of Dansk Kulturfilm'. Thus any argument that the directors had been appointed on the basis of their skill – they were indeed the 'cream of the Danish short-film community' at the time (Kobberrød Rasmussen) – was immediately circumvented by the accusation in the press that Danish informational filmmaking was a communist cabal regardless. It was true enough that Karl Roos and Theodor Christensen had been members of the Communist Youth League and had written for left-wing newspapers. On the other hand, as Neergaard pointed out, the drafts of each film had been 'monitored and vetted by so many different bodies and persons that slipping in communist propaganda would have been impossible, if any of the directors had actually been trying to do so' (quoted in Kobberrød Rasmussen 2013).

The ECA did not withdraw fully from the collaboration, wishing to retain the rights to the films and to take responsibility for overseas distribution, as previously planned (Nørrested and Alsted 1987: 287). Moreover, half a dozen representatives of the ECA in Denmark attended the screening of the first cut of the four films in October 1950, and imposed a long list of corrections and alterations (288–9). Notably, the ECA's Press Attaché in Denmark, a Mr Madden, re-wrote the script for *Fabrikken Caroline*. His version mentioned Marshall Aid no fewer than eight times, and attributed the post-war growth of Danish agriculture directly to US aid (289–90). This was factually wrong, and resisted as such by both Ebbe Neergaard and the Agricultural Films Committee; more interestingly, such a script flew in the face of the ECA's own guidelines regarding light-touch promotion of Marshall Aid in its sponsored films. The original script was eventually reinstated (290).

The Danish experience of the Marshall Plan scheme was thus unusually complex and negative, but it did serve a domestic purpose of forcing filmmakers to come to terms with the idea that Dansk Kulturfilm and its functionaries were not deliberately repressing filmmakers' freedom of expression, but were caught up in a complex network of power and obligation. The filmmakers got to experience projects run by the studios themselves and under a project manager, Witte, of whom they all approved, but their scope for freedom of expression was hardly improved by the framework and priorities imposed by the American funders. In his role on the three-man committee, Ebbe Neergaard, too, experienced being a 'hostage' caught between two conflicting sets of interests: the Marshall authorities and the Danish filmmakers (Nørrested and Alsted 1987: 292).

These UNFB and Marshall projects are not particularly acute examples of the suppression of freedom of expression, but they are nodes of conflicting pressures. They also show how Dansk Kulturfilm and MFU were caught up in a fast-developing international film scene, in which informational and documentary film was an important tool for different iterations of internationalism, which were sometimes at odds with each other. They are also interesting examples of how agencies took chances, acted pragmatically and were dependent on interpersonal connections. The next case study investigates a film project initiated by Dansk Kulturfilm in response to another fast-moving instance of international cooperation, this time specific to the Nordic region.

ANIMATING NORDIC COOPERATION: *SOMETHIN' ABOUT SCANDINAVIA*

The camera ... glides over a frieze which depicts the countries' respective visual arts, crafts, architecture – from different eras, all the way back to ancient times ... The camera rests at last on a Viking ship. From the edges of the ship, lines begins to emerge, which become an aeroplane. The plane flies away across a globe ...

(Barfod 1954: 8)

The trope of SAS aircraft as modern-day Viking ships, which we witnessed in *They Guide You Across*, crops up again in Bent Barfod's animated ten-minute film *Noget om Norden* (*Somethin' about Scandinavia*, 1956). As the title suggests, this film presents the principles of Nordic cooperation to an audience construed as domestic and international, but it was commissioned, produced and funded in Denmark. The film thus constitutes not only a snapshot of the most salient aspects of economic and cultural integration in the Nordic region as defined by activists and creatives in the mid-1950s, but also exemplifies the unexpected complications of distributing a film to Denmark's closest neighbours. *Noget om Norden* is thus less obviously a product of international cooperation than *They Guide You Across* and *Alle mine skibe*, but it sets out to represent – and thus intervene in – the regional, intergovernmental integration which has shaped the Nordic countries during the last half century.

Pre-dating the formal establishment of the Nordic Council in 1952 was a pressure group, Foreningen Norden (the Nordic Association) which had established branches in all five Nordic nations from the 1910s, and still exists today (Foreningen Norden 2016). The five national branches of Foreningen Norden met in Reykjavik in early August 1949 to discuss the shape and scope of future Nordic cooperation. On the agenda was a list of measures which later came to characterise the ambitions of the Nordic Council from 1952: economic cooperation to ensure global competitiveness, a common Nordic labour market, harmonisation of social security legislation and lawmaking more generally, and cultural cooperation. Two concrete suggestions in the cultural sphere captured the attention of the press: a common Nordic postage stamp, and a colour film presenting the Nordic countries and the work of Foreningen Norden (Anonymous 1949). The proposed film project made it into the headlines of the Danish newspaper *Kristeligt Dagblad* and Sweden's *Svenska Dagbladet*, and as a result, clippings of the articles were sent from the state press cutting service to Dansk Kulturfilm. It is unclear whether these reports seeded or crystallised the idea for a film on the Nordic region, but in April 1952, Koch-Olsen wrote to the Danish branch of Forening Norden to ask for its feedback on a draft treatment for such a film. This letter indicates that the initiative for the film had not come from Forening Norden itself, but from internal discussions within Dansk Kulturfilm and MFU. Koch-Olsen asked for the association's opinion on the extant draft and on which topics should be covered in such a film (Koch-Olsen 1952a). Separately, and at the same time, he wrote to Foreningen Norden's Danish director, F. W. Wendt, to provide more context to the request. Koch-Olsen expressed doubts about the animated film format which had been proposed and whether it would reach the right audience, though MFU liked much of the content; at this point, they wanted input from Foreningen Norden before taking the project further (Koch-Olsen 1952b).

The treatment of the film project which Koch-Olsen sent to Foreningen Norden had been provided by Carl Th. Dreyer, who had been asked for suggestions and was convinced that an animated film was the appropriate way to tackle the subject of the Nordic region. He argued that the material was so complex and 'undramatic' that it would be necessary to substitute 'baroque and surprising situations' for drama, and that animation would enable the complexity of the information to be compressed into abstractions (Dreyer 1951a). In late 1951, as he worked on the treatment for *Noget om Norden*, Dreyer was awaiting confirmation that he had been appointed to the directorship of the Dagmar cinema and requested a statement of support from Dansk Kulturfilm confirming that he had administrative experience of managing productions (Dreyer 1951a). This appointment was indeed confirmed shortly afterwards and it obviated the need for Dreyer to work on any more informational films. In 1955, while *Noget om Norden* was still under development, Dreyer's penultimate production, *Ordet* (*The Word*) premiered – his first feature film for a decade. A cynical interpretation would be that it is probably no coincidence that Koch-Olsen again insisted on crediting Dreyer in the opening titles of *Noget om Norden*, in a memo of 1955 (Koch-Olsen 1955b). On the other hand, several ideas in Dreyer's treatment do seem to have influenced the finished film, the SAS planes being perhaps the clearest example of this:

> We see a map of Scandinavia. Aeroplanes fly in elegant curves between cities. Their aeroplanes with Viking names bring the message to the whole world of *small nations* which, by pooling their resources, manage to achieve big results. (Dreyer 1951b: 4, my emphasis).

Either way, a statement that the film is based on an idea by Carl Th. Dreyer actually appears above the animator's name in the opening sequence. A decade after Dansk Kulturfilm strategically integrated his work into the *Social Denmark* series, then, Dreyer was still enough of a name in Scandinavia and abroad to make it advantageous to highlight his comparatively marginal involvement in *Noget om Norden*. Coverage of the film in the magazine of Foreningen Norden's Swedish branch suggests that this had been a good move:

> There is a new film about Nordic cooperation! An animated colour film, made in Denmark by the young artist and filmmaker Bent Barfod and based on an idea by none other than the famous Carl Th. Dreyer. The film, which is called Noget om Norden, premiered in conjunction with Nordic Day and was a great success. It is not a long film, only ten minutes, but it is funny, instructive and the very opposite of formal. Why, 'ingenious' is the best word to describe it. (Nordens Tidning 1956)

As the Swedish review notes, the animator chosen to take the film project further was Bent Barfod (1920–2007). Barfod made around 250 films in a career that began in the late 1940s, and established Denmark's first dedicated animation studio (Hjorth Nielsen n.d.). He had previously produced graphics and diagrams for Danish informational films, including *They Guide You Across*. Also recruited as a consultant on the film was journalist Mogens Lind (1898–1967), who provided comments on Barfod's draft and produced a draft of the voiceover.

A strategic measure which emerged early on in the process was to use a child actor to narrate the voiceover, and for the voiceover text to mediate the film's information in a childlike way. We can compare this to the recurring strategy of dialogue and 'useful idiots' in *kulturfilm* voiceovers. The idea of using a girl's voice appears as early as August 1954, in a handwritten note from Koch-Olsen on Mogens Lind's comments on Barfod's second draft (Lind 1954b). This would, it was felt, pre-empt any strategic, diplomatic or political complications around the Nordic region (Koch-Olsen 1956a). Nevertheless, at a critical time for the development of Nordic cooperation, there was potential for misunderstandings and offence. In addition to input from Foreningen Norden, the involvement of a number of ministries crops up in the production files, notably a screening for the Minister for Economy and Employment, whose remit was crucial to negotiations on the common Nordic labour market which had been inaugurated in July 1954. Coinciding with the production of the film *Noget om Norden* were negotiations on a Nordic common market, which were abandoned in 1959 in favour of membership of the European Free Trade Association (EFTA). Also sensitive was the recent accession of Finland to the Nordic Council. Finland had been unable to take up membership until relations with its neighbour the USSR thawed after Stalin's death, and so participated for the first time in the Council's January 1956 session (Nordic Cooperation n.d.).

ABSTRACTING POLITICAL CONCEPTS

Some of these political tensions are mediated in *Noget om Norden* and/or emerged as points of contention during the development of the film. Looking closely at the draft and finished versions of the film is revealing precisely because the discussion of the representation of abstract ideas in animated form entails an articulation of priorities and (mis)conceptions about those ideas – in this case, how Nordic cooperation works and how its elements should be symbolised.

Noget om Norden begins with five cartoon Vikings attempting to lift a rock, first individually, and then succeeding through cooperation. The rock fills the screen while the opening credits are shown, and then the camera pulls out to show the five Viking shields, which transform into a map of the Nordic region. Both in Dreyer's treatment and Barfod's drafts, there is an emphasis on the smallness of the Nordic countries and on how this can be mitigated by teamwork and critical mass. The opening sequence was the basis for an alternative title for the film, which almost stuck. *At løfte i flok* relies on a set phrase which has no exact cognate in English; literally, it means 'to lift as a flock', but its pragmatic meaning is to manage a difficult task by working together. There is also the echo of the verb's alternative meaning, 'to vow'. While the opening sequence with the rock-lifting renders the metaphor literal, the film also concerns the mutual assurances which the Nordic countries have entered into, in

Figure 6.3   Tariff barriers depicted as Viking forts in *Noget om Norden*
(Bent Barfod, 1956).

order to lift each other up. In the end, the more straightforward *Noget om Norden* relies only on alliteration, but is stymied, on the other hand, by the lack of an equivalent noun in English for Norden, and by the connotations of racial supremacy which 'Nordic' and its derivations had acquired in English during the previous decades (Marklund and Petersen 2013: 250–1). As the writer Elsa Gress commented of her translation of the voiceover for the US market, there was really no alternative to *Somethin' about Scandinavia* (Gress 1959).

A particularly challenging topic for the film was the concept of tariff barriers. In Dreyer's treatment, these were represented by striped toll barriers lifted or cast aside one by one by each nation (Dreyer 1951b: 3). As the voiceover explains: 'then the domestic market is so large that the cost of production can be reduced to a level where it's possible to compete on the international market'. Lind's comments on Barfod's storyboard of mid-1954 focus on the representation of trade tariffs, and suggest that they and other barriers to Nordic cooperation could be depicted as slips of paper which blow away more or less easily, the papers marked 'tariffs' breaking up stubbornly before the image fades; this was presumably meant to allude to the ongoing multilateral negotiations (Lind 1954b: 1). In Barfod's film, the toll barriers are envisioned as five small fortresses full of fish, trees and other raw materials (see Figure 6.3). The fortresses crumble in the face of the sound made by five Viking horn-blowers sounding their instruments in unison, after several attempts, and are transformed into kiosks and then a merry-go-round which sends the products spiralling off into ships and out into the world (Barfod 1954: 4–5). Lind suggested that the fortresses should meld together into one fortress around Scandinavia and thence to a north star (Lind 1954b: 3). The kiosks seem to have been concocted by Wendt and Dansk Kulturfilm's production manager Agnar Hølaas, building on the notion that this was how inter-Scandinavian trade first began in medieval times (Hølaas 1954c: 1).

This sequence had the potential to render the film unusable when negotiations on a Nordic Customs Union and Free Trade Area were discontinued in July 1959, when the majority of Nordic states opted to join EFTA and/or prepare for application to the European Economic Community (EEC). When consulted, however, Wendt was of the opinion that the film's treatment of economic integration was so general that it was still applicable to the current situation. Even if the Nordic countries joined the emerging European trade blocs, barriers to trade in the Nordic region would still fall. Wendt therefore recommended that the film remain in SFC's catalogue (Wendt 1959).

The common Nordic labour market and harmonised social security, already in place at the time the film was made, was a concern for Dreyer and Barfod's later drafts. Dreyer emphasises the possibility of hospital care for his influenza-ridden Danish worker in Sweden (Dreyer 1951b: 6), while in Barfod's version, his migrant worker has injured himself skiing (Barfod 1954: 6–7). Another concept that featured in drafts of the screenplay and in discussions was a bridge over the Øresund between Copenhagen and Malmö. In reality, such a bridge was opened in 2000, but it had held sway in the popular consciousness for decades. Lind's comments on Barfod's early draft suggested that the bridge from Denmark to Sweden should be depicted as a bridge of clouds (Lind 1954a: 1). This suggestion may have been inspired by Dreyer's proposed sequence showing sculptures from the piazza of the Konserthus in Stockholm flying on clouds to Denmark to visit Thorvaldsen's Museum (Dreyer 1951b: 6). Hølaas was quick to reply to Lind that the bridge should be retained in the film as something more concrete than clouds, for instance, as an engineer's drawing, as it was more than a dream, though not yet realised (Hølaas 1954c: 1).

DISTRIBUTION AND VERSIONS

Noget om Norden was distributed in Danish cinemas as a *forfilm*, initially partnered with the feature *En kvinde er overflødig* (*A Woman not Wanted*,

Gabriel Axel, 1957). Later (illustrating how incongruous *forfilm* and feature pairings could be) it circulated with a West German sex education film, *Sexuallægen* (*Eva und der Frauenarzt*, Erich Kobler, 1951). Between 1957 and 1964, *Noget om Norden* reached an estimated 280,337 cinema-goers, not counting another hundred one-off cinema screenings (Achton Schmidt 1968). After its theatrical run, the film was added to SFC's film library and was the second most popular Danish film in 1959–60 (SFC 1960a). It was loaned out 1500 times by SFC up to the late 1960s, and copies were sold to the Danish army's training section, to the national tourist board (Achton Schmidt 1968) and to the OEEC (Organisation for European Economic Cooperation, formed in 1948 to administer US Marshall Aid) (MFU 1958c). *Noget om Norden* was screened at a long list of film festivals, including Edinburgh, San Francisco, Vancouver, New York, Palermo, Stratford, Oberhausen, Stockholm, Lübeck and West Bengal (Achton Schmidt 1968). More disparate loans and screenings recorded by SFC – listed here to give a sense of the types of institutions using such films, as well as their global reach – included Melbourne University, Deutsch-Scandinavischer Verein, Hamburg, Kvikmyndasklubber Listafélagsins (the Film Club of the Icelandic Art Society), Polish television, Warsaw's Danish-Polish Association, the German-Nordic Union, the Nordic Press Attachés in Bonn, a screening in Ankara, Grenzakademie Sankelmark school in Flensborg, Instituto Cubano del Arte e Industria Cinematográficos (ICAIC, Cuban Institute of Cinematographic Art and Industry) and the Danish High School in Argentina (Bü 1968).

Ironically, given the film's subject matter, distribution of the film in the Nordic region proved rather less straightforward. In Iceland, the Danish ambassador in Rekjavik reported that he had tried to promote *Noget om Norden* via a private screening in the Nyja Bio cinema. However, neither distributors nor cinema owners had any appetite for buying the film (Knuth 1956). Two copies sent to the Norwegian national film library (Kommunernes Filmcentral) had been sent back to SFC by return, as the film could not be exempted from tax (MFU 1957). And *Noget om Norden* almost caused a major breach between Danish state-sponsored film production and the Swedish film company SF (Svensk Filmindustri), which, unusually, undertook the distribution of this film in Sweden. The CEO of SF, Carl Anders Dymling, wrote incensed to SFC to complain that the Danish Embassy in Stockholm, at the behest of the Foreign Office, was advertising free hire of the Danish-language version of the film 'in newspaper after newspaper' (Dymling 1957). Meanwhile, SF had invested in making a Swedish-language version which would circulate in cinemas together with a suitable feature, as well as stocks of a narrow-gauge version which had been promoted to schools. These measures were compromised by the competition from the Danish Embassy; in effect, the Danish state (in the form of its diplomatic corps) was competing with a foreign business (SF) which had entered into agreement with another Danish state organ (Statens Filmcentral). This exemplifies how incompatible overseas distribution arrangements could sometimes arise, given the involvement of both Statens Filmcentral and the Foreign Ministry's Press Bureau in placing films abroad. Koch-Olsen summarised the advantages of flexibility on the part of the Foreign Office thus:

> As things stand now, with the ongoing disagreement with SF, I think the first step must be to raise the issue of revising the not very clear agreements between the Foreign Office and the Justice Ministry [where MFU was located] on foreign distribution ... The Foreign Office and anyone else who is interested in the overseas distribution of Danish film must look kindly upon the film being versionised in Swedish at no cost to us, that it is distributed by Sweden's biggest film company, and that it is screened in Swedish cinemas as a *forfilm*. As soon as its run in cinemas has finished, the Foreign Office can distribute the film as it wishes ... One could organise events in Stockholm in conjunction with the official premiere, and probably that would do a lot more for the film's publicity than isolated screenings in the Embassy and so-called cultural screenings. (Koch-Olsen 1957b)

The production of a range of different language versions of the film was also a factor in the foreign distribution arrangements. In this respect, too, the discussions around arrangements for *Noget om Norden* tell us something about the norms, insofar as this film deviated from them. The production of foreign-language versions was both facilitated and complicated by Bent Barfod having his own film company. Barfod thus took the initiative to make an English-language version in the first instance for use at screenings abroad (MFU 1958c). This version did not review well amongst North American educational film users. Comments forwarded to Dansk Kulturfilm from the Educational Film Library Association in New York included:

> Inappropriate narration, poor sound. The artwork is nice, but the rest of the film doesn't live up to it.
> This might have been excellent, really first rate, with a different narrator. Our kids probably couldn't understand a word said.
> Excellent color and photography. Too rapid a presentation which probably adds to uninteresting presentation. Dialogue difficult due to accent. (Educational Film Library Association Inc., n.d.)

The involvement of Svensk Filmindustri in the film's distribution in Sweden also resulted in a Swedish-language version at no cost to MFU, but the disagreement with Dymling about competition from the Danish Embassy in Stockholm engendered extensive discussion at home about best practice regarding foreign language versions. For Koch-Olsen (1956b), if the version could not be made under the auspices of Dansk Kulturfilm or the filmmaker, it was crucial that the new versions were at least approved by MFU, a copy of the Swedish text provided by SF and that the filmmaker could supervise the sound mixing. In West Germany, *Noget om Norden* attracted the attention of the Zentrale für Heimatsdienst (an organisation promoting democratic values in the Federal Republic of Germany) and the Europa-Unionen, a society promoting European integration. Via the Danish Foreign Ministry's Press Bureau, several approaches were made to gain permission to produce a German-language version of the film for use in promotion of international cooperation along Nordic lines. The film, commented a Dr Feineis of Zentrale für Hematsdienst, provided the clearest and most persuasive explanation of the benefits of economic integration that he had seen (Hvass 1956; Kristensen 1957b) – an assessment which does seem to confirm that the confusion amongst US viewers was caused by poor sound quality rather than exposition.

CONCLUSION

These three case studies illustrate several aspects of the production and distribution of *kulturfilm* around 1950. Each illustrates a different dimension of the burgeoning and various international networks that sponsored and distributed informational films. They illustrate three different facets of a general commitment to the idea of film as an internationalising force, a commitment that can be construed as idealistic and/or instrumentalist, even cynical and propagandistic. And this commitment is often undermined by inadequate sound technology, which gets in the way of effective communication across language barriers.

The production histories are exceptions that prove the rules in the sense that most films were; solutions to problems of distribution were often responsive to shifting and fast-moving opportunities and problems, including in regard to sponsorship. On the other hand, this flexibility could and often did spill over into squabbling about incompatible values and practices. What all three films show, as well, is that the imagology of Danishness as it circulated in the outside world often overlapped with Scandinavianness or Nordicness, and that this was actively exploited at times for the sake of mediating the message, the flying Viking ships of SAS being a case in point. The key trope is the national as a metonym of the international. Concomitantly, the films could and did function to explain aspects of regional and national identity to domestic and international viewers. We now move on to consider a sample of films made more exclusively for a domestic audience.

7. CITIZENS OF THE FUTURE: INFORMATIONAL FILM AND THE WELFARE STATE

The Grand Old Man of Danish documentary, Theodor Christensen, again looms large in this chapter. Indeed, the title is inspired by a 1946 film directed by Christensen: *Fremtidens Borgere* or *Citizens of the Future*. The citizens in question are the Danes themselves. Although films made for domestic use did sometimes circulate internationally in foreign-language versions, their primary purpose was to inform the domestic populace about national institutions and infrastructure and to instruct viewers as to how to behave as citizens. The films thus tend to construct the nation imaginatively as a space and as a social organism, but they also imbue it with futurity in a range of ways.

The national future was uppermost in the thoughts of the authors of the Danish Social Democratic party's manifesto of 1945, which bore the title *Fremtidens Danmark* – Denmark's Future (Socialdemokratisk Forbund 2017). This document was essentially a blueprint for the party's vision of a welfare society, influenced by Keynesianism and aiming to build on the social progress of the interwar period, some of the achievements of which had been depicted in the *Social Denmark* films discussed in Chapter 5. The welfare state would rest on economic growth, full employment, democracy, equality and social security (Jespersen 2008a: 16). But the welfare state described in *Denmark's Future* lay, indeed, in the distant future. While the Social Democrats dominated the government through much of the two decades after the war, the conservative party Venstre was in power for two years from November 1945 and again for three years from October 1950. Not until the 1960s did Denmark see a dynamic decade of explosive economic growth, urbanisation, improved living standards, rapid and radical change in socio-cultural mores and substantial government investment in social infrastructure. The 1950s, on the other hand, have generally been regarded by Danish historians as a much more static period, during which development was hampered by post-war economic reconstruction and the cultural and political effects of the Cold War (Jespersen 2008a: 12–13). By 1957, an economic upswing was apparent, a platform for the growth of the 1960s (15). Nonetheless, and by the same token, the 1950s can be seen as a period of preparation, rationalisation and planning, the value of which may have been underestimated by historians of the post-1968 generation (21).

The Social Democratic Party's 1945 manifesto makes explicit mention of the role of film in the education of the populace, along with theatre, music and radio. Concerning film in particular, an appendix to the manifesto states that its production and promotion should be organised in such a way that its 'artistic and democratic qualities' can fully flourish (Socialdemokratisk Forbund 2017). However, it is important to emphasise that the manifesto regards culture as an end in itself, not as a means to an end. The purpose of economic politics, the manifesto declares, is to create conditions in which the people's cultural life can develop and deepen. Accordingly, neither the films analysed in this chapter nor state-sponsored film more generally in the period should be construed as a programmatic attempt to influence public behaviour and loyalty in line with developments in the nascent welfare state. In some cases, the films are indeed responses to new legislation or technologies, but more often they are instigated piecemeal by social institutions or ministries in response to perceived gaps in public knowledge or behaviours that have emerged over the longer term. Overall, then, there is a non-linear relationship between key political developments and the production of films on cognate topics. As we have repeatedly seen in previous chapters, the struggles between stakeholders, production managers and filmmakers, as well as the struggles between social facts and film technologies, can be traced in the commissioning and production process. This is where the tension between the theory and practice of the welfare state becomes tangible. When assessing the role of informational film in shaping the welfare society, looking for what is subversive, misplaced and misunderstood in the films is at least as fruitful as focusing on their mediation of a pedagogical national narrative.

Nonetheless, as films aimed at influencing the behaviour of the people of a small, culturally homogenous nation state, the productions discussed in this chapter do rely to varying extents on the shared and assumed knowledge of the implied audience. This runs the gamut from images of landmarks, to allusions to historical events, to culturally specific humour, to non-verbal or multisensory forms of knowledge, such as touch, smell and taste.

These films of the late 1940s and early 1950s, then, explain and celebrate contemporary progress and opportunities in a range of aspects of national institutions and infrastructure. In many cases, they gesture to the perils and pleasures of a new world in the offing – a new world which would flicker across the television screens of the 1960s. For the time being, narrow-gauge film remained a primary medium through which Danes engaged in life-long learning.

VISUALISING A NATIONAL RAIL NETWORK

'Hallo, hallo! *Here are the railways*. This film is about life on the Danish railways. It is produced by Dansk Kulturfilm in collaboration with Danish State Railways and filmed by Nordisk. Screenplay and mise-en-scène by Theodor Christensen, photography by Fritz Olsen and Jørgen Roos, music by Kai Rosenberg, sound by Børge Hallenberg, and this is Fredericia Station and Svend Pedersen speaking!'

Eschewing opening titles for an unorthodox announcement over Fredericia railway station's tannoy, *Her er Banerne* (*Here are the Railways*, Theodor Christensen, 1948) is an example of a profoundly local and Danish film which nonetheless self-consciously inserts itself into the international documentary tradition. *Her er Banerne* was commissioned by Dansk Kulturfilm in collaboration with Danske Statsbaner (DSB, the Danish National Railway) to celebrate the centenary of rail travel in Denmark.[1] The film was conceived as a documentary that would depict modern rail travel, rather than a historical film (Koch-Olsen 1947d). Fredericia station, at the western end of the bridge over the Little Belt between the island of Funen and Jutland, was quickly identified as a suitable subject, being the destination for trains from all the points of the compass. And the converse: as the voiceover declares, 'trains roll away from Fredericia in every direction'.

Her er Banerne is a classic of Danish documentary, its status comparable to *Night Mail* (Basil Watt and Harry Wright, 1936) in Britain. The two films are not only comparable in terms of canonicity. The Danish film director Jon Bang Carlsen reminisces that the resemblance between them is so striking that it is as though

the two directors had the same brain and the same eye. The tempo, the nearly identical perspectives in this shared history of speed through the landscape of duty. As though it was the same hand plucking the strings of reality. Was it reality? (Bang Carlsen 2014)

Aside from its British predecessor, *Her er Banerne* owes much to an earlier film directed by Christensen, on which Ingolf Boisen also worked: *Iran – Det nye Persien* (*Iran – The New Persia*, 1939). The film was co-directed by

Christensen, Boisen and Axel Lerche for Minerva Film, and by Tove Hebo, Boisen's first wife, who later married Christensen. It was commissioned by the engineering company Kampsax, which built the trans-Iranian railway from the Caspian Sea to the Bay of Persia between 1933 and 1939. *Iran – Det nye Persien* was described by Boisen as the first proper Danish documentary film (Boisen 1977: 86), though it is technically an industrial film. It is marked by the fluid energy that one senses in 1930s British documentary, and ends with a balletic, almost surrealist montage of trains on the tracks laid by Kampsax. Again, the tempo is reminiscent of *Night Mail*, but this may be an effect of the shared subject; the choreography of shots might just as well be compared to the manipulation of city space in Walter Ruttmann's *Berlin: Symphonie einer Großstadt* (*Berlin: Symphony of a City*, 1927, Germany). In 1939, Christensen was sent to London with his film about Iran to screen it for John Grierson, Basil Wright, Paul Rotha and other luminaries. Legend has it that at the end of the screening, there was an awkward silence provoked by the film's resemblance to *Night Mail*, before Grierson remarked: 'in Scotland, we kill people for less than that' (Roos 1968: 150).

Christensen himself considered the conclusion of *Iran – Det nye Persien* to be psychologically unsatisfying, as the final shot leaves the viewer at a hundred kilometres an hour in a tunnel. A decade later, for *Her er Banerne*, after discussion with Koch-Olsen, he decided to tone down the originally planned locomotive 'ballet' and instead end with a sense of peacefulness, an 'anticlimax' to round off the film's 'drama of movement' (*bevægelsesdramatik*; Christensen 1947c). Nonetheless, *Her er Banerne* devotes a good deal of its twenty-six minutes to the study of the trains' choreography in and around Fredericia station. The most striking of these sequences is ostensibly a demonstration of how goods wagons are herded into a side yard, coordinated by the station master, but is breathtaking in its cinematography. The cameraman is a young Jørgen Roos, whose Oscar-nominated short *A City Called Copenhagen* (1960) is the focus of Chapter 9. For *Her er Banerne*, he joins the railwaymen as they run in front of train wagons to throw brake blocks on to the rails at the appropriate spot (see Figure 7.1). One shot is filmed alongside a railwayman waiting to link two wagons together as one wagon careers into frame and one set of buffers smacks into the other. The disoriented viewer gets privileged access to the perilous work of the sanguine railwaymen as wagons and engines lumber and screech terrifyingly all around.

Throughout *Her er Banerne*, tempo and movement are employed to communicate how the daily rhythms of Fredericia station tie the nation's railway lines together, and thereby its towns, people and products. This is a function of the synergies between the film's narrative structure, its editing and the movement of trains, people and technologies within the frame. Roos later claimed that Christensen learned the train timetable inside-out during filming, so that if they

Figure 7.1   Railway workers and wagons in Theodor Christensen's
Her er Banerne (1948).

had to go out onto the tracks to film, they could safely do so with confidence
(Roos 1968: 150). Whether or not this is apocryphal, Christensen builds the
film's structure around the ebb and flow of arrivals and departures through the
day. To minimise disruption at Fredericia station, the shoot was painstakingly
planned to last no more than twelve days. To ensure a reasonable but not overwhelming level of passenger footfall, filming was to take place in mid-August,
towards the end of the holiday season. Planning the production was more
complicated than Theodor Christensen expected; certainly more complex than
filming medical operations, he commented (Christensen 1947b).

A conceit in the film relies on the idea that the progress of trains through
the station is represented by the movement of lights across a signal board
in the control room known as Post II. Cross-cutting between train and control
room then serves to build a complex and suspenseful temporality, mediating
the complexity of operations and the oscillation between quiet and congested
periods throughout the day. It was not possible to film the signal board in
situ in the control room, and so it had to be replicated and filmed on set
(Christensen 1947d: 1). The control room is one element in the wider montage
that builds up to a dramatic climax in the film, the 'midday group' of trains

scheduled to arrive around 2 p.m. Again, movement within and between shots increases in pace, showing cleaning ladies readying their buckets, the restaurant laying out quantities of beer, coffee and pastries, trolleys waiting on the platform for luggage and mail, and passengers spilling from the nearby ferry port (Christensen 1947d: 5). The ensuing frantic activity around 2 p.m. gives way to a stillness in the station that the manuscript admits is unrealistically sudden, but undercut by shots of the thundering express trains heading north, south and eastwards (6).

Some of the film's images were not captured at Fredericia. Evidence of Arthur Elton's continuing connections with the Danish documentary scene is provided by correspondence in winter 1947–8, in which Christensen asked Elton to secure some footage of the 'Nordekspress' train in Hamburg, where he was stationed at the time working for Welt im Film (Christensen 1947a). In return, Elton requested footage of ice breakers and the train ferry over the Great Belt, were it to freeze up, or of German refugees being returned home to the British zone. This exchange arrangement was to be regarded as 'an exception' (Elton 1947), but it does illustrate how international collaboration between documentarists shaped film content.

One of the film's working titles was *Vi er Banerne – We are the Railways*. This would have reflected the film's emphasis on Fredericia station's workers and passengers, a focus that chimes with Christensen's interest in working people. However, the people working in and passing through the station also have an important role to play in the carefully planned rhythm of *Her er Banerne*. Christensen explains in his manuscript that the opening sequence of aerial pictures of an empty station is designed to ensure that when people arrive for work they are noticed over the cacophony (literal and metaphorical) of machinery and technology; that they can start to inhabit the images (Christensen 1947d: 1). A planned montage sequence shows ticket sellers, train drivers, cleaning ladies, controllers and other workers beginning their shifts and makes snatches of their conversations audible, the tempo of movements, noise and cuts gradually increasing before the film shifts its focus back to the trains themselves (Christensen 1947d: 2).

The attention to the station's rhythms is what evokes the complexity of its operations: the sheer number of people involved, their specialisms and efficient interactions, and their dance with machinery and communication technology. By the same token, Fredericia station emerges as a microcosm of the nation, a node in the networks of transport and class weaving together an island nation, in much the same way as *Night Mail* connected north and south in a long, narrow land. *Her er banerne* is thus a much more sustained exercise in the visualising of national networks that characterised Christensen's *Gammelt Metal – Nye Varer!* (see Chapter 4) half a decade previously, repurposed for national imaginings in peacetime.

THE PUBLIC LIBRARY AS IMAGINED COMMUNITY:
SCREENING THE SCREENING ROOM

Another film of the late 1940s maps a quieter but no less significant national network. *Biblioteket er åbent* (*The Library is Open*, Søren Melson, 1949) reflects on the libraries which are a condition of possibility for informational film distribution in Denmark. In doing so, the film brings its viewers face to face with their compatriots, collectively engaged in cultural consumption and life-long learning.

Just before Christmas 1946, the Chair of Danmarks Biblioteksforenings Bestyrelse (the Governing Council of the Danish Library Association) wrote to Dansk Kulturfilm to suggest that a short film be made about the country's libraries for theatrical screening (Lassen 1946). This initial approach outlined an unusually clear goal for the film project, and the Library Association proved itself to be unusually pro-active in developing the film project. The aim would be to draw viewers' attention to the idea that it was not only 'casual entertainment' one could find in libraries, but that users could also orientate themselves on particular subjects or improve their general knowledge. In mid-January 1947, a screening was organised for a committee of library stakeholders so that they could consider a previous film on Danish libraries and an American film on the Library of Congress (Nielsen 1947). A committee was formed by the Library Association to oversee the film project in liaison with Dansk Kulturfilm, consisting of librarian Ida Bachmann, Sigfred Hjort Eriksen, editor of the professional journal Biblioteks-Nyt, and Carl Thomsen (1894–1971), a State Librarian whose life's mission was to popularise and democratise libraries (Mlvr 2011). This committee produced a draft outline for the film from which the filmmakers could work (Thomsen 1947). Unusually, the resulting film script is attributed to Bachmann and Hjort Eriksen.

The finished film is unexpectedly ambitious in terms of visual and aural style. While the voiceover is businesslike, reciting statistics, rules and a litany of book titles and the libraries that stock them, the rather dry information from the 'voice of god' is supplemented with the comments, queries and audible thoughts of library users and librarians on a wide range of issues. Two sequences are particularly striking in their use of voice. Firstly, a patron reading a musical score begins to whistle the tune and conduct an imaginary orchestra. There follows a quick-fire montage, cutting between close-ups of other library users and librarians saying 'shhhh!', making fun of the popular cliché. Another distinctive sequence ends the film. The camera circles a grand and anonymous room, tracking clockwise in medium close-up across a series of readers seated and concentrating on their respective books. They represent various 'types', from schoolchildren to a bearded grandfather reading aloud to his grandson, who leans entranced over the back of his armchair. Most are reading silently, but we hear what they are reading to themselves for a few seconds before the camera moves on, into the space of the next reader. The closing sequence thus stages the pleasure of the intimate encounter between reader and text that will be available to the film's viewers courtesy of their local library, as well as the simultaneity and multiplicity of experience essential to the imagining of community. This closing sequence dominated discussion after the screening to the stakeholders of the rough cut of the film (C.o.p. 1948). It was agreed, for example, that Melson would cut one of the books, on the cultivation of tulips, and replace it with a book on family history, to be provided by the Royal Library in Copenhagen. This is a neat example of the kind of micro-level intervention by stakeholders which could be accommodated as films acquired their final shape.

Meanwhile, the camerawork imbues a film about an otherwise static subject – books and libraries – with a sense of dynamism. From the opening titles, the camera is on the move, tracking towards the right across a set of bookshelves stocked with leather-bound volumes. The camera then pans to a woman engrossed in a book and from her it whip pans to her mischievous child, who hares off down the staircase from the mezzanine. The books have thus immediately been associated with the state of intense attention they inspire in people. This is further underlined about halfway through the film, when a nursery teacher is reading aloud to her young charges. Their rapt attention is communicated not through their faces, but by slow tracking and panning over the backs of their heads, a study in concentration.

A switch from horizontal to vertical panning is conspicuous in a sequence which exemplifies the array of libraries across Denmark and beyond, and how they are connected by inter-library loans. Library buildings modest and grand, modern and baroque, are displayed in a montage soundtracked by different voices specifying the book each place has sent and for whom. The perpendicular panning abstractly connects the libraries and the books they exchange; if the books are the warp thread of national culture, the libraries are the weft. The sequence of buildings includes one of the libraries of Oxford University, with a corresponding English voiceover. It had been decided to include footage of one of the major British libraries to illustrate the wider international tradition of loans, and footage of the Bodleiean Library in Oxford was sought via contacts in London. Before the images arrived, Hjort Eriksen wrote to say that he had discovered that the choice of library was inappropriate, as borrowing was not allowed there (Hjort Eriksen 1948), but the insert remains in the film; the price of correcting the factual error would have been to re-edit the script and soundtrack. In addition to visualising the network of inter-library loans across the country, then, the same sequence also projects the library map onto the map of Denmark by showing footage of a representative sample of local libraries and state or national institutions.

The mobile library service, *bogbilen*, is also included in the narrative; the cameraman even films from the back seat at one point, as the book wagon drives from one village to another bringing the fresh stocks of books that one local patron has just been complaining he lacks. In the book van are the librarians responsible for the script, though they are in shadow and therefore playing the part of 'every-librarian'. Details of the shoot around Denmark are provided by filmmaker Søren Melson in an account of an excursion undertaken by him and cameraman Poul Pedersen in May 1948 to western Jutland, in a jeep loaned by Nordisk Films Kompagni (Melson 1948). The tour combined filming at a number of regional libraries for *Biblioteket er åbent* with several shoots in fishing villages and on tuna boats off the west coast. The document shows that filming took place at several local libraries in the towns of Nyborg, Kolding and Vejen, travelling 408 kilometres west across the country in the space of a day, followed by filming in the larger library in Aarhus. This itinerary is a reminder that the imaginative trope of Denmark as a 'little land' is predicated on geographical reality; even small-budget, short-order productions can feasibly include documentary footage of a representative selection of locations in order to map aspects of national infrastructure. While *Her er Banerne* relies on the trope of railway lines extending from a metonymic node, *Biblioteket er åbent* exploits the possibility of displaying authentic images from across the nation.

As we know from Chapters 1 and 3, libraries were a crucial part of the network of distribution of mid-century informational film in Denmark. *Biblioteket er åbent* directly engages the cinephilia of the film-goers who would have encountered it as a *forfilm* before their feature of choice, highlighting film as one of the resources available at their local library. Rows of spectators are shown sitting rapt in the dark with light playing on their faces; again, the tracking motif is used to tie the film screening in this sequence to the more papery resources highlighted in the rest of the film. The camera ends up at the back of the room with the 16mm projector, which is screening the Lumière brothers' *L'arrivée d'un train* (*Arrival of a Train*, 1895), enhanced by a commentary in Danish. The voiceover explains that the screening is provided to enhance the film-focused study group we have just seen pictured with a practical demonstration. While cinema audiences would previously have come face to face with themselves as spectators in other films,[2] the composition of this shot seems calculated not just to inform cinema-goers about the substantial presence of film in their local library, but also to *confront* them with it in this self-reflexive sequence (Figure 7.2).

Biblioteket er åbent is an interesting example of a film whose distribution within Denmark demonstrates that the system was open to ad hoc adjustments – the exceptions mentioned in this film's production files help us to understand the rules that applied more generally. One instance of special treatment was

Figure 7.2   In *Biblioteket er åbent* (Søren Melson, 1949), library-users look back at cinema-goers from the projection room.

the involvement of the State Librarian's office in theatrical screenings. Statens Filmcentral was asked to coordinate with Carl Thomsen regarding the film's screening schedule in cinemas, so that a campaign promoting the work of libraries more generally could coincide with screenings around the country (Petersen 1949). There also arose a controversy when the filmmaker found out that the film had been cut to suit the needs of the Palads Cinema, and asked for (and was given) a guarantee that this was an exceptional measure (Melson 1949). Also exceptionally, the Danish Library Association and Library School were permitted to show the film at a private screening, as long as no members of the press were invited (Koch-Olsen 1949b). Appropriately, another exception was made regarding distribution of the film to libraries; copies of the film could be added to the permanent narrow-gauge collections at larger libraries, provided that it was not made available for loan before its theatrical run was complete (Koch-Olsen 1949b). This results in a fascinating *dispositif* for a film originally designed as a cinema *forfilm*, which would now be watched in the very surroundings it reflects back to the viewer.

Rationalising the Housewife, Nationalising Home Economics

Another example of the late 1940s depicts another national educational network, this time provision of training in home economics for the nation's brides-to-be.

In May 1949, Erik Witte at Minerva Film sent the bill for production of *Peter må vente* (*Peter has to Wait*) to Dansk Kulturfilm. The film had overshot its budget by thirty-four per cent, primarily because the director, Svend Aage Lorentz, had required intense use of lighting on large sets such as a church. The detailed invoice requested as a result lists a number of expensive props, including a wedding gown, veil and bouquet. The producers had planned to return the gown to the shop and had had it cleaned, explains Witte, but on account of the length of the hire, and the wear incurred by the dress during use, this proved not to be possible. The dress was therefore at Ib Koch-Olsen's disposal, he concludes tartly (Witte 1949). Whether Koch-Olsen collected the gown is unrecorded, but the itemised list of bridal paraphernalia on this invoice is an amusing material metaphor for the institutions of marriage, family, home and womanhood on which *Peter må vente* relies for its persuasive force.

Peter må vente was initiated by a letter of December 1946 to Dansk Kulturfilm from Foreningen for danske Husholdningslærerinder (the Association of Danish Home Economics Teachers). The Association had enquired a year earlier about the possibility of a film promoting the value of formal training in home economics, but a film about training for housekeepers was planned, and so it was feared that this project was too similar. As the latter film had come to nothing, the Association now wanted to propose their own film project again. It was argued that the economic context of the immediate post-war period – acute shortages of crucial products and the need to reduce consumption of meat, eggs, milk and cheese – made a practical and theoretical education in Home Economics essential for every young Danish woman. Yet only ten per cent of girls took advantage of the training available via evening classes and colleges. It was this training which the Association wanted to promote (Juul Andersen 1946).

Ideas for the film were thrashed out with a small committee from the Association, and Koch-Olsen offered the film to director Astrid Henning-Jensen in the first instance; whether it was felt appropriate to offer this particular film to a woman director is not made explicit (Koch-Olsen 1947e). Henning-Jensen had just won the Prix International at the Venice Film Festival for the feature film *Ditte Menneskebarn* (*Ditte Child of Man*, 1946), on which she had been Assistant Director with husband Bjarne as Director, and was too busy. Regardless, Koch-Olsen's 'rough notes' in his letter to Henning-Jensen about the home economics film are very suggestive of the notions of gender and class underlying the training for young wives that the film's commissioners wished to promote. It is proposed that the film begin with a montage of housewives awakening across the land:

> The alarm clock rings. – Town housewife gets up. – Alarm clock in the sink. Different kinds of alarms. – Pocket watch. – Telephone. Different types of housewives. – Rural housewife. – Town housewife. – Worker's wife. – Middle-class wife. – Upper-class wife. Difference between central heating and stove. Coffee pot. Pictures switch between the four types. One house where the husband is helping. – Another where the husband is not helping. A factory worker takes her child to daycare. A wife goes back to bed after a night shift. – One planning her day. One that goes back to bed after the husband leaves. Follow the two types through the day with shopping, cooking, cleaning etc. In one of the homes, the children should have their own small tasks (a pedagogical pointer). (Koch-Olsen 1947e)

The notes continue to emphasise that the different classes of housewife in town and country should be contrasted, some with household help, some without. The film should cover the art of grocery shopping, cleaning, laundry and mending, cooking, childcare, budgeting and purchase of kitchen equipment. Though particular visual techniques are not specified in this sketch, it is clear that the film as originally conceived closely links gender, class and nation, imagining (and imaging) Danish housewives in all their limited diversity, moving through the 'homogenous empty time' of a typical day. This emphasis on clocked time, when combined with the film's interest in the 'techniques' of grocery shopping and cleaning, chimes with the focus on efficiency and rationalisation of labour which we witnessed in the Marshall films discussed in the previous chapter.

The finished film, though, eschews the structure as originally outlined, but it does play with time in a different way. After Astrid Henning-Jensen declined the project, Svend Aage Lorentz was brought on board as director, and author Susanne Palsbo was asked to write the screenplay. Palsbo had recorded the voiceover for *Denmark Grows Up* (1947, discussed in Chapter 5), wrote the song lyrics for *Kartofler* (*Potatoes*, 1944–6, discussed in Chapter 4) and the script for Søren Melson's Marshall film *Fabrikken Caroline* (1951, see Chapter 6). Palsbo was expecting a baby around New Year 1948, and as a result the manuscript was delayed until that summer. Koch-Olsen reports that Palsbo commented of motherhood: 'there's just so much to do, until you work out how to do it' (Koch-Olsen 1948e). Thus, while it is tempting to be cynical about the contracting of women directors and writers to a film on home economics, there is circumstantial evidence that this script was infused with first-hand experience of the domestic labour it tries to police.

Palsbo's screenplay begins with a quick-fire montage alternating between young men and women in a variety of apprenticeships – a welder, a hairdresser, a bricklayer, a (female) carpenter and a trainee chef – all of them said to take around four years (Palsbo 1948b: 1–2). Then the narrative settles on a young couple, Peter and Lene, who are seen at their wedding then returning from their honeymoon. A voiceover provides a running commentary on Lene's unsuccessful attempts at a range of housework: cooking an omelette, cleaning the bathroom, scrubbing pots, doing the laundry (3–4). Peter is patient for a time, comments the voiceover; that's how it is when people are newly married. But a plate of burnt *frikadeller* (meatballs) is the last straw, and he storms out (5). Lene is left bereft in her disordered kitchen, which the screenplay describes as full of piles of dirty crockery, casserole dishes and bottles lying around. 'There sits the little wife, lonely and abandoned in her messy kitchen, and she doesn't know what to do.' At this point, Palsbo's screenplay makes an unexpected move, which is not included in the finished film in its full complexity: Lene looks directly into the camera, breaking the fourth wall, and snaps: 'Won't you stop preaching for a moment and tell me what to do?' (6). The voiceover responds: 'I can tell you what you should have done', going on to insist that housekeeping requires specialist training like any other job. The film then surprises again with a self-reflexive move: while Lene looks astonished, the voiceover explains that precisely because this is a film, events can be re-wound and the wedding delayed until Lene has taken the right training. The bride and her father are seen walking backwards down the aisle, down the steps and into the waiting carriage, while the wedding march plays in reverse, a musical composition which Palsbo renders in musical notation in her draft (7). Peter, the husband, is left to wait at the altar while Lene investigates housekeeping classes. The screenplay continues to gesture knowingly to itself as a film. When Lene finds out that there are free evening classes for full-time workers, a thud is heard: the voiceover explains that what we just heard was a weight falling from Lene's chest (10). But there is also concrete information about the new one-year course in housekeeping which the Association of Home Economics Teachers wanted to promote. The voiceover delivers this information while we watch Lene learning to cook and how to wring out a floorcloth, before embarking on two six-month internships as a housekeeper's assistant in the city and in the countryside (13–14). During a class on childcare, Lene has had enough, and walks into shot, right in front of the camera, asking (again breaking the fourth wall) if she can go and get married now (Figure 7.3)? The voiceover acquiesces and Lene marches out of the classroom. Along the way, her work clothes transform into a bridal gown in a jump cut, she collects her father, and they ride in the horse-drawn carriage from the countryside into Copenhagen and towards the church, where her relieved husband-to-be is still waiting (16–18).

Figure 7.3   Lene breaks the fourth wall to demand her freedom (*Peter må vente*, Svend Aage Lorentz, 1949).

Aside from some factual updates about housekeeping courses, Palsbo's screenplay served as the basis for Lorentz's film. Palsbo was concerned that the role of Lene was 'not so easy' and should be played by a 'proper actress' (Palsbo 1948b). The role went to Jytte Ibsen (1929–2015), a nineteen-year-old stage and screen actor who also appeared in Dansk Kulturfilm's feature *For Frihed og Ret* (*For Freedom and Justice*, Svend Methling) the same year. Ibsen imbues Lene with a quirky, determined, girl-next-door glamour reminiscent of Hollywood screwball comedies, and with its staging of the marriage (and re-marriage) and its self-awareness, *Peter må vente* exploits recognisable tropes of the screwball genre to seduce and persuade its target audience of young women.

Peter må vente was screened both in Copenhagen and the provinces together with a selection of other short films finished around the same time. The programme in Kalundborg on 22 April 1949, for example, consisted of *Peter må vente*, *Biblioteket er åbent*, *Bondegården* (*The Farm*, Nic. Lichtenberg), *Æventyret om en by* (*Fairytale of a City*, Ove Sevel) and two films by Jørgen Roos: *Opus I*, an animated film made by scraping patterns into black film, and *Mikkel* (about a fox fostered by a family). The next evening, *Peter må vente* was screened to members of the Association of Danish Home Economics Teachers, followed by *smørrebrød* at the National Scala restaurant, and Dansk Kulturfilm's office manager Helene Nielsen attended (Nielsen 1949). Through 1949 and into 1950, *Peter må vente* toured Danish cinemas as the *forfilm* to a Swedish romantic drama, *Flickorna i Småland* (*The Girls in Småland*, Schamyl Bauman, 1945), with an estimated audience of 272,000 across 195 cinemas (SFC 1951).

Although *Peter må vente* was commissioned in connection with the development of new housekeeping courses and thus might be assumed to become quickly irrelevant, it continued to be hired from SFC by clubs, societies and schools into the 1960s: for example, it was hired 161 times in 1953–4 and 209 times in 1959–60 (SFC 1954; SFC 1960a), with school loans representing an increasingly large proportion of the total as the decade went on. This could suggest that school teachers preferred to play safe by hiring tried and tested films that had passed their pedagogical use-by date, but it also illustrates a broader point about the non-linearity, and indeed the slow pace, of the impact of films and their ideologies on the population.

SELF-ACTUALISATION AND LABOUR MARKET PLANNING

While *Peter må vente* was still on the programme of provincial Danish cinemas in winter 1949–50, the Social Democratic government moved to tackle a set of issues around the national labour market. Arbejdsmarkedskommissionen (the Labour Market Commission) was established in December 1949, with a remit to analyse employment patterns and report on means of planning and rationalisation of the labour market (Jespersen 2008b: 445). To maximise employment in an era of urbanisation and economic change, Denmark would need to mitigate certain structural hindrances in its employment culture. These included a lack of geographical mobility amongst workers and businesses, and a propensity to over-specialisation partly caused by an inflexible apprenticeship system (447, 450). The Commission's complex remit gave rise to a bewildering number of reports on problems ranging from seasonal work, to support for disabled workers, to reduced working hours, and, naturally, on various aspects of education and training. This, then, was the broader context for the development of a national careers advice service for young people in the early 1950s, a project which triggered the commissioning of a film encouraging the use of careers advisors. The result was Theodor Christensen's *Hvad skal jeg være?* (*What should I be when I grow up?*, 1955).

The question of professional opportunities for women and girls that underpins *Peter må vente* also lies at the heart of *Hvad skal jeg være?* The film's central message, as underlined in the press release announcing its premiere, is the answer to the question in its title: 'talk to your careers advisor before making any decisions!' (Dansk Kulturfilm 1955). An interesting theme in the film, though, is the tension between parents' wishes for their children, based on outmoded gender norms, and the aptitudes and interests of the young people themselves. In other words, the film suggests that the self-actualisation of the individual is a matter for state intervention, thus privileging the relationship between the individual and society, wrested free from the pressures of the family unit. The film's 'happy ending' is a victory for the logic of the rational, planned labour market over parental ambitions: the young protagonist, Søren, persuades his father to let him train as a machinist, while his more intellectual sister Lise is allowed to leave her job as a secretary and pursue her dream of further education.

The film project was discussed at an MFU meeting of late 1953. The importance of incorporating a gender perspective into the film was raised at this meeting by board member Hanne Budtz (1915–2004), a lawyer, politician and women's rights campaigner. Budtz herself remained involved in the film project as a consultant, but another woman more directly linked to contemporary efforts to reform careers advice was also invited to advise: Grethe Philip (1916–2016), a leading figure in the development of careers advice and planning in Denmark. Philip was Denmark's first woman to graduate with an MA in Economics (Cand. Oecon.), later spent nineteen years as a member of parliament, advocated for changes in taxation and family law to promote gender equality, and worked extensively in finance. In 1951, Philip had been appointed an advisor at Copenhagen's Centralarbejdsanvisningen (Central Careers Service). Her focus was on careers advice for young women, and her perspective was both economic and social. She moved to the Danish Labour Market Commission in 1954 (Haastrup 2003). Grethe Philip helped to shape *Hvad skal jeg være?* from the outset, providing an advance copy of her report on the establishment of a state careers service, and advising on successive drafts, along with representatives from the Ministry of Labour and Society (Hølaas 1953; Hølaas 1954b). Philip's involvement is an example of Dansk Kulturfilm's ability to secure consultancy from the relevant figures of the day. Conversely, *Hvad skal jeg være?* can, for the same reason, be seen as a concrete example of the use of state-sponsored film in the promotion of new government projects.

Through summer and autumn 1954, Christensen revised the manuscript. Two significant changes were made along the way: the film's running time was doubled from the originally proposed six minutes to twelve minutes, and the content was 'dramatised' more, the latter measure with a view to making the film easier to place with cinemas (Hølaas 1954a). A final version was agreed with Dansk Kulturfilm and consultants from the government's Employment Directorate, plus Grethe Philip, in early November 1954. A few final, handwritten changes to that screenplay indicate that the consultants had wanted to hammer home the message about individual fulfilment from the school careers advisor even more explicitly: 'It's your future that these decisions are concerned with. You yourselves must use your eyes, you yourselves must gather knowledge about the kind of work you think you may like to do ... It is, and will be, your future at stake' (Christensen 1954: 8–9). These words are contrasted with the pleas of Søren's father that he should take his high school exams first. The careers advisor's mantra continues to echo in Søren's head as he unwillingly goes to school and hangs out at the dockyard in his spare time: 'let no-one else decide for you' (15). After Søren unleashes a family crisis by stowing away on a ship, it is the careers advisor who resolves the situation by persuading the father to let both his children pursue their dreams and their talents. Voicing the bewilderment of the Danish everyman, the father admits that he had no idea the careers advice service existed. 'Well, now you know!' retorts the careers advisor, closing the door to his office, and thereby the film.

As in *Peter må vente*, much of *Hvad skal jeg være?* unfolds in a family home. However, the resonance and function of the respective homes are quite different. In *Peter må vente*, the kitchen and dining table serve only as visual metaphors for Lene's dysfunctional housekeeping and its threat to the institution of marriage. In *Hvad skal jeg være?*, the home is a more complex space in which family politics are played out as a microcosm of social tensions. As illustrated in Figure 7.4, blocking allows for the rivalry between brother and sister to play out in abstract spaces such as the door frame. The *mise-en-scène* constructs an anonymous middle-class Danish home in all its paraphernalia: coffee pot, modern lampshade, mid-century furniture. The dining room is the venue for a family dinner celebrating Søren's high school graduation, shot from the perspective of a dinner guest to maximise the claustrophobia. The living room is the setting for a prologue to the film, when the parents of Søren and Lise discuss their ambitions for their children's future, even though Søren, as we hear him comment in a voiceover, is not yet born. Søren's and Lise's trajectory away from the gravitational pull of their family's expectations is thus given more dramatic impetus by rooting its centre of gravity in that same homely living room. Of no little significance in this conventional setting is Lise's strikingly modern pageboy hairstyle, her fringe as sharp as her sarcastic remarks to the truculent Søren about the educational chances he has had. But the necessary contrast to the family home is the machinery at the docks and in the ship's engine room. Here, Christensen employs his long experience in industrial filmmaking to communicate Søren's fascination with the engine. Thus the film's *mise-en-scène* also functions to sustain a tension between the family home as material space and its analogue writ large, the welfare state as 'people's home'.[3]

Hvad skal jeg være? premiered on 22 December 1955 as part of a complete film programme; it was not, as originally planned, distributed to cinemas as

Figure 7.4   Søren and Lise discuss careers with their father in *Hvad skal jeg være?* (Theodor Christensen, 1955).

a *forfilm* attached to a feature film. Instead, the film toured forty cinemas in Denmark together with Bjarne Henning-Jensen's forty-minute colour film about a boy growing up in a modernising Greenland, *Hvor bjergene sejler* (*Where Mountains Float*, 1955),[4] and Astrid Henning-Jensen's *Ballettens børn* (*Children of the Ballet*, also 1955). By mid-1956, the three-film programme had been seen by an estimated 240,000 viewers (SFC 1956: 10). *Hvad skal jeg være?* took much longer to penetrate the annual list of the top fifty most frequently hired narrow-gauge films, reaching number thirty with 154 hires in 1961–2. This pattern again testifies to the tendency of school teachers to stick with older, tried and tested films, and to the longer-term impact of mid-1950s careers advice policy.

Debating Leisure: Amateur Club Culture and Professionalisation

As discussed in Chapters 1 and 3, clubs (*foreninger*) are a distinctive and crucial aspect of social and cultural life in Denmark. The very constitution of Dansk Kulturfilm from the mid-1930s was based on this building block of Danish society: the interests of end-users of films were represented via the

Figure 7.5   A nation watches itself play sport in *Enden på legen* (Theodor Christensen, 1960).

inclusion of a broad range of specialist associations on Dansk Kulturfilm's Board. Clubs and associations were, as we have repeatedly seen, a crucial audience for the filmic output of Dansk Kulturfilm throughout its history. Our final case study in this chapter focuses on a film which throws into sharp relief not only the *foreningsfilm* – films made specifically for use in clubs and societies – as a genre of informational film, but which also thematises the Danish culture of *foreninger* itself. Theodor Christensen's *Enden på legen* (*The End of the Game*, 1960) explores the tradition of amateur sports and leisure, their role in community-building and health, and portrays the professionalisation of sport as a social threat (Figure 7.5).

As in the other Scandinavian countries, sport in Denmark has been organised since the mid-nineteenth century in ways that chime with the welfare model, specifically as 'a large popular movement, anchored in a legacy of voluntarism and idealism, upheld by voluntary club structures and sport governing bodies ... which are mobilised in unified confederations' (Persson 2013: 168). In terms of ethos, grassroots sporting organisations share with the social-democratic welfare society more broadly a discourse of democratic participation, fair play, egalitarianism and the importance of access to health-promoting activities. As a result, involvement of children and adults in sport is relatively high in Scandinavia by international standards (Persson 2013: 170). At the time *Enden på legen* was made, for example, the allied association for shooting, gymnastics and leisure (De danske skytte-, gymnastik- og idræts-foreninger), just one of the larger confederations of sports clubs, could boast 370,149 members spread over some 1700 local clubs (D.D.S.G. & I. 1960: 3), equating to approximately eight per cent of the Danish population of around 4.5 million in 1960.

The emphasis on voluntarism and grassroots participation has historically generated a certain hostility to the professionalisation of sport in Denmark, so much so that by the late 1950s, the national football team was the last remaining amateur team in Europe (Jakobsen 2009: 31). The production of *Enden på legen* thus coincided with a period when public debate about amateurism versus professionalisation in sport was particularly intense, though the issue was current enough to have inspired the original film commission half a decade earlier. Throughout the 1950s, it had become increasingly clear that Denmark's policy of disqualifying footballers who played professionally with foreign teams from the Danish national soccer team was unsustainable; it was a running joke that despite two potential world-class national teams scattered around the world, Denmark had to field its third-best squad, the ones who had stayed at home (Jakobsen 2009: 32). Nonetheless, Denmark qualified for the football competition at the 1960 Olympic Games in Rome and won silver. In the pre-match excitement, the emerging teenage star striker Harald Nielsen (1941–2015) predicted that Denmark might win gold, an ambition that was regarded as thoroughly un-Danish by the press at home. Nielsen's comments earned him the nickname he bore for the rest of his life – 'Guld-Harald' (Golden Harald) – an epithet that spoke as much to the collective discomfort with success in the public sphere in Denmark as it did to his gilded talent on the field (Jakobsen 2009: 127). That summer was also marked by a tragedy for Danish football, when a small plane transporting amateur footballers to Jutland for try-outs for the national Olympic team crashed into the Øresund, killing all eight players on board. The roll-call of the deceased poignantly included the occupations of the footballers: butcher, engineer, industrial apprentices, soldier (Helleskov Kleiner and Heisz 2010). Like their colleagues who tragically died in the Øresund plane crash, the national team sent to the Olympiad in Rome consisted of men who had day-jobs and had attained mastery of the game through training with amateur clubs, the same local sports clubs that blanketed the country and were organised into larger national confederations. 'Golden Harald' signed for Bologna in 1961 and as a result was never eligible to play for the national team again. The ban on professional players was not lifted until the 1970s, despite campaigning by figures such as Harald Nielsen and the national team trainer, Arne Sørensen (1917–77).

This, then, was the social and media context in which *Enden på legen* premiered in late summer 1960. The initial request for a film about the ethics of sport had come from Dansk Folkeoplysnings Samråd (Danish Council for Popular Enlightenment) in January 1954. The Council regularly put forward suggestions for film topics, with a view to increasing the choice of 'enlightening' films available to clubs and interest groups. Together with a request for a film about 'sport today (leisure for better or worse)' came suggestions for films on democracy, on housekeeping and mental health. A year later, the Council chased up the request, as none of the films it had suggested in the previous few years had come to fruition. Its letter underlined that neither school films nor films designed as cinema *forfilm* were suitable for use by clubs and interest groups whose mission was to enlighten their members through discussion and instruction supported by film (Dansk Folkeoplysnings Samråd 1955). From the beginning, then, *Enden på legen* highlights an important – if sometimes ill-defined – distinction between, on the one hand, the need for longer, more complex films that would provoke discussion amongst club members and, on the other, the impetus towards drama as a means to engage cinema-goers, as with *Hvad skjal jeg være?* While the *foreningsfilm* as a genre required a discursive approach, *Enden på legen* has also been seen as one of the first examples of the mission of social critique that came to characterise a new generation of Danish documentary from the beginning of the 1960s (Bondebjerg 2012: 48, 209), a development that we glimpse before the end of this book.

Not until autumn 1958 did serious discussions about a film on the topic of sport commence, and it is the minutes of the January 1959 meeting of Dansk Kulturfilm's Board that confirm that pre-production was underway (Dansk Kulturfilm 1959). The project had been discussed informally with Theodor Christensen, and the services of an expert in the field had been secured: Knud Lundberg (1920–2002). Lundberg had written the book that had inspired the idea for the film, *Idræt på godt og ondt* (*Leisure for Better or Worse*, 1951), and had recently tried a stint in local government, but was even better known in Denmark for having represented his country in all three of the national football, handball and basketball teams (Team Denmark 2005: 12). Lundberg was consulted on successive drafts of Christensen's screenplay as it developed through 1959, including approval of the final version of the voiceover (Hebo 1960). Aside from some practical corrections, Lundberg felt that the film should emphasise that sport and leisure in contemporary Denmark was built on a very broad popular basis (Pedersen 1959c).

More crucially for the film and for the context in which it circulated, however, is that Lundberg was notorious for his opposition to the professionalisation of sports, a stance which was developed in his book and in his own practice. In some of his revisions to the script, he is careful to control how this point is expressed, insisting on this phrasing, for example: 'With financial professional sport we're well on the way to squeezing the life out of sport, and state professionalism distorts its meaning' (Lundberg 1959). Christensen himself was sympathetic to this point of view. For example, after a screening at the 1961 Berlin Film Festival in August 1961, he expressed his own philosophy to the newspaper *B.T.* as follows:

> With Enden på legen, I want to ... emphasise that sport is healthy, as long as it is a game ... a very necessary game, which has incredible relevance for mental hygiene in any society. It would be impossible to replace sport. But sport must not be mis-used. The same moment that the amateur turns professional and earns money for his hobby, it's dangerous, and in the same second sport is exploited for propaganda or politics, which is of course the norm with dictators, something healthy is transformed into something sick. (B.T. 1961)

The subject of the film is, then, the evils of the commercialisation and politicisation of sport. It warns against national 'hysteria' over sports stars and warmly supports retention of Danish 'amateur status' (Nielsen 1960: 486). Crucially, given that the film was commissioned to serve as a stimulus to debate at club meetings, and made with state funding, its approach to the subject as well as its context of consumption must be understood through the lens of the role of sport and leisure as a facet of the welfare society – like access to culture, a facet of the healthy and enjoyable life that was an end of the welfare state. Precisely because it was a *foreningsfilm* with a remit to inspire discussion, *Enden på legen* was the subject of a number of articles in the relevant press organs. For example, a magazine for evening and continuing education provides a succinct review of the coverage and perspective of *Enden på legen*:

> Amateur sport versus the rough and tumble of professional sport (financial interests and exploitation by the state); the creation of sports stars; the passivity of spectators and national hysteria; nerve-shredding pursuit of the competition and searing matches are the chief themes. In a provocative form – to which the fine photography and inventive editing contribute – these themes are laid out for the viewer. A rather good voiceover also leaves its mark; each time the film explores a situation from the shadowy side of sport and leisure, the voiceover throws its mantra 'A healthy mind in a heathy body!' back at us. The goal has to be 'healthier people in a healthier world'. For if we don't hold on to that vision (and avoid falling into an unsportsmanlike ditch), it'll be the end of the game. (Aften- og Ungdomsskolen 1960)

In the magazine of De Danske Gymnastikforeninger (the Danish Gymnastics Associations) Mads Nielsen reviews the film at length and nuances some of its positions. He makes the point that *Enden på legen* undermines its message about the dangers of professionalisation by actually showing the less salutary aspects of the amateur system: the stands filled with empty beer bottles after a football match, for example, or the acceptance by radio commentators of ungentlemanly tactics in international matches (Nielsen 1960: 487). The same reviewer worries that although the filmmakers clearly regard the profession-alisation issue as an urgent one, the film's obsession with speed, tempo and technical tricks might obscure its pedagogical function (486).

There is no doubt that *Enden på legen* is a highly stylised film. In part, this is due to the work of the editor, Ole Roos, who cut the film while Christensen was alternately indisposed and overseas during the later stages of production (Hebo 1960). While quickfire editing works with the movement of bodies, shuttlecocks and balls to communicate the dynamics of sports games, the precision editing also carries us across and between sports to construct montage sequences comparing and contrasting their respective tempos and the social 'types' who participate in them or watch them. The film is a profoundly affective experience, also, in part, generated by the tempo within and between shots, as well as the close-up attention to sweat and mud on skin, grunting and shouting, the smack of shuttlecock on racket strings and the thud of flesh against leather or grass.

The same essay in which reviewer Mads Nielsen critiques the didactic clarity of *Enden på legen* was re-printed by Statens Filmcentral as part of a facilitation pack later developed to support discussion and learning during film screenings. The brochure designed to accompany *Enden på legen* also contained a lengthy essay on the film by editor Ejnar Johansson, an extract from a radio programme on press coverage of sport, some statistics relating to the involvement of Danes in sports broken down by age and gender, and a list of further reading. This mix of extant and dedicated material thus gives us a glimpse of what might have been discussed amongst attendees at screening evenings. Here we see the relationship between Dansk Kulturfilm's Board membership as representatives of end-users come full circle, as the idea at the heart of the original film commission is taken up for debate at grassroots level, mediated through artistic decisions, expert advice and government-sponsored teaching aids. Fuelled by coverage in association media organs and by the contemporary relevance of its subject matter, *Enden på legen* was a popular film for hire amongst schools, clubs and associations, entering the 'top fifty' list at number seven in 1960–1 (hired 272 times), and rising to the sixth most frequently hired film in 1961–2, with 325 hires (SFC 1961b, 1962).

Enden på legen transcended its origins as a debate-film, however, by dint of its artistic qualities and the reputation of its director. It was screened in

Copenhagen together with the American documentary *Jazz on a Summer's Day* (Bert Stern, 1960). It also had the dubious honour of being the only film to represent Denmark at the Berlin Film Festival of 1961. Unfortunately, due to dwindling funding, it was screened with English rather than German subtitles, which hindered comprehension amongst the festival-goers (Brandt 1961: 217). Moreover, a sequence drawing on footage of massed ranks for German sports spectators during the reign of Hitler elicited gasps and grumbles from the Berlin audience (B.T. 1961).

THE END OF THE GAME?

An undignified episode in 1963 entangled *Enden på legen* in a legal dispute over the use of footage of some of the sportsmen featured. The film was broadcast on television in July 1963, much to the chagrin of two professional boxers who had staged a boxing match for the cameras – smeared with grease and fruit juice as fake sweat and blood – under the impression that the footage was for the use of doctors and other specialists. Lundberg as advisor and Statens Filmcentral were the targets of the lawyer hired by the boxers' promoter (Art 1963). The irony of the representatives of professional sport suing state-sponsored filmmaking drives home just how high the stakes were for amateurism in Denmark in the early 1960s. The slow corrosion of grassroots sports culture which *Enden på legen* attempted to warn against can be read as an allegory for the contemporary erosion of another aspect of the social-democratic social order: state-support for informational film itself.

In this chapter, a representative selection of informational films has enabled us to explore some of the ways in which a range of dimensions of the national community were imaged and mapped out in films meant to inform and persuade. By dint of their subject matter, the films both point backwards towards shared values and traditions, but also point forward towards increasingly rational and planned ways to organise social life. Overall, and especially in the later two films, there is a sense of increasing criticism towards social norms. This subtle shift in documentary practice is consonant with a sea-change in Dansk Kulturfilm's mission and support structures in the latter half of the 1950s. In the next chapter, we trace the multiple pressures faced by Dansk Kulturfilm through the 1950s and its eventual mothballing towards 1965. Our focus is a particularly contested strand of the agency's activity: the art film and, more broadly, the question of documentary versus art.

NOTES

1. The distribution of *Her er Banerne* was complicated by the historical curiosum that Danish State Railways operated their own cinema in Copenhagen's Hovedbanegård

(Central Station). The director of the 'Kino', as the cinema was called, requested a theatrical-length version of *Her er Banerne*, but this was refused by Koch-Olsen, who thought it would be a shame to cut the twenty-four-minute version down, especially since non-theatrical audiences liked films of around half an hour (Koch-Olsen 1948d).

2. Feature films which included images of cinema audiences for this informational film to 'trigger', and would likely have been fresh in the memory of Danish audiences, included *Brief Encounter* (David Lean, 1945, UK), released in Denmark in early 1947. Many thanks to Richard Farmer (and other Facebook friends) for their suggestions.

3. In Swedish parlance, the concept of *folkhemmet* (the people's home) has applied this metaphor to the welfare state since the early twentieth century, but the Danish equivalent does not have the same historical resonance.

4. A synopsis of *Hvad skal jeg være?* in Greenlandic is included in the production files, suggesting that the film was circulated in Greenland, though I have not been able to find any record of this. Such an initiative would, however, fit with the Danish state's policy of 'Danicisation' of the Greenlandic populace in the 1950s.

8. A FREE HAND:
THE ART FILM VERSUS THE ART OF
DOCUMENTARY

'Remember: we detest *l'art pour l'art*!' So wrote Mogens Skot-Hansen to Søren Melson during the production of the *Social Denmark* series, in an attempt to persuade him to edit out the controversial footage of plump ladies in bathing suits from *People's Holiday* (Skot-Hansen 1947). Melson was appalled at the cuts eventually imposed on the film without his permission and approached the newly established filmmakers' union, Dansk Filmforbund, for back-up (Melson n.d.). While making his department's preferences clear, Henning Friis at the Labour and Social Ministry admitted that a filmmaker's authority over his film was a matter of principle that had to be determined by Dansk Kulturfilm and MFU (Friis 1947). Throughout the history of Dansk Kulturfilm, the extent to which the filmmakers contracted by the state were given artistic licence is often expressed in terms of the metaphor of 'a free hand'. This principle is exploited to different ends in the discourse surrounding the production of a range of films, but in general, the artistic quality of the informational film is regarded as a means to an end: to communicate the message outlined in the commission.

The interest amongst Danish documentarists in what Skot-Hansen playfully dismisses as '*l'art pour l'art*' was intense enough to be remarked upon by Arthur Elton, who was familiar with the Danish milieu after his consultancy work on *Social Denmark*. Elton did not see the artistic aspirations as an unequivocal strength:

> When one is with the Danish documentary people, as likely as not they
> will be discussing the technical side of their craft, the proper timing of a

mix, the weight and effectiveness of a cut, the juxtaposition of a word and a visual, the structure and build of a sequence. This love of film for its own sake is something which I admire and respect, although sometimes it can go too far. The consequence has been that, though technically many of the Danish films are superb, and achieve a blend of picture, voice and music that any country may envy, some of them lapse into virtuosity for its own sake. (Elton 1948: 9)

This chapter picks up the recurring issue of artistic freedom for Denmark's informational filmmakers, with particular focus on a film genre – the art film – which became a touchstone for the debate about creativity versus documentary in informational film among professionals, public and press for much of the 1950s. After outlining the concept of the art film as it emerged from initiatives by UNESCO around 1950, we consider two Danish films of the late 1940s (Dreyer's *Thorvaldsen* and Hagen Hasselbalch's *Shaped by Danish Hands*) which awakened the ire of the Danish press because of their failure to correspond to international standards of the art film – though they each advanced the broader genre of the *kulturfilm*.

Apparently blind to the multiple pressures shaping commissioned films, the Danish press was incensed that no state-sponsored films on art were shortlisted for UNESCO's 1950 congress on art films and fulminated about Dansk Kulturfilm's 'fiasco'. The perceived gap in domestic production of art films (as opposed to films about applied art) was plugged by the Director of Thorvaldsen's Museum and other dignitaries who organised film screenings through the 1950s and published a catalogue of available films of the genre for schools and clubs. The art film is thus a useful example of the various rival organisations whose work promoting film intersected with that of Dansk Kulturfilm, and also throws up a variety of unexpected screening contexts such as museums. For some filmmakers, including Theodor Christensen, the intractability of Dansk Kulturfilm on the twin issues of artistic and ideological freedom for its directors was rooted in an institutional structure which was unfit for purpose by the late 1950s.

This chapter ends with an analysis of a later art film, *Herning 65* (Jens-Jørgen Thorsen and Novi Maruni, 1965). One of Dansk Kulturfilm's final productions, *Herning 65* more obviously belongs to the art film genre and, as such, prompted discussions on the relative value of art films versus the fate of the informational film as an art form. In turn, these discussions anticipate the replacement of Dansk Kulturfilm by new state-supported structures better suited to developing film as a creative industry for the new decade.

UNESCO AND THE ART FILM

In 1948 and 1950, the first two International Congresses of Art Films were held in Paris and Brussels, and the newly established UNESCO prepared a catalogue of some 150 films on different branches of the arts from a wide range of countries. The notion that certain films about art could become works of art in their own right began to take root. Writing shortly after his stint at UNESCO's Mass Communications Section ended in 1949, the New Zealand film censor Gordon Mirams explained how certain films of the period transcended their function as films *about* art to become films *as* art. Such films treat the painting or the sculpture or even the historic piece of architecture not as an indivisible whole but as an object whose qualities and design and aesthetic conception could be revealed brilliantly by the film itself through skilful cutting and cross-cutting, selection and juxtaposition of details, music and commentary. The result in one or two cases had been something which, dealing with an established work of art in another form, comes close to qualifying as a new work of art in itself (Mirams 1950: 19). Steven Jacobs identifies a German film of 1935 from Ufa Studios, *Steinerne Wunder von Naumburg* (*The Wondrous Stones of Naumburg*, Rudolph Bamberger and Curt Oertel), as the first to realise the potential of a mobile camera to offer a dynamic encounter with art, in this case the stonework of Naumburg Cathedral. The art documentary first developed as a specific genre, however, after the Second World War, and enjoyed a golden age during the late 1940s and early 1950s before its power was usurped by the spread of television (Jacobs 2011: 2–3).

An International Congress on Art Films took place in Paris in summer 1948, and UNESCO prepared a catalogue of some 150 films on different branches of the arts, published in 1949 as *Films on Art*. A permanent International Federation for Art Films was established, and a second Congress was held in Brussels in February 1950, at which forty art films made since 1948 were exhibited. While Denmark was represented at the 1948 Congress by five experimental shorts, at the second Congress in 1950 only one of the films it sent was selected for screening by the jury: an independent film about the painter William Scharff made by a young director, Mogens Kruse (Anonymous 1948b). Much to the chagrin of the Danish press and art critics, neither of the Danish films nominated for inclusion – Dreyer's *Thorvaldsen* (1949) or Hagen Hasselbalch's *Shaped by Danish Hands* (1948) – made it through the selection process. Members of the jury dismissed the Danish entries as neither serious nor filmic enough (Vinding 1950). Journalists were incensed at this Danish 'fiasco' and urged the national film bodies to invest more in the development of the Danish art film (Pierre 1950). If we now turn to consider these two films and their circulation, we might be tempted to conclude that the Danish press need not have been so critical – the two films were among the most widely circulated of all Dansk Kulturfilm productions. Though they may not have been judged artistic enough within the narrow parameters of the art film at UNESCO's Congress, they both fulfil the remit of the art film by offering the viewer a richly intermedial encounter with the art forms they explore.

SHAPING *SHAPED BY DANISH HANDS*

As an institution responsive to the needs of professional, trade and civic organisations, it was an obvious task for Dansk Kulturfilm to produce films on Danish craft and design. Applied arts such as silverware, pottery and furniture manufacture constituted important aspects of national cultural heritage and were (and remain) important export goods. This was a topic which lent itself well to the principle of double-coding of films for domestic and international consumption. Films such as *Shaped by Danish Hands* and Hasselbalch's later project on the same topic, *D ... For Design!* (1956) demonstrate how a number of 'hands' shape the *kulturfilm* and its construction of 'Danishness' for consumption at home and abroad: the artistic 'free hand' afforded the filmmaker; the exigencies of funders' demands; the material instantiation of culture (the objects filmed) and its impact on film style and narrative; and the changing technological contexts in which the films circulated and were viewed (including, in this case, trade fairs and North American television markets).

What was to become *Shaped by Danish Hands* was not commissioned by an arts and crafts organisation, but rather seems to have grown from MFU's wish-list towards the end of the war. On 19 December 1944, for example, a discussion of films for export more broadly advances the idea that films about Danish industries could have the knock-on effect of promoting Denmark abroad (SFC 1941; see also Nørrested and Alsted 1987: 247). The content and focus of what at that time was known as *Kunstindustrifilmen* (the Applied Arts Film) were sketched out at a meeting in January 1947. Present were Koch-Olsen, Hasselbalch and advisors Boisen (presumably Ingolf) and Gunnar Biilmann Petersen, a prominent designer, graphic artist, academic and architect. Petersen agreed to act as consultant on the screenplay as it developed and to act as liaison with his colleagues in the industry. The discussion is a glimpse into which facets of Danish applied art were considered marketable abroad at the time. Silverware, ceramics, hand-weaving, mosaic work and lampshades are all mentioned; possible shooting locations are also discussed, including Brüels ceramics, Kaare Klint's red chair and exhibits at Kunstindustrimuseet (the Danish Museum for Applied Arts). Hasselbalch intervenes from the filmmaker's point of view to point out that a black and white film should concentrate on 'colourless' things. He suggests including footage of silver-polishing in the world-famous Georg Jensen's workshop and the phenomenon of *moseeg*, or bog-wood.

Hasselbalch provided two one-page treatments, each taking a slightly different approach to the brief. The first is summarised by Hasselbalch as follows:

> Throughout this film, lighting, editing and camerawork should underline the quality and individual particularities of the artefacts, as well as the artistry and skilled practice of their creators. To allow for later versions in other languages, dialogue will be avoided totally, but we will create possibilities for 'imitating' dialogue through short sound-synchronised sequences. The rhythm of the images is calm and flowing. (Hasselbalch 1947a)

The film should open with titles that are formed from silver or wood, and the viewer is to be welcomed by a 'wonderful girl' into a living room full of Danish design objects. Only the girl's shadow or hand is seen in the rest of the film as she presents the artefacts one by one to the viewer, and the film explores how they came into being.

As an alternative, Hasselbalch sent a second treatment which picks up on Koch-Olsen's suggestion that the film could include a historical perspective on the applied arts. This treatment takes the viewer back to Viking times, before visiting a modern Danish home full of design objects. This film would describe the 'development, ingenuity, initiative and the artistic urge to create. It should be characterised by humour ... the tempo vivace. There will be no detailed descriptions of production methods etc., only an account of essential technical and artistic features' (Hasselbalch 1947b). Successive working titles give us a richer picture of the intended scope, focus and theme of the film. The working title oscillates between *Dansk Formgivning* (roughly, *The Danish Craft of Form*), *Ler, Træ og Sølv* (*Clay, Wood and Silver*), and *Stof tager Form* (*Material takes Form*). But Hasselbalch's two proposals are also revealing in that they echo two recurring tropes that obtained into the 1950s (and arguably today) in the promotion and reception of Scandinavian arts and crafts: a narrative of continuity with historical practices, versus engagement with the form of the artefacts themselves (Guldberg 2011: 49, 53). This is a point we shall return to towards the end of the discussion of *Shaped by Danish Hands*.

In the meantime, word had spread in the arts and crafts community about the proposed film. A letter arrived in late January from Viggo Sten Møller, the head of Landsforeningen Dansk Kunsthaandværk og Kunstindustri (the Danish Society of Arts and Crafts and Industrial Design). Møller was nonplussed that Dansk Kulturfilm had not contacted the Society about the film, and offered to meet with Koch-Olsen to discuss how it could contribute to this and other projects (Møller 1947a). As can be surmised from the January meeting to draft the film's content, Dansk Kulturfilm was using an academic design specialist as consultant on the film, rather than formal representatives of the relevant national professional body. Møller was invited to view an unfinished version of the film in mid-September 1947 and was displeased. In particular, he criticised the exclusion from the film of branches such as textiles, book binding and design, glass and jewellery, and expressed his expectation that more films about some of these subjects would be made (Møller 1947b). In a move perhaps consonant with Møller's influence in society – he was gaining a reputation for his energetic promotion of Danish crafts and would be made a Knight of the Dannebrog in 1951 (Harding and Hiort n.d.) – within a week, his recommendations for revisions had been applied to the film. Specifically, footage of the furniture designer Kindt-Larsen was added, as was a section on Børge Mogensen's FDB furniture and one on ceramics from Saxbo. Coverage of the furniture designer Kåre Klint and of the sculptor and toymaker Kaj Nielsen was reduced (Koch-Olsen 1947b). Unfortunately Møller was not entirely happy with the changes; he commented after a private screening of the finished film that the images of Kindt-Larsen's furniture were not as inspiring as the products deserved, probably because he had forced the inclusion of this content, he mused (Møller 1947c). After Hasselbalch's draft had been approved, the Danish text was sent for English translation. Comparison of the two documents reveals that a few sentences have been left out or added in the target text. The changes seem broadly to correspond with Møller's requested revisions; for example, an explanatory comment that Berthelsen executes Kindt-Larsen's designs is included.

Møller's intervention is interesting because it illustrates not only the influence of Denmark's professional associations, but also the rather flexible process by which input from stakeholders was sought by the producers at Dansk Kulturfilm and sometimes, as in this case, was thrust upon them. Furthermore, the correspondence around the production of this film makes explicit a tension which runs like a red thread through the history of state-sponsored filmmaking in Denmark: on the one hand, the notion of filmmakers as public servants funded by the public purse and therefore beholden to institutions such as professional associations, and, on the other hand, the commitment to informational filmmaking as an art. It is rare for the issue to arise so explicitly in the archival material as it does here in Ib Koch-Olsen's correspondence with Viggo Sten Møller. Appropriately for the title of the film in question, the metaphor that is used by both gentlemen is 'a free hand' (literally, 'free hands', or *frie hænder* in the Danish). In response to Møller's request for edits, Koch-Olsen wrote the following:

> I should also like to avoid misunderstandings, and so I shall reiterate, as I have also mentioned in person, that it has been essential for us to give the director *a free hand* with this material. This is so that he can make a film that is as it should be in filmic terms, that is, prioritising

artistic considerations. Our general principle when it comes to films to be screened abroad is that they first and foremost must be good films – in the same way that you give your sculptor free reign, when you have shown him to his place. (Koch-Olsen 1947b, my emphasis)

Another aspect of the principle of 'a free hand' is developed in further correspondence. Møller (1947c) argues that publicly funded films ought to be planned in collaboration with the appropriate professional societies. It is his impression that this has been the model for producing and distributing tourist films. Koch-Olsen (1947c) again employs the metaphor of 'a free hand' when he replies that tourist films have been made independently of the Tourist Board and placed abroad via the Foreign Ministry; the 'free hand' afforded the directors extends to their freedom to seek specialist advice as they wish. Nonetheless, many directors did not feel that they had enough artistic freedom in their work for the state. Indeed, Hagen Hasselbalch himself wrote vehemently, and rather wittily, on just this matter in *DF-Bulletin* (the Danish film workers' trade union magazine) in early 1948, that is, around the same time. He exhorted Dansk Kulturfilm to fund each director to make a film on a freely chosen topic once a year. This would foster the development of filmmaking as an art and give the public access to films on topics more challenging than 'nuts and bolts and sea urchins'. Such topics could include – he rounds off inventively – natural cycles, a white hyacinth, the new world just dawning, world peace, the dangers of democratic choice; '– just make a film' (quoted in Nørrested and Alsted 1987: 250).

Such discussions, and the title of Hasselbalch's film, actually give us a useful metaphor for the multifarious influences on each Dansk Kulturfilm production. Many people and institutions have a 'hand' in shaping the film text, and the degree to which the director has 'a free hand' in the endeavour emerges as a point of contention, as it did with *They Guide You Across* – though the stakeholders are domestic rather than international.

Mediating Tactility and Texture

The film was ready for screening at the end of February 1948, and in the first instance was available only in the original English version. Its purpose was 'to give the outside world an impression of Danish craftspeople and their work in clay, wood and silver' (Koch-Olsen 1948a). Free or not, this is a film full of hands. In line with Hasselbalch's first treatment, *Shaped by Danish Hands* opens with a striking animated title sequence in which wooden cow figures trundle across the screen, a modernist chair clatters to the foot of a staircase and a lump of clay splats against a tabletop. While individual craftspeople throughout the film are often allowed to appear and even be interviewed in

Figure 8.1   A clay pot is formed in *Shaped by Danish Hands* (Hagen Hasselbalch, 1948).

medium-shots or pans around their workplaces, it is the encounter of hands with artefacts that emerges as the dominant trope. In the opening sequence, the voiceover explains that ancient pottery lies under the earth of Jutland, and we watch as an old lady shapes, dries and smokes a clay pot. An inspection of the finished artefact dissolves to hands covered in clay throwing a pot. Later, teapots and vases made on the island of Bornholm are held and inspected in close-up, and turned to reflect the light against a black background. We see hands painting and toy designer Kaj Bøjesen's hands cutting paper into new shapes. This visual pattern is underlined by a statement in a voiceover by Finn Juhl: furniture should give the user the urge to feel the wood; fingers should tingle.

The film ends with a montage of hands working a range of crafts and objects (Figure 8.1), until a metal vase apparently shaping itself (in stop motion) announces the end credits. The self-shaping of the vase from flat metal sheet to voluptuously curved jug is an ingenious artifice which draws attention to the role of the many craftspeople whose handiwork (pun intended) has featured in the film. The traces of the intervention of whichever artist is creating this *objet d'art* can be seen to coax the metal through a number of stages of its formation, from the edges of the metal plate concertina-ing upwards and inwards to create a vase shape through to the trimming of the top edge and lip. Furrows, curves and even finger prints can be seen to mould the metal and then be erased as the object takes form. The full import of the film's title thus emerges in the occlusion of hands from the final sequence.

Much has been written in recent years about the proximal senses – touch, smell and taste – in cinema (see, for instance, Marks 2000; Marks 2002; Barker 2009). As an audio-visual medium, film cannot communicate the other senses directly to the viewer, but it has various tools at its disposal to trigger sense memory and thus help the viewer to approach a sensory experience in an 'asymptotic' way, evoking 'tactile forms of knowledge' (Marks 2000: 132). This kind of approach to the film text is usually associated with recent experimental or intercultural filmmaking, but here we have an example of a mid-twentieth-century informational film whose communicative power cannot be understood without an account of its emphasis on hands and touch. The frustrating inability of film to communicate taste and smell is actually tackled explicitly in Hasselbalch's unused treatment for *Shaped by Danish Hands*. The 'wonderful girl' who functions as narrator and hostess sits down and pours a glass of Cherry Heering liqueur into her Danish-designed Holmegaard wine-glass. Addressing the viewer directly, she says: 'I assure you that our liqueur is good, too. I'm just sorry I cannot offer you any. Film technology is not so advanced yet. But don't be envious of these cigarettes. I'm not so proud of our tobacco' (Hasselbalch 1947b). This suggests not only that Hasselbalch himself was interested in the limits and possibilities of depicting the senses in cinema, but that he fully expected his audience to grasp the irony of mediating multi-sensory experiences – promoting tactile objects and delicious drinks – using the audiovisual confines of black-and-white film.

The finished film's resort to 'tactile forms of knowledge' is less surprising if we consider its remit: to bring Danish design to foreign viewers, who may have no personal experience of such artefacts and perhaps a limited understanding of the film's English voiceover. The viewer is repeatedly asked to encounter these material objects through the proxy hands of the artists and inspectors. Light is made to play over the objects, sometimes against a black background, evoking surface texture or smoothness or volume. The stop motion animation over the opening and closing credits transforms inert objects into pulsating volumes and surfaces, in line with one of Hasselbach's working titles: 'matter takes form'. And while the close-ups never dissolve into what Marks (2000; 2002) would call a haptic image, whereby depth and perspective are sacrificed to surface texture of image or screen, the viewer is regularly invited to understand the artefacts as having been crafted by hands and to be apprehended by hands (see Figure 8.2). This point is evocatively nuanced by Eve Kosofsky Sedgwick, who thinks that in touching we understand that we are not the first

Figure 8.2   A craftsman's hands mimic the joists in the table he has made (*Shaped by Danish Hands*, Hagen Hasselbalch, 1948).

to touch an object: it has been formed by other hands or machines or natural forces, and that 'to perceive texture is to hypothesize whether the object I'm perceiving was sedimented, extruded, laminated, granulated, polished, distressed, felted, or fluffed up' (Sedgwick 2003: 14).

While the camerawork (as planned by Hasselbalch) often glides over the ceramics and silverware in the film, singly or in rows or piles, there is another visual pattern which sets furniture in motion. From the falling chair in the opening sequence, furniture is associated with movement: a tree falls in the forest and is sanded into the elegant lines of a Kåre Klint chair; an occasional table and a net for warming nuts pop out of a set of convertible furniture; the designer Børge Mogensen is awakened by his cat in a bed that slides in and out of a skylight, and sets to work. Again, Sedgwick is helpful here in thinking through how this dynamism of furniture and objects, combined with the viewer's privileged access to their surfaces, communicates the experience of an embodied encounter with them: 'to perceive texture is to know or hypothesize whether a thing will be easy or hard, safe or dangerous to grasp, to stack, to fold, to shred, to climb on, to stretch, to slide, to soak' (Sedgwick 2003: 15).

Arguably, then, *Shaped by Danish Hands* reveals that the definition of art film was predicated on a focus on the fine arts, not the applied arts. If the criterion was – and indeed ostensibly seems to have been, for example for Mirams – that the film engages with the art subject to create a new amalgam, then this film's exploration of the formation of artefacts in the skilled hands of the craftsperson would fall into that category.

Hands across the Ocean

Perhaps it was this compelling aesthetic strategy that allowed *Shaped by Danish Hands* to serve as an act of cultural diplomacy, a marketing film and an art film. It was seen by larger audiences than any other Dansk Kulturfilm production to whose exhibition records I have had access, by dint of the burgeoning interest in Scandinavian design in the North America of the 1950s.

Shaped by Danish Hands was sent to the Edinburgh International Film Festival in 1948 and to Venice in August 1949. It was screened at a Danish cultural exhibition in London in October to December 1948 (Dansk Kulturfilm 1949b: 9). Thereafter it continued to circulate widely in the UK. The Embassy of Denmark in London took responsibility for reporting on its distribution and reported 898 screenings during 1950, of which the vast majority – 817 screenings, accounting for 49,020 viewers – were the result of loans from the UK's Central Film Library (Udenrigsministeriet 1951), the relationship which Arthur Elton had facilitated a few years before. *Shaped by Danish Hands* also circulated widely in South America. Hagen Hasselbalch travelled there himself with a copy to show informally (Koch-Olsen 1948b), but a new trade agreement between Argentina and Denmark coincided with the film's release in French (*Formé par les mains danoises*) and Spanish (*Obra de artesanía danesa*), and resulted in 438 screenings in Argentina (SFC 1949). A slightly shortened Danish-language version of the film, *Skabt af danske hænder*, had been seen by some 230,000 people in clubs, schools and events in Denmark by 1952 (SFC 1952).

A game-changer for *Shaped by Danish Hands* in terms of audience reach was its adoption in November 1953 by the North American educational film distribution company Films of the Nations, whose mission was 'Promoting Peace through Films'. *Shaped by Danish Hands* was one of three films about Denmark in the company's 1954 catalogue. The titles of the other two – *Picturesque Denmark* and *Fairytale Tour through Denmark* – are suggestive of general overviews or tourist films, so the inclusion of applied arts as a topic seems somewhat incongruous. For comparison, the same catalogue listed nineteen films under Sweden, two under Finland and one under Scandinavia as a whole (Films of the Nations 1954: 2–3).

Films of the Nations both sold and rented its films. *Shaped by Danish Hands* is listed as available for sale at $40 or rent at $2.50; colour films in the catalogue are notably two or three times more expensive to buy, which presumably reflects the inflated costs of duplicating colour film at that time. According to figures provided to the Danish Foreign Ministry (Kristensen 1955), each copy sold was estimated to result in ten showings per month, and attendance was based on a nationwide average of 122 persons. Copies sold per quarter in 1954 ranged from one to twenty-nine, and loans hovered around fifty per quarter. Films of the Nations also acted as agent for television screenings across North America, which increased the number of viewers exponentially. In the fourth quarter of 1954, for example, 550,000 viewers saw the film on television in the Montréal broadcasting market and an estimated one million in and around South Bend, Indiana. The grand (estimated) total number of viewers of *Shaped by Danish Hands* through film hire or purchase in 1954 was 594,750, with an estimated television audience of 2,790,000 (Kristensen 1955). A revised version, slightly shortened and with an American-accented voiceover, was proposed and prepared in late 1953, but a memo indicates that this plan was not executed (Minerva Film 1953). Films of the Nations proposed the next year that the US version should be used as the basis for a Spanish-language version for Cuban television (Udenrigsministeriet 1954), attesting to the widespread and enduring appeal of the film.

An important factor in the exceptionally wide circulation of *Shaped by Danish Hands* was the travelling exhibition 'Scandinavian Design', which toured two dozen cities in the USA and Canada between 1954 and 1957. 'Scandinavian Design' was a multimedia event involving not just the exhibition itself but locally organised Scandinavian cultural weeks, lectures, film screenings, readings of Scandinavian literature on the radio, and so on; total visitor numbers were estimated at 660,000 (Guldberg 2011: 42–3). Jørn Guldberg's analysis of images and texts in the exhibition's programme reveals how the event contributed to the emergence of a discourse of 'Scandinavian' modernity in North America, a conflation of the individual nations' cultures into a narrative of 'continuity and contiguity ... a discourse of absence – the absence of polarities, dramatic changes, demographic and cultural differences, and segregation within the product cultures and so on' (49). Regardless of the increasing conflation of the Nordic nations in the North American mind, the economic impact of the exhibition on precisely the national economies and their constituent industries was considerable; the Danish Consul General reported in 1954 that exports of Danish furniture to the USA had doubled in one year and increased forty-four-fold since 1950 (Guldberg 2011: 55, n. 26).

This, then, was the cultural and economic wave which *Shaped by Danish Hands* surfed in North America and to which it inevitably contributed. At home, however, the Danish newspapers whined that the film was out of date and an embarrassing ambassador for the country at the 'Scandinavian Design' exhibition. Søren Hansen, Viggo Sten Møller's successor as head of Landsforeningen Dansk Kunsthaandværk, explained that the film was no longer current; it was five years old, and there had been various developments in artistic form since it was made. Another issue was that the voiceover featured an English accent, not an American one, which distracted the audience. The association would like a batch of new films to be made, but did not have the funding (Ekstrabladet 1953). But discussions about a new film were already underway, and Hagen Hasselbalch was engaged to make *D ... For Design!*, a new short completed in 1956 and featuring the 'wonderful girl' he had dreamt up a decade before.

THE HAND OF THE ARTIST: DREYER'S *THORVALDSEN*

We have repeatedly seen how the international reputation of Carl Th. Dreyer made it politically sensible for Dansk Kulturfilm to engage him to make informational films, but that the results were often uninspiring. Arguably, two or three of Dreyer's *kulturfilm* projects harness his artistic abilities and result in art films that at least gesture to the principle that the amalgam of filmic medium and art form should generate an intense encounter with the art work for the viewer. The productions I have in mind are *De naaede Færgen* (*They Caught the Ferry*, 1948), *Thorvaldsen* (1949), and *Storstrømsbroen* (*The Storstrøm Bridge*, 1950).

Commissioned by MFU for a road safety campaign, *De naaede Færgen* is arguably tangential to the discussion of art films, in the sense that it is an adaptation of a novella, rather than a response to visual or plastic art. However, this film is one of the few *kulturfilm* which, anecdotally, I have found is remembered in contemporary Denmark, and has the distinction of having featured on a commemorative postage stamp in 1989. During its theatrical run along with *The Bandit of Sherwood Forest* (Harry Levin and George Sherman, 1946), Dreyer's short was seen by 270,000 cinema-goers in Denmark, and it was hired more than 3000 times by schools and clubs over the next decade, placing the film consistently in the top ten hires (SFC 1949–1960).

De naaede færgen is an adaptation of a novella by Johannes V. Jensen (1873–1950), a Dane awarded the Nobel Prize for Literature in 1944. Dreyer's achievement in the film is to render visceral Jensen's literary account of speeding on a motorcycle. Evidence of Dreyer's direct engagement with Jensen's prose includes the presence in Dreyer's research materials of an essay on motorbiking by Jensen:

> Yes, we see in a different way, to a different tempo, flashes of things closeby, the trees lining the road, the ditches, vehicles ... What is new is how

the more distant views and horizon are visible; the foreground rushes past, but the background, the land itself, begins to live in a peculiar way, moves in rhythmic lengths, one horizon opens out onto another, the relief of the landscape unfolds, not in fixed planes, but in movement. (Jensen 1944: 10)

Accordingly, Dreyer's screenplay pays exquisite attention to the rhythm of the combustion engine and its effect on vision: shot 24, for example, specifies that the roadside trees are filmed as the motorcyclists see them, as 'flickering lines'. The shot list specifies four times (shots 23, 31, 44 and 84) that the 'rhythm' of the engine's 'explosions' must match the speedometer (Dreyer 1948).[1]

The second film mentioned explores the structure of the bridge over the Storstrøm channel between the islands of Falster and Masnedø, south of Zealand. The bridge was opened in 1937, and for a time was the longest such bridge in Europe. Aside from an opening title card detailing the bridge's vital statistics, *Storstrømsbroen* is free of voiceover, consisting only of a series of perspectives on the architecture of the bridge, and a final gesture to narrative as a ship sails under the bridge, filmed from below in such a way that the attentive viewer may hold her breath in anticipation of a collision. The film drives the *kulturfilm* format to an extreme of impressionism, weaving together music and images of the bridge from a dizzying variety of angles, its steel architectonics contrasting with the organic textures of water and clouds (McFarlane 2011). A good deal of research material for this film has survived in Dreyer's archive: his exploratory readings and conversations with engineers are woven into poetic segments that have been quite literally cut up into paper strips so that different compositions can be tested out. The aim is

> a film about the dynamics of lines and surfaces, a film that shows the bridge's greatness and simplicity and the beauty that emerges when iron and concrete are employed in the right way. (Dreyer 1947c: 1)

In an example of just how pervasive the influence of the commissioning organisations could be on a film, the archive also includes a portfolio of images and postcards of the bridge taken by the local tourist board. Many of these images mirror shots in the film with absolute exactitude. It is not clear whether the images pre-date the film and were used as part of the brief, or were stills from the production later used as images by the tourist board. This nonetheless neatly encapsulates the task of the *kulturfilm*: to set existing enterprises in motion, and thereby to move the viewer.

A more complex film, and one of Dreyer's most widely seen shorts, was *Thorvaldsen* (1949), a ten-minute film marking the centenary of Thorvaldsen's Museum. Bertel Thorvaldsen (1770–1844) was a sculptor of Dano-Icelandic extraction who spent most of his career in Rome achieving worldwide renown, before donating his sculptures and plaster cast collection to the city of Copenhagen and retiring to Denmark around 1840. The museum built to house his works was erected next to the national parliament as Denmark's first museum and its layout, as well as the murals decorating the facade and interior of the building, remains more or less untouched today. Dreyer's film begins with a short narrative summary of Thorvaldsen's life, against a background of the facade of his museum. The film then explores the genesis of a selection of his best-known statues and reliefs. The final sequence traces the development of Thorvaldsen's *Kristus* (Christ) figure for Vor Frue Church in Copenhagen, showing how the sculptor first sketched out the statue's hands in various positions before finding the right gesture to immortalise in marble.

During the film shoot, Thorvaldsen's sculptures were set in motion in a concrete sense. The artistic decision to have the camera move around the sculptures while they rotated on a plinth, thus creating a sense of contrapuntal motion, necessitated that a number of sculptures be moved from the positions in which they had stood since the 1840s and into the museum's entrance hall. This operation was fraught with risk for the sculptures; correspondence between the Director of the museum, Sigurd Schultz, and Ib Koch-Olsen reveals that the museum's head porter had suffered palpably under the strain of relocating the marbles into the entrance hall and safely back into ther original places in time for the museum's centenary celebrations. However, Schulz cheerfully observed that the project had given the curators a fresh perspective on the sculptures as they related to the museum space:

> On the one hand, we are very aware what this film might mean for the museum, and on the other hand, it was quite an experience for us to see some of the statues pulled out into the entrance hall and standing in that big open space. They looked so good, and their plastic effect was so strong while they stood there, free and with so much air around them! There is no doubt that it would improve Thorvaldsen's reputation as an artist if they could always be exhibited like that in this place, instead of with their backs pressed up against the walls in the small rooms of the museum. (Schultz 1948)

Schultz was a visionary figure (see Thomson 2016b) with a firm grasp of how the encounter between camera and sculpture can render visible new dimensions of the artwork's plasticity. However, as Thorvaldsen's Museum was designed around the sculptures, its integrity required their return to their allotted positions. The sense of encounter with the sculptures in open space which Schultz had enjoyed became the task of Dreyer's film. Accordingly, while *Thorvaldsen*'s use of slow, gliding camera movements, dissolves, chiaroscuro effects and its arguably sensuous treatment of the sculptures' surface are recognisably Dreyerian, scrutiny of Thorvaldsen's production history reveals that the film was shaped by a series of interventions by other filmmakers, and by Schultz himself. The most prominent of these is the film's cinematographer, Preben Frank, whose eponymous company also produced the film for Dansk Kulturfilm. Frank struggled to assert his right to be co-credited with Dreyer, and died of cancer shortly after completion of *Thorvaldsen* (Kimergård n.d.b).

The appointment of Dreyer as director of this film was not uncontroversial. One peer review of the manuscript is signed J.R. – possibly Jørgen Roos? – and suggests that the combination of Dreyer and Thorvaldsen was unfortunate since neither was an expansive or full-blooded personality, and so the result was likely to be 'cold, irrelevant, negative, uninteresting, unfilmic, unobjective' (J.R. 1948). Theodor Christensen also reviewed Dreyer's first draft as likely to result in a boring film which would perpetuate Thorvaldsen's unjustified reputation as anaemic. However, he acknowledged that it would be opportune to have Dreyer make a film on Thorvaldsen (Christensen 1948: 1–2) and recognised Dreyer's genius as a creator of the intense filmic experience ('*intensitets-film*') (2–3). Comparing Dreyer's original draft to the finished film suggests that the chief revision between draft and shoot was to excise a distinctive feature: that images of each sculpture be preceded by the respective preparatory sketch or model. In the finished film, only the 'Kristus' statue is preceded by close-ups of the pencil sketches, with dissolves indicating the transition between renderings of the figure in different media. Dreyer's initial interest in the transmediation of sketch to sculpture would seem to indicate a preoccupation with the contrast between two- and three-dimensional objects on film. Otherwise, the film's emphasis on Thorvaldsen's 'rhythmic musicality' is already apparent in the draft, and the camera's role in teasing out the movement immanent in the sculptures is clearly laid out:

> In [the Priamus relief] as in all Thorvaldsen's art, it is the rhythm that gladdens us. He had a peculiar ability to build up the movements of the figures into rhythmic and self-contained harmonies ... From the left, in the bowed stance of the slaves, there is a falling movement down to the kneeling king, so we feel how deeply he is humbling himself before his enemy, the sitting Achilles, the victor. Then the gaze flows further to Achilles' two friends behind the table, where the mood chimes with their sorrowful, still position. The rhythm unconditionally forces the attention towards the two main figures in the middle. (Dreyer 1947a: 2)

It will be noted how the draft does not obviously distinguish between the spectator's eye, and concomitantly his or her 'reading' of the tableau, and the camera's movements. In a similar vein, the draft comments that in 'Venus med

Æblet' (Venus with Apple) the goddess' face is expressionless, in line with Thorvaldsen's reputation for coldness. But it was normal in Antiquity, explains Dreyer, that feelings should be expressed through the sculpture's 'movements' alone (Dreyer 1947a: 2). Again, there is a rhetorical conflation of the reading of the sculpture's rhythmic composition and the more literal 'movement' with which the camerawork will later imbue it: the emotion of each work would be released by the motion of the camera, moving the sculpture in order to move the spectator.[2]

Dreyer himself was clear-minded about the purpose of the film. The film should 'with the help of the most popular and easiest to understand of his works ... bring the ordinary person to see and understand what is special about Thorvaldsen's art generally' (Dreyer 1947b). In other words, the film was for a general audience, not those with an established interest in sculpture. Much of the press coverage after the film's first screening in January 1949 suggests that reviewers understood its mission in the same way. For example, one reviewer praised *Thorvaldsen* as 'a very beautiful and instructive thing with an easily understandable text that in many places is quite revelatory for the non-expert' (Ulrichsen 1949). By 1953, figures collated by the Danish Information Office indicated that *Thorvaldsen* had been shown 429 times in Danish clubs, schools and other venues to an estimated public of 52,338 (Johansen 1953). The film was also distributed in Danish cinemas to be shown with the feature film *The Macomber Affair* (Zoltan Korder, 1947), bringing *Thorvaldsen* to around 330,000 cinema-goers across the country between April 1949 and mid-1951.

Thorvaldsen was also distributed exceptionally widely abroad. The film's first overseas screening, with English voiceover, took place at an exhibition of Danish culture in London in late 1948. Erick Struckmann, who had acted as consultant on the film, was keen for it to be finished in time for the exhibition because it would be impossible to exhibit Thorvaldsen's sculptures themselves, and so Thorvaldsen would otherwise be rather modestly represented. British contacts had expressed an interest in screening the film, he wrote (Struckmann 1948). Nonetheless, the 'somewhat static' *Thorvaldsen* was not rapturously received at the Edinburgh International Documentary Film festival the next year (Hardy 1949: 18). In the fast-developing television markets of North America, the film was screened ten times by 1953, reaching an estimated audience of just over 9 million viewers (Johansen 1953). Versions with French and German voiceovers were made on 35mm and 16mm film respectively for use by embassies and other agencies abroad, and were still available for hire in 1960 (SFC 1960c: 20–1). Foreign-language versions of Dansk Kulturfilm productions were a common occurrence, but *Thorvaldsen* is unique in that a copy of the Danish version was custom-made in 1951 for distribution in Iceland, and this copy is the commercially available one today: it had been realised that the standard version did not acknowledge the sculptor's Icelandic father in the opening text.

ART FILM EXHIBITION IN 1950S DENMARK

As 'devices for cultural and educational reconstruction' (Jacobs 2011: 2), art films grew out of the same internationalist idealism that drove the foundation of UNESCO in November 1945. Jacobs also observes a connection between the flourishing of the art film and a growing engagement with the arts amongst the lower and middle classes. This certainly chimes with press interest in the art film in Denmark around 1950, and with evidence of widespread enthusiasm for art film screenings. Such screenings were not primarily facilitated by Dansk Kulturfilm and Statens Filmcentral, however.

It is telling that in 1948, SFC issued a press release advertising the premiere of 'art films' which it had acquired from six different countries. These included a film about Dutch clog dancing, Baroque architecture in Prague, Macbeth, Mary Aubusson, the paintings of Repin and a film of Mary Wigman dancing which had been abandoned by the German occupying forces at the Liberation. The somewhat incongruous and scrappy collection speaks to the contemporary understanding of art films as films about art broadly conceived, rather than as a genre with its own style and function (Anonymous 1948a).

That the function of art films was to provide an experience of the artwork rather than simply reporting on it seems to have been well understood within the broader discourse of cultural life in Denmark around 1950. For example, the regional newspaper *Østsjællands Folkeblad* picked up on an article by the artist and director Børge Høst in SFC's newsletter for members. A small selection of films by the Italian filmmaker Luciano Emmer had been acquired by SFC and would now tour various screening venues around the country, introduced by Høst. The article explains that Emmer's films do something new: they 'dramatise' art for a broad public. The films are not just well made and interesting; they are *kulturfilm* in the literal sense, comments Høst. They provide an 'intense experience' of the artworks they depict – an experience which does not require extensive study to achieve (Anonymous 1951). Around the same time (the year of publication is illegible), an article in *Berlingske Aftenavis* discusses the nature of the art film at some length in connection with a successful run of screenings and talks at Thorvaldsen's Museum:

> Thorvaldsen's Museum has just completed its biannual series of film screenings and lectures, which this time had even greater success than any previous series. It is very clear that there is an ever-greater need for this newest form of museum visit, and everything points to there being an increasing demand for films that can be used as a supplement to regular

museum visits. Efforts in recent years to make museum treasures accessible and understandable for the widest possible public have created a
new, open space for the *kulturfilm*, and special, carefully constructed
exhibitions have encouraged the use of film in museum work ... In the
last twenty years or so, *kulturfilm* whose artistic and educational properties are equally impressive have been made abroad, as well as here in
Denmark in the last half dozen years or so. (Anonymous 195?)

It will be noted that the term '*kulturfilm*' is used interchangeably in the above
quote, and indeed elsewhere, with the notion of the art film as a specific genre.

The role of Thorvaldsen's Museum, and especially that of Sigurd Schultz as
museum director, in the circulation of art films in Denmark is worthy of note.
While Dreyer's film about Thorvaldsen was in production, Schultz arranged
a series of art film screenings at Thorvaldsen's Museum by a young director,
Mogens Kruse. The run of free screenings at the museum was intended to mark
its centenary with a new experience for the general public. In a letter to Koch-
Olsen later that winter, Schultz reiterates his belief that Dreyer's *Thorvaldsen*
would set the standard for future films on the challenging subject of sculpture,
but he also takes the opportunity to argue that Dansk Kulturfilm ought to take
on the task of fostering a Danish art film scene. The Danish public, he writes,
should not have to make do with imported films about foreign art (Schultz 1949).

The screenings of Kruse's experimental films turned into a regular series at
Thorvaldsen's Museum, with two seasons of art films a year until the early
1960s. Though a 16mm copy of Dreyer's film had been gifted to the museum,
Thorvaldsen was only shown once as part of the screening series, in winter
1950 (Schultz 1962); the emphasis was on a diversity of international films
about art. In an interview with the newspaper *B.T.* (Morten 1952), Schultz
details the principles behind this initiative and the benefits for the museum.
In the November 1952 series, so many people had flocked to the screenings,
around 600 per evening, that the programmes had to be repeated. The increase
in visitor numbers as a result was noticeable, claims Schultz; the ground floor
of the museum was kept open, and most film-goers chose to visit the sculptures too. Despite the potential for profit from this popular event series, the
museum, as an institution dedicated to public education, offered free entry
to screenings. It hired films and projectors from Statens Filmcentral and gave
a small honorarium to invited speakers; it had no ambition to compete with
cinemas. Again, Schultz uses the interview to make an appeal to state film institutions for more art films to satisfy public demand, an appetite which his own
screenings were doing something to satisfy, and probably to whet. It is important to note here that the museum's entrance hall was not simply being used
as a cinema, with immobile viewers consuming moving images in the dark.
On the one hand, the screenings were predicated on the opportunity to walk

around the museum before or after. On the other hand, the focus on art films suggestively brings the museum's exhibits into conversation with the art forms animated on the screen. To allude to Mirams again, the essence of the 1950s art film was to create new artistic syntheses by using film's medium-specific properties to illuminate dimensions of the works explored.

Aside from the long-running series of art film screenings at Thorvaldsen's Museum, other associations and organisations hosted screenings and talks. In October 1952, for example, the left-wing newspaper *Social-Demokraten* reported that Arbejdernes Kunstforening (the Workers' Art Club) was planning at least three art film evenings that winter, after six similar events had sold out the year before. The season's first event would consist of a screening of a film about the Danish painter J. F. Willumsen and a talk by Sigurd Schultz (Anonymous 1952). These events took place in the context of Arbejdernes Oplysnings-Forbund (the Workers' Enlightenment Union), a country-wide organisation that had its own film library and thus functioned in parallel with Statens Filmcentral.

From 1956, Schultz chaired a new Dansk Komité for Kunstfilm (Danish Committee for Art Films), established at the invitation of the Fédération Internationale des Films d'Art. Members included representatives of film institutions, museums and art associations. The Committee commissioned and published a brochure listing art films currently available for loan in Denmark to schools, clubs and other interested parties. The Committee's work thus supplemented that of the state film distribution agency Statens Filmcentral, exemplifying the intensity of enthusiasm amongst a range of interest groups in mid-century Denmark for the use of film in schools and lifelong education. By the late 1950s, then, Schultz's quarter century of experience with audience expansion furnished him with the authority to pronounce on how the Danish state's cultural institutions were failing to support a specific sub-genre of the *kulturfilm*, and to lead by example on how the art film could be fostered as a practice and made available to the public.

HERNING 65: DANSK KULTURFILM'S SWANSONG

The press and public debate about the art film and Denmark's lack thereof spilled over into the production and reception of what was to be Dansk Kulturfilm's last film: *Herning 65*. Technically, the final stages of production were transferred to Statens Filmcentral while Dansk Kulturfilm was being wound down, but for that very reason, the film allows us to witness the impact on this and other institutions of the shifts in film policy that occurred in early- to mid-1960s Denmark. Woven into this transition is a more existential debate about the role of state-sponsored film in documenting the arts, versus its role as art.

The town of Herning lies in the mid-West of the Jutland peninsula, and for the average Dane is synonymous with two activities: the textile industry and modern art. This somewhat incongruous pairing was fostered in the mid-twentieth century primarily by Aage Damgaard (1917–91), an entrepreneur who invited contemporary artists to take up fully funded residences in his shirt factory. His business, Angli Skjorter, thus used patronage of emerging artists, including the likes of Piero Manzoni, notorious for his 'Merda d'artista' (1961), as a means to build up an art collection. Damgaard saw the collision of art and factory environment as a way to improve (or at least enliven) the working lives of his employees. Damgaard's art collection formed the basis of the internationally recognised Herning Art Museum, established 1977, which moved to new premises and adopted the name HEART (that is, HE[rning] ART) in 2009 ('Historien om heart' n.d.).

The museum's original premises were built in 1965–6 to house the growing Angli shirtmaking business, and the factory was designed in the 'A' shape of the company logo. The inner wall of the complex's courtyard was painted with a 220-metre ceramic mural by the artist Carl Henning Pedersen entitled 'Fantasiens leg om livets hjul' (Fantasy's Game with the Wheel of Life, 1966–8) and this artwork still stands today ('Angligården' n.d.). This courtyard and factory building, Angligård, replaced an earlier factory known as 'Den sorte Fabrik' (the Black Factory), which had housed the business until the building was sold in 1965. In the course of the previous decade, a long-term residence by artist Paul Gadegaard had transformed the Black Factory into a living mural and sculpture. Gadegaard was an exponent of the 'Klar Form' (Clear Form) movement and a member of the art collective Linie II; his work was resolutely non-figurative and non-narrative, exploring the pure form of shape and colour to play with dimensionality. He was also interested in the role of art in society and public space, concerns which his collaboration with Damgaard allowed him to explore at will. Gadegaard also decorated Damgaard's other factory buildings, but the Black Factory was his masterpiece ('Paul Gadegaard' n.d.). Nowhere else in the world had such an experiment, inspired by Klee and Chagall, been developed in such a holistic way ('En film om en fabrik' 1966). After the factory was sold in 1965, the artwork was not preserved and the building was demolished ('Paul Gadegaard' n.d.).

While HEART Museum's current website states that Gadegaard's Black Factory has been lost, it was in fact recorded for posterity in the medium of film. In January 1965, news of the imminent sale of the Angli Factory prompted a trio of filmmakers, artists and musicians to appeal to the newly established Statens Filmfond (the State Film Fund) to finance a short film which would not only immortalise Gadegaard's concrete masterpiece but actually 'use its union of art and working environment for the last time' (Maruni et al. 1965: 1).

Figure 8.3   An Angli factory employee playing at work in Gadegaard's mural (*Herning 65*, 1965).

The film's synopsis (Maruni *et al.* 1965: 2 ff.) describes an encounter with a complex form of painting which spreads rhythmic shapes out into the factory space, over tables and benches, through cupboards and machines. The artwork also exists in time, and the film can tease out this dimension of it by panning over the contours of Gadegaard's shapes in close-up. The logic of the film will be to reveal the workers gradually, through a hand or arm working at a machine (see Figure 8.3). As details give way to a more holistic sense of the factory as a space of work and play, so too will the colours emerge as constitutive of the space. Slow pans will give way to increasingly fast cutting, ending by ejecting the viewer into the factory's most 'fantastic' space, its office. Maruni and his colleagues also explain that they will invite established jazz musicians such as Niels-Henning Ørsted Pedersen to compose a soundtrack from the noise of typewriters, sewing machines and local accents, recorded *in situ*, which will be edited in time with the rhythm of images. Finally, the colour needs special consideration in order to preserve the authentic tones of the artwork; overall, the effect of key parts of the film should be 'of such intensity and speed that the function of the eye is affected absolutely and dazzlingly'.

The details of this proposal describe quite precisely the finished film and its effects. The final minute-and-a-half of the film lives up to the original aspiration of the filmmakers that the eye should be dazzled: technically, the super-fast montage is produced not by editing but by running twenty-four still images per second through the projector ('En film om en fabrik', 1966).

One unforeseen aspect of the production process was that Gadegaard's colours were so intense that filming could not take place during the day (such that daylight was supplemented with lighting rigs). Instead, the shooting had to take place at night so that the colours could be entirely lit artificially by 50-kilowatt lamps – which almost overwhelmed the building's electrics ('Avanceret jazzteater på Alléscenen søndag' 1966).

THE PREMIERE OF *HERNING 65*

Compared to the usual cinema premieres of Dansk Kulturfilm's productions, *Herning 65*'s launch was as experimental as the film itself. The event took place on a Sunday afternoon in late January 1966 at the small Fredriksberg theatre Allé-scenen. Previously the Betty Nansen Theatre, a name which it also bears today, the venue was a youth theatre in the period 1964–75 (Rask n.d.) and held a regular jazz programme, into which *Herning 65* was incorporated. The programme for the evening (Musik og Ungdom 1966) featured several well-established creatives, including the popular poet and lyricist Benny Andersen, painter, poet and CoBrA member Jørgen Nash, and composer Niels Viggo Bentzon. It was organised around a sequence of seven acts, bringing jazz into conversation with other art forms: jazz and theatre, dance, a collective sing-song, poetry, film, music, sound and painting. *Herning 65* came fifth on the programme, with an introduction by its director, Jens Jørgen Thorsen, and an 'epilogue' by Gadegaard. Statens Filmcentral planned to screen the film on its portable 35mm projector just off the balcony (Elvius 1966).

Herning 65 was described as the 'high point' of an evening that presented an unusually successful fusion of the arts, with the film's electronic soundtrack singled out for praise ('Moseholms jazzteater' 1966). The same reviewer commented that the theatre was full of young and lively attendees. The reviewer in *Politiken* (J.L. 1966) concurs that the film was the most worthy part of the evening, though it was only tenuously connected to jazz as such. The same reviewer gives a sensitive assessment of the film's visual style:

> The film extends in an imaginative and artistically controlled way Gadegaard's thoughts about art as the environment for daily existence. Never before have I seen a film that works so consciously to affect the eye – it is a 'visual' film in a very concrete sense. The camera moved very cleverly in a continuously gliding movement, which emphasised the

rhythmic in Gadegaard's masterpiece, and the cuts brilliantly drew connections from things to people. So too was the rhythm of editing used in a radical way, sometimes accelerating violently. This is one of the most valuable art films Statens Filmcentral has acquired, not least in light of the fact that Gadegaard's life's work will soon disappear, because the Angli Factory has a new owner. (J.L. 1966)

For the sake of balance, we might let the last word on *Herning 65* go to a reviewer in the magazine *Kirke og film* (*Church and Film*):

We read in the introduction to the film that Gadegaard has realised constructivism's call for the usefulness of art. The film itself must fall under the concept of destructivism, and if the decoration of the factory is as horrifying as the film, one can only be thankful that it is about to disappear. And let's shove the film to the back of the shelf and forget it; so much money is wasted in modern society. (Porsby 1967)

In light of the publication in which this charmingly curmudgeonly review appeared, we can assume that it merely gives expression to a conservative reluctance to use taxpayers' money on the arts. Nonetheless, it also hints at a feeling that the social democratic, instrumentalist compact between state and the short film was, at that very moment, under review in Denmark, and the wind was blowing in a direction of which Mr Porsby would not have approved.

What is to be Done with Dansk Kulturfilm?

In January 1958, around a year before he started working on *Enden på legen* in earnest, Theodor Christensen tackled the question of state support for informational film in Denmark in an article in the Danish cinema journal *Kosmorama*. Christensen reminds the reader that only eight years had passed since Arthur Elton's report for UNESCO (Elton and Brinson 1950) had praised Danish governmental support for documentary to the skies. Now, in 1958, the government had ordered a report on the organisation of film in Denmark which was rumoured to recommend the amalgamation of Dansk Kulturfilm, MFU and SFC with the Film Museum under one manager. The reasons for this, Christensen claims, have to do with the lack of artistry in the films produced by these organisations and their lack of connection to their end users. This set of issues has nothing to do with a lack of good directors, he explains; the talent of the outstanding post-war generation of Danish documentarists has been squandered by an organisation that keeps the users (the associations and interest groups) separated from the filmmakers by the wrong kind of functionaries and middlemen. To re-invigorate documentary culture in Denmark, a completely new organisation was needed: one in which the production of films would be overseen and administered by filmmakers and associated specialists themselves (Christensen 1958: 107). He compares the heyday of the G.P.O. Film Unit and Crown Film Unit in Britain with the increasing government intervention in the National Film Board of Canada, offering both as examples, respectively, of the artistic and political freedom accorded (or not) to filmmakers engaged in the work of state-sponsored documentary. Christensen concludes by warning against dismantling the current system before a replacement has been organised, and summarises his basic principle thus:

> The more permanent one wishes to make the administrative leadership of a production organisation, the more necessary it is to ensure full freedom for filmmakers, within the relevant administrative parameters. (Christensen 1958: 108)

A conviction that a set of genre-specific aesthetics was fundamental to the effective communication of information was a *sine qua non* of the British documentary movement generally, by which Christensen was influenced. Basil Wright, too, was fond of reminding festival goers that documentary film 'was not founded on the verbal delivery of facts and information, but revelation through the affective power of the image' (MacDonald 2013: 457).

A more concrete expression of this transition can be discerned in the production file for *Herning 65*, which bears witness to ongoing confusion, arguments even, throughout the summer and autumn of 1965 as to which state institution was responsible for the film. The production company Minerva eventually took on the project. The proposal and production took place precisely at the time when Dansk Kulturfilm was still technically active in conjunction with Statens Filmcentral, but about to be rendered defunct by a new Kortfilmråd (Short Film Council), which was established in September 1965 after a recommendation from a committee set up three years previously to consider how to rationalise and strengthen short film production in Denmark (Larsen n.d.). Another institution established by the Film Law of 1964 was a new Filmfond (Film Fund), which centralised all state support for the film industry and was advised by Filmrådet (the Film Council) (Dam n.d.b). The urgency of capturing Gadegaard's artwork before it disappeared had led to the new Statens Filmfond asking Dansk Kulturfilm to adopt *Herning 65* in its final production plan. The film project had been deemed worthy of support (Filmrådet 1965), but as yet there was no new body to oversee production.

This game of institutional musical chairs was the surface manifestation of a deeper transformation of the relationship between the state and the short film in the early 1960s. A significant driver for this institutional and conceptual shift was the increasing presence of television in the media landscape. The heyday of the short 16mm film as a vehicle for education and enlightenment was coming to an end; shorts were increasingly screened on television and in cinemas, and their function was less instrumental and more artistic (Larsen n.d.). Ib Bondebjerg, too, has argued that the transition from the classic documentary film to the modern in Denmark has a basis in this contradiction between an institutional need for information and the application of artistic and creative freedom in relation to concrete tasks (Bondebjerg 2012: 42–3).

Christensen's frustration with the lot of informational filmmakers in Denmark chimes with John Grierson's conviction that documentary film as art is best facilitated through an administrative leadership committed to that principle. In an essay of 1960 – thus almost the same time as Christensen's article – Grierson wrote:

> How do you break through to where the artist in film can become practi-cally and fully engaged? I think there is one inevitable formula. You need a patron from your government authority or your public authority or your industrial authority who is himself imaginatively dedicated to what he does. It is not always an individual. It may be a few people thinking together. But I associate the greatest moments of collaboration with individuals. I am sure there are many who do not ordinarily associate themselves with poetry as such but they are poets-extraordinary in their own estate. (quoted in Hardy 1979c: 175)

With Grierson's words in mind, we can also observe that another driving force in this transformation and transition was an individual, Werner Pedersen, who had become director of Statens Filmcentral and thereby of Dansk Kulturfilm and MFU in 1961. Pedersen was an advocate of the short film as an art form in its own right, and was a keen supporter of emerging filmmakers influenced by the British Free Cinema movement, such as Tørk Haxthausen and Henning Carlsen (Nørrested and Alsted 1987: 434–5). The latter directed an adaptation of Knut Hamsun's *Sult* (Hunger) to wild acclaim just a few years later, in 1966. Essentially, Pedersen was convinced that the short film as a genre and as an industry could not live by sponsored film alone. He expressed this view in a press release addressed to the Ministry of Culture in 1962, listing three reasons why the state should support artistic experiments among makers of short films. Firstly, reliance on state- and commercially spon-sored films was preventing the recruitment a new generation of talent amongst directors and writers. Secondly, stimulating the short film as an art form would revitalise short films as a tool for education and information. Thirdly, Pedersen claims that the short film can only function as an effective training ground for emerging filmmakers where 'free' film art is also supported, such as in France and Poland (cited in Nørrested and Alsted 1987: 437–8). It is important to note here that Pedersen is arguing for a symbiosis between the informational and artistic dimensions of the state-sponsored film; developing the art of the *kulturfilm* does not entail producing art films. Pedersen, after all, had taken on the editing of the first catalogue issued by the Dansk Komité for Kunstfilm (Pedersen 1959b). It is noticeable that quite a number of the relatively few films produced under Pedersen's watch in the early 1960s are *kulturfilm* – as opposed to art films – about artistic figures: *PH Lys* (*PH Light*, Ole Roos, 1964) is a portrait of Poul Henningsen's design work (see Thomson 2013a), and one of Dansk Kulturfilm's very last productions was an eponymous bio-pic of Carl Th. Dreyer (dir. Jørgen Roos, 1966). The distinction between art film and documentary about art is also clear from Pedersen's response to the first cut of *Herning 65*, when he advises Jens Jørgen Thorsen and Novi Maruni to make the film less experimental:

> What you have there is a wonderful story and beautiful images, which in all modesty can contribute to expanding the viewers' experience of the world, if you'll allow me to be a bit pretentious. But you're using all this in a form which corresponds to the well-trodden paths of the so-called experimental film, and it suggests that you are much more concerned with your own interesting masterpiece than with the story that needs to be told, or the people who need to hear the story. You could have made an original documentary, but you're making an unoriginal experimental film – and the result is, in my opinion, that the film does not communicate. (Pedersen 1965)

As we have seen, filmmakers themselves had long been keen to gain more support and freedom to develop the short film form artistically. This, then, was a principle adopted in the constitution of the new Kortfilmrådet, of which Pedersen was appointed the first Director of Production from 1967. Thirty per cent of the available funding for short films was allocated to so-called 'free' (*frie*) films, and the rest to films on commissioned topics, along the lines of Dansk Kulturfilm and MFU (Larsen n.d.). Before we herald the 'End of the Game' for Dansk Kulturfilm, however, we examine what is arguably its finest hour.

NOTES

1. For a more extensive analysis of *De naaede Færgen*, see Thomson 2015b.
2. For further discussion of the aesthetics of *Thorvaldsen*, see Thomson 2010 and Thomson 2016b. The latter essay also explores Sigurd Schultz's public engagement work more broadly.

9. SYMPHONY OF A SHORT FILM: *A CITY CALLED COPENHAGEN*

'What is a city?' This question preoccupies the voice that guides us through the streets of the Danish capital in Jørgen Roos' twenty-minute short of 1960, *A City Called Copenhagen*. Sometimes erudite, sometimes jocose, the narrator conjures up a dichotomous city poised between old and new, art and industry, order and playfulness. Overwhelmingly, this is a city of people: street-cleaners, artists, schoolchildren, architects, jazz fans and cyclists; people riding roller-coasters, counting banknotes, sifting through rubbish, tending allotments. But the film is haunted and structured by an (as yet) uninhabited space that looms over the city: the SAS Royal Hotel, the great Gesamtkunstverk of architect and designer Arne Jacobsen (1902–71).

Roos' film and Jacobsen's tower are almost exactly contemporaneous. Both were commissioned in the mid-1950s and completed in 1960, and shooting on *A City Called Copenhagen* coincided with the final stages of construction of what was to be Denmark's first skyscraper. Not only does the almost-finished hotel feature in the film as a gleaming counterpoint to slum clearances, baroque landmarks and the chaotic choreography of the streets, it also serves as a device to invest the city with a new verticality. While the glass and aluminium curtain wall was being installed on the facades of Scandinavia's then tallest building, a temporary cage elevator stretched up the front of the block. Roos was thus able to shoot the closing sequence of *A City Called Copenhagen* as a vertical tracking shot, treating the viewer to a perspective on the Rådhus (Town Hall) and its neighbouring spires that would have been unthinkable just a year before (Steinthal 1960a). As the camera rides upwards, floor by floor, and the credits roll, the voiceover muses: 'What is a city? Well, maybe we can't define it. But anyway, there is a city called Copenhagen.'

'What is a city?' The notion of the undefinable city was of its time. On the other side of the Atlantic, 1960 saw the publication of Kevin Lynch's classic work *The Image of the City*, a book that transformed understanding of how people and planners made sense of the urban environment. At home in Copenhagen, a ground-breaking book of poetry was about to appear, one which would galvanise Danish literary modernism with its exuberant scrutiny of the everyday, the urban, the technological: the twenty-eight-year-old Klaus Rifbjerg's *Konfrontation*. Jørgen Roos' vision of the city as a palimpsest of old and new, amenities planned and lives lived, appealed to cosmopolitan cinephiles overseas, and also assuaged the apprehensions of Copenhageners about the impact of the new tower on the city skyline and about the pace of social, cultural and architectural change at the dawn of the 1960s.

In Chapter 7, we saw how *kulturfilm* for domestic audiences of the 1950s constructed a sense of a future-oriented, progressive national community. The decade from 1960 would see increasing prosperity, improved housing and a raft of social legislation, consolidating the egalitarian welfare state which we associate today with the golden age of the Nordic model. In 1960, the DC-4 Skymaster Dan Viking, whose flight across the Atlantic we witnessed in Chapter 6, was already a thing of the past; the SAS hotel and its air terminal annexe had been commissioned to provide the modern design and comfort that befitted passengers of the new jet planes. Similarly, *A City Called Copenhagen* was conceived from the start as a production that would transcend the tourist film genre. Its task was not just to sell the city as a holiday destination but to enlighten the outside world on the subject of Danish modernity – indeed, to be an expression in its own right of that cultural modernity. When the narrator of *A City Called Copenhagen* declares that 'the future's already here', Jacobsen's SAS tower looms into view on the screen, enacting the ambivalence and ambition of this historical moment.

'What is a city?' Most of the films we have encountered in this book have posed, implicitly or explicitly, similar questions. What is art? How does this machine work? What does this organisation do? How should I behave as a citizen of Denmark? We have seen how the answers to these questions coalesce in the process of commissioning and making films, how concepts crystallise as effects of the interplay of power, institutional practices, and material and technological contingencies. In this final chapter, *A City Called Copenhagen* is offered as a case study not just because the voiceover explicitly articulates the question that underpins the film, but also because the process of resolving that question, on the cusp of the 1960s, can be traced in particularly rich detail. This film is distinguished by an unusually long gestation period, an exceptionally detailed commission, a rapturous reception at home

Figure 9.1   The invitation to the premiere of *A City Called Copenhagen.*

and abroad (including a nomination for an Academy Award), and an afterlife as one of the first Eastman Color films to be digitally restored by the Danish Film Institute, some fifty years after it was made. The film's production files hold a raft of information on the gradual development of the brief and its interpretation by Jørgen Roos and various stakeholders, giving us a particularly detailed insight into the interplay of aesthetic, financial, technological and practical concerns that shaped the finished film at a particular (though extended) historical moment.

Like the SAS tower rising over Copenhagen, though, this film also ushers us into the future. *A City Called Copenhagen* was the only film produced by MFU in 1960 (Nørrested and Alsted 1987: 360), and heralded the beginning of the end of MFU and of Dansk Kulturfilm's active life. Moreover, as one of only a handful of films made in colour by these twin organisations, Roos' short exemplifies a generation of films that pose a particular challenge for posterity, one that was unforeseeable in 1960: the restoration of parts of the national cinematic heritage that have undergone 'magenta shift' and other kinds of deterioration. In what follows, then, we use archival material to reconstruct the various pressures that shaped this landmark film, but we also pay attention to what it can tell us about the short film production practices that had crystallised by 1960, and the factors that were about to transform informational filmmaking in Denmark as the nation and its cultural policy entered a new era.

The SAS hotel features on the invitation to the premiere of *A City Called Copenhagen* (Figure 9.1), issued around New Year 1960 to the usual guest list of journalists, functionaries, the film's stakeholders and cultural movers and shakers. In the image that decorates the cover of the invitation, the hotel is obviously still under construction. The temporary elevator from which Roos shot the closing sequence is clearly visible and the building's revolutionary curtain wall is only half-finished. In the foreground stands one of the legendary city horn-blowers whose sculpted forms decorate the roof of the Town Hall, visually underscoring the productive and poignant tension between old and new that is at the heart of the film. The premiere took place on 2 February 1960 in the Palladium Cinema, appropriately located on the corner of Vesterbrogade and Rådhuspladsen (Town Hall Square), a stone's throw from the SAS hotel.

Newspaper reviewers from around the time of the premiere communicate something of the excitement with which *A City Called Copenhagen* was received, and we can glean our first impression of the film's style and structure through their eyes. Reviewer Herbert Steinthal was particularly enthusiastic. In a piece entitled 'Now that's Copenhagen!' ('Dét er København!'), he explains how the audience was initially wrong-footed by an inventive false prologue:

> The very first frames of the film reveal the authentic, subtle Copenhagen humour that shines through the whole film. Any evening in Copenhagen has to end in Tivoli, says the American voiceover – it was the American version that was screened to an invited audience at the Palladium yesterday – and a series of fun colour shots of the nightly firework display illustrate his words. And suddenly we see on the black screen: The End ... Then the presentation of the town really begins, with slides in postcard colours of all the things the tourist wants to see ... The viewer is immediately amused by this unconventional introduction. It makes him open his eyes and look more closely at the city and its inhabitants, who actually don't want to be taken too seriously. (Steinthal 1960a)

After the playful opening gambit described by Steinthal, the film goes on to explore a variety of aspects of everyday life in what the voiceover refers to as 'the capital of a democracy'. The engagement with ordinary people and hidden corners of the city drew fulsome praise from contemporary critics:

Clichéed tourist attractions can be beautiful. But in order to imbue all this ornament with meaning, the everyday must also be portrayed. Roos has a good eye for the street sweeper, the pensioner sitting on Blaagaards Square, the afficionados at the jazz club, nursery school children on municipal potties, a bust of Dante on display in front of a junk shop, seagulls over a rubbish dump, the conscientious city planners, and much, much more. (Politiken 1960)

Roos' many strengths – as writer, cinematographer, editor and director – were also praised by critics:

If he is a delightful cinematographer, so too is he a brilliant editor. When he has shown us what citizens' money is spent on – social care, roads, etc. – and that we are happy to pay our taxes, he immediately cuts from the grumpiest taxpayer imaginable to a plaice being filleted at the market, and then a gallery of fish heads. (Steinthal 1960a)

One particularly perceptive reviewer identifies a crucial factor in the film's success at the premiere: the audience left the screening feeling more cheerful than they had been twenty minutes earlier. The film simply bubbles over with the humour of this 'little land', he writes, and this is all the more striking in light of the film's prestigious sponsors:

Insofar as it is carefully emphasised that the Danish Government, the Danish Government Film Committee, Copenhagen City Council, Copenhagen Harbour Administration and, as producer, Statens Filmcentral are behind the project, the foreign audience which the film targets will truly get the impression that humour is something we are very good at in *the little land of Denmark*. The film demonstrates in its own right that humour is related to wisdom; there is something fresh here that will make itself felt in the film's worldwide charm offensive. (V-r 1960, my emphasis)

The screening at Palladium was introduced by the then Mayor of the city, Sigvard Jensen Munk. Several reviewers were struck by the Mayor's admission that there had been some nervousness amongst the commissioning bodies when Roos and his co-writer Roger Maridia presented their treatment. Having seen the finished product, however, the funders had no regrets about giving the filmmakers 'a free hand' (Stg. 1960). This is a term we have encountered before in discussion of how much artistic liberty the directors of informational film should expect. As we saw in Chapter 8, for example, the same expression was used a decade earlier to describe filmmaker Hagen

Hasselbalch's remit for *Shaped by Danish Hands*. Nonetheless, with *A City Called Copenhagen*, the concept of a free hand for the filmmaker takes on new significance. When the reviewers resort to adjectives such as 'unconventional' and 'fresh' and laud the film's playful humour, this represents the fulfilment of a concerted effort from Roos and the film's stakeholders to achieve a specific quality in the film, something they couched in terms of 'renewal'. If we now go back to the beginning of this story of this film, and follow the funders, producers and Jørgen Roos himself as they thrash out what a film about modern Copenhagen should be, what we actually witness is a slow, piecemeal renegotiation of the projected Denmark we have seen crystallise in the state-sponsored short film since the late 1940s. Put differently, with *A City Called Copenhagen*, the Danish informational short becomes resolutely modern, at precisely the same moment as the city it depicts.

TOURIST FILM OR ART FILM? THE COMMISSIONING PROCESS

A City Called Copenhagen is distinguished by the longest commissioning process of all the films discussed in this book (and indeed the longest commissioning process of any film whose files I have had access to). The paper-trail behind the film gives an insight into just how nuanced the expressed wishes and strategic considerations of the bodies involved in commissioning films could be. In particular, this film's gestation illustrates how stakeholders negotiated the distinction between the *kulturfilm* and genres such as, in this case, the tourist film. The possibility of commercial sponsorship arises and is rejected, showing a sustained commitment to the principle of funding *kulturfilm* for the public good. Also apparent in the records is the increasing feasibility and desirability of filming in broad gauge and colour, and of adopting different running times, in order to reach cinema and television audiences worldwide.

As we have repeatedly seen, issues of film genre and aesthetic strategies are negotiated during the commissioning and production processes, and *A City Called Copenhagen* is no exception. The principle that there should be a 'concept' behind the film was championed by Sigvald Kristensen of the Foreign Ministry in particular, but interventions from various stakeholders can be seen to influence the project's eventual form as an experimental art film whose purpose was not so much to sell the city, but rather to communicate something of its essence.

As we have seen in previous case studies, the impetus for Dansk Kulturfilm's projects often grew from a confluence of factors, and *A City Called Copenhagen* is a marked example of a commission with multiple drivers. In this case, demands from Danish embassies and consulates abroad coincided in the mid-1950s with an offer of sponsorship from a local industry, as well as strong (if somewhat dissolute) interest from Copenhagen City Council. Already in these two stimuli we see two competing, but not mutually exclusive, pressures: on the one hand, the demand amongst foreign audiences for an informative film about the city, and on the other, the infiltration of the *kulturfilm* genre by local businesses as a means to sell Danish produce as well as the city itself as a tourist destination. This dilemma considerably delayed the production of *A City Called Copenhagen*. On the other hand, the film eventually directed by Jørgen Roos is distinctive (and arguably very successful) in its exploitation of the tension between these two pressures for comic effect.

A City Called Copenhagen was more than six years in the making, as evinced by the first filed correspondence about the nascent project. In late 1953, Ib Koch-Olsen, Head of Dansk Kulturfilm, caught wind of an offer to finance a film about the city from an unlikely source: the manufacturer of the well-known Danish liqueur Cherry Heering (Koch-Olsen 1953). Koch-Olsen expanded on the idea later that winter in correspondence with the then Mayor of Copenhagen, Hans Peter Sørensen (Koch-Olsen 1954). The Heering company was willing to invest 35–50,000 kroner in a short film, on the condition that it was of high artistic quality, and that the company premises were shown and mentioned during the credits. As Koch-Olsen pointed out, the latter condition was less outlandish than it might seem, as the Heering headquarters were located in a historic merchant's house dating from 1785 in the Christianshavn area of the city (Nordea-Fonden n.d.). Koch-Olsen declared himself broadly in favour of giving the offer serious consideration, given that there was an acknowledged appetite overseas for a new film about Copenhagen.

This international demand had been identified by the Foreign Office's Press Bureau, which was responsible for disseminating knowledge about Denmark abroad. Some months after Koch-Olsen had outlined Heering's offer, Foreign Ministry official Sigvald Kristensen also wrote to Mayor Sørensen, explaining that there was a gap in the market for a film about Copenhagen that would 'give foreign audiences an in-depth insight into life and work in a modern, democratic capital city' (Kristensen 1954). The Foreign Ministry's Press Bureau was being bombarded by requests from embassies and consulates worldwide for such a film, explained Kristensen. Unfortunately the only films available about the city were an eight-minute silent production *Copenhagen* (Gunnar Wangel, 1950), and two reels distributed in the UK by Peak Productions. These options were 'very dated' tourist films (Kristensen 1954). What Kristensen wanted was a new film that showed life in the capital from the average citizen's point of view:

> The film ... ought to be concerned with his living conditions, his responsibilities and rights as a citizen, his efforts in the workplace and as a member of the community and the results of these efforts: a democratically-run,

modern city, where the constant goal is to create better conditions for the individual citizen. (Kristensen 1954)

It is striking that in the same letter, not only does Kristensen provide guidelines for the film's point of view and focus, but also characterises the anticipated audience in unusually precise terms:

> The film should, first and foremost, target an engaged audience in schools, continuing education and interest groups around the world, whose interest in and respect for the Danish way of life we would like to win. The Press Bureau is convinced that such a film will also be able to serve the interests of the tourist industry more effectively than a tourist film of a more conventional type. (Kristensen 1954)

Here we witness a very clear statement of faith in the *kulturfilm* model: that by prioritising film's ability to enlighten, the secondary mission of selling Copenhagen as a tourist destination will also be more effectively served. From the very beginning of the commissioning discussions, then, the principle is established that this film ought to distinguish itself from the tourist film genre in terms of its pedagogical content and artistic quality.

Concomitantly, as far as the Foreign Ministry was concerned, the film should be made with public money. Kristensen was not keen on the idea of sole sponsorship by Heering, for two reasons: the sponsorship might compromise the filmmaker's artistic freedom, and other businesses and organisations that were not featured in the film might raise objections. He suggested that the City approach a range of businesses to ask for their support. While the sponsors were entitled to be named in the credits, they should not expect their businesses to be featured in the film (Kristensen 1957a).

The project languished at committee stage at the City Council until mid-1957, when Kristensen again raised the subject with Sørensen's successor as Mayor, Sigvard Jensen Munk. This time, a meeting was organised, bringing together Kristensen from the Foreign Ministry, the Mayor's Chief of Staff Otto Berg, and representatives from Copenhagen's Tourist Board, the Copenhagen Harbour Administration and Dansk Arbejde (a precursor to the Danish Export Association). The minutes of this meeting (Berg 1957) provide a detailed account of the perspectives of these various bodies as they thrash out how the film should be funded, the possibilities for its format and distribution, and its audience and aims. In other words, this meeting gives us a good sense of how a range of interested parties fed into the process of drafting a brief for a film to be actioned and how, in doing so, they are implicated in the ongoing work of defining genres, putting emerging technologies to work, and determining how and where cinema could be most useful.

As far as funding is concerned, it is striking that several small sums of money were available to be pooled by participants in the meeting, because they had already been secured for anticipated film projects. As we have seen before, 'useful' filmmaking was undertaken by many organisations and individuals in this period, far beyond the institutional confines of Dansk Kulturfilm and Ministeriernes Filmudvalg (The Danish Government Film Committee or MFU). The export association Dansk Arbejde, for example, had received a contribution of 2500 kroner towards the production of a film on Copenhagen from Tuborg breweries. The Copenhagen Harbour Administration had a pot of 10,000 kroner earmarked for its own film, a project abandoned as it would have cost four or five times as much. And the City Council's Committee on Continuing Education would contribute up to 5000 kroner.

This was a start, but nowhere near the ballpark figure of 90,000 kroner calculated at the meeting as the cost of a narrow-gauge colour film of seventeen to eighteen minutes in length. This format was settled on as half as expensive as an Academy format film, but was also expedient for potential screening on television (as we saw in Chapter 8, this was crucial for any film with ambitions for North American distribution). Distribution in cinemas was considered by most participants in the meeting as targeting too broad a public, and as too ambitious, given that North American distributors sold pre-selected shorts to cinema owners as part of feature packages. Four language versions were planned at the meeting: French, German, Spanish and British English, with the possibility of an American-English version. It was also suggested that businesses could sponsor further versions in the languages of the countries to which they exported goods, underlining the film's subsidiary role in promoting Danish trade.

The minutes indicate a certain degree of consensus around Kristensen's earlier concept of the film as something more than a tourist film. It should be a film about 'the living city', reiterates Kristensen at the meeting, 'not just a series of images of traditional tourist things. There must be an idea behind the film', and it must be made by a real 'film-poet' ('*filmdigter*'), such as the Swede Arne Sucksdorff. Ejler Alkjær, representing the Copenhagen Tourist Board at the meeting, displayed a nuanced appreciation of the distinctions between the tourist film genre and films for other purposes. While the City Council might be interested in a film that would create goodwill amongst Copenhageners, or which presented the city to the world, or which promoted local businesses, the Tourist Board could only support a true tourist film. Specifically, this meant a film which inspired viewers to visit Copenhagen. In contrast, an *oplysningsfilm* (enlightening film) which presented information about the city to overseas audiences could serve as a substitute for a visit. This clear-minded intervention seems to have helped the participants decide to prioritise the latter. The distinction was certainly echoed in a press release of January 1960 announcing the forthcoming premiere: 'It is not meant to be a tourist film, to whet the appetite and tempt guests to the city, but its more profound depiction is designed to provide an impression of Copenhagen for people who might never have the chance to visit' (SFC 1960a). By MFU's first Board meeting of 1958, Kristensen was able to confirm that the City Council had accepted that the film should not be 'a banal tourist film' but that the filmmakers should have 'a free hand to shape it artistically' (MFU 1958a).

That this set of considerations constituted a firm brief for the film is underscored by the consistency of the message that made it through to the final draft of the manuscript, prior to the start of shooting in summer 1959:

> What was wanted was not a film based on the traditional notion of the city as a tourist destination. On the contrary, the film should try to capture the city's special atmosphere, say something about the people who live here every day, their work and their pleasures. At the same time, social conditions should be covered, and the harbour should be brought into the picture. (Roos 1959: 1)

The Swedish filmmaker Arne Sucksdorff had been mentioned, as we saw above, in discussions about the type of film that should be commissioned. Sucksdorff was approached as the first choice of director, but turned down the commission as he did not want to make the film on 16mm, as was planned at that stage (MFU 1958b). Jørgen Roos was then asked if he would like to take on the task, in early March 1958. He too was disappointed that the shooting format was to be 16mm, and took a few days to consider (Nielsen 1958a), before accepting the commission. Roos was already recognised as 'one of Danish film's most talented young men' (Steinthal 1960b), working exclusively in the short film format. Still only thirty-five years old when appointed to this project, Roos had over twenty short documentaries and experimental films to his name as director. He had also worked extensively as cinematographer and editor for renowned directors such as Carl Th. Dreyer and Theodor Christensen (see Chapter 7), and belonged to a family that had produced several key figures in Danish cinema.

The project finally had funding, parameters and a director. Now it needed a screenplay.

'THE MOST DANGEROUS OF ALL FILM MODELS': THE CITY SYMPHONY GENRE

Though Roos as director was assured a 'free hand', the production files show that Sigvald Kristensen was a driving force behind the artistic development of *A City Called Copenhagen*. This is an unusual case of a stakeholder intervening in the creative process not with the purpose of specifying details to be included or correcting matters of fact, but to contribute his knowledge of cinema and his considerable experience of marketing Denmark abroad. Having pinned down the parameters of the project, from mid-1958 onwards, Kristensen can be seen working with the filmmaker's ideas to nuance and sharpen them. What is particularly interesting about Kristensen's vision for the project is how he draws on the established genre of the city symphony genre to frame the film.

That the city symphony was an important precursor to this film project is already clear, albeit not explicitly articulated, in the discussion of Arne Sucksdorff as a possible director. Sucksdorff was well known for *Människor i stad*, his filmic portrait of Stockholm, which had won the Academy Award for Best Short Film of 1948. While the title of Sucksdorff's film translates literally as *People in [a/the] City*, the film was distributed internationally with various titles including *Symphony of a City* and *Rhythm of a City*. There is, however, an even stronger indication in the production files of *A City Called Copenhagen* that a city symphony was what the stakeholders had in mind. In mid-April 1958, a private screening of three films was organised in Gutenberghuset, the building which houses today's Danish Film Institute on Gothersgade. Present were Jørgen Roos, now committed to the project, Sigvald Kristensen, Otto Berg from the Mayor's office, and a small number of other colleagues from MFU and the Town Hall. Three examples of the city symphony genre were shown for the benefit of the sponsors and director: Walther Ruttmann's *Berlin, Symphonie einer Großstadt* (*Berlin: Symphony of a City*, 1927, Germany), Sucksdorff's *Människor i stad*, and John Eldridge's *Waverley Steps: A Visit to Edinburgh* (1948, Great Britain). The trio of films presumably inspired discussion after the screening, but this is not recorded. The selection is consistent with the repeated refrain in previous meetings that there ought to be a 'concept' behind Roos' screenplay, and betrays a degree of ambition to create a film that would write itself into an established and lauded European genre. Unusually, then, in the case of *A City Called Copenhagen* we have a record of at least some of the film's intertexts, and of how the commissioning process drew on the wider European film heritage as well as the more practical needs of the sponsors to develop the brief in collaboration with the filmmaker.

What we cannot assume, however, is that this small knot of functionaries and film connoisseurs wanted a straightforward interpretation of the city symphony formula. Roos was faced with a quandary: how to satisfy the brief of making a film with a 'concept' behind it, when the city symphony genre was built on re-hashing the same tropes in city after city? As early as 1937, John Grierson had been scathing about the proliferation of such films:

> Symphonies of cities have been sprouting ever since [Ruttmann's Berlin], each with its crescendo of dawn and coming awake and workers' proces-

sions, its morning traffic and machinery, its lunchtime contrasts of rich and poor, its afternoon lull, its evening denouement in sky-sign and night club. The model makes good, if similar, movie [sic]. (Grierson 1966b: 205)

The foundational texts of the city symphony genre date from the 1920s and include Alberto Cavalcanti's *Rien que les heures* (*Nothing but Time*, 1926, France), Dziga Vertov's *Man with a Movie Camera* (1929, USSR), Joris Ivens' *Regen* (*Rain*, 1929, The Netherlands), and of course Ruttmann's film of Berlin. The impetus behind these early city symphonies, as Laura Marcus puts it, was to 'renew the [film] medium – and to turn away from commercial and narrative cinema – by returning to cinema's origins in the documenting of reality, but with the particular twist given by the perspectives and angles of modernism' (Marcus 2010: 30). As the nomenclature suggests, typically, the films are structured into symphonic movements, tracking the life of the city over a single day, or rather, a 'composite day' (MacDonald 1997: 3). There is a tendency to offer a taxonomy of occupations, classes, neighbourhoods, and so on, constructing an Olympian perspective on an unfathomably large and complex social organism. In this sense, too, the notion of a symphony works as a metaphor for the principle of *e pluribus unum*, whereby 'the individual contributions of millions of people (working with technologies that have developed over centuries) are subsumed within the metropolis's megapartite movement through the day' (MacDonald 1997: 4). The city's population is nonetheless revealed, often through shifts between micro- and macro-levels, to exist in structured, modern and homogeneous spacetime, a 'self-sufficient miniature cosmos' (Stein 2013: 4).

A calling-card of the genre is self-conscious use of montage, which enacts the cities as machines of rhythm and pattern. Erica Stein explains that it was precisely these aesthetic strategies that soon made Ruttmann's *Berlin* in particular a target for politically inflected critique: 'The legibility lent to the usually overwhelming onslaught of technology, industry, and spectacle that compose the quotidian reality of the modern urban dweller produces a corresponding erasure of the socioeconomic order's alienating, exploitative qualities and its historical context' (Stein 2013: 3–4). Notably, Grierson abhorred the seductive effect of rhythmic abstraction in Ruttmann's *Berlin*, commenting that the spectacle of 'tempo and rhythm' had effects comparable to a military parade, and that documenting the movement of a machine was of little use without insight into its operator and his 'underpaid labor and meaningless production'; this was 'the most dangerous of all film models' (Grierson 1966a: 151–2; see also Stein 2013: 1).

As for Jørgen Roos, he had served his apprenticeship in a milieu heavily influenced by British documentary culture, not least as cameraman for

Theodor Christensen, and it is unlikely that Grierson's scepticism about the city symphony had escaped him. Nor was he minded to make a film that would conceal the lived experience of workers and ordinary city folk behind a veneer of sophisticated montage. As discussed in Chapter 7, in films such as *Her er banerne* (*Here are the Railways*, 1948) Christensen had harnessed the exhilarating rhythms of Ruttmann's *Berlin* and of Watt and Wright's *Night Mail* (which Grierson narrated) in order to render visible not merely the abstract patterns created by trains and the railwaymen who tended them, but the embodied skills and collective efficacy of the workers. And it was Jørgen Roos, together with his fellow cameraman Fritz Olsen, who had risked life and limb to scramble between train tracks and moving wagons to capture that industrial ballet.

Roos' film, then, would have to find a balance between gesturing to the city symphony canon and interrogating that genre aesthetically and politically. Finding this balance took three attempts. The production files contain an initial treatment from Roos and two further drafts of the screenplay, as well as detailed feedback from Sigvald Kristensen. As with other aspects of this film's production history, we are privy to an unusually detailed glimpse into the screenwriting process.

'This is an Experiment': Developing the Screenplay

The first treatment dates from 28 May 1958, about six weeks after the screening of the city symphony films. This proposal (Roos 1958a: 1) begins by stating that a city can only be depicted through the people who live in it. This approach has been adopted in many films, continues Roos, by letting the viewer experience the city through the eyes of a number of typical citizens or tourists, but it is worn-out and dated. Another possibility is to choose a defined slice of time and construct a fictional cross-section of the city's life, but this has also been done many times. Though he does not say so, he is referencing the strategies adopted in *Waverley Steps* and *Människor i stad* respectively. Roos proposes a different method of centring a film on the people of the city: persuading a number of well-known residents to be recorded talking about what the city means to them (2). The interviews would then be edited and form the basis of a screenplay. The verbal commentary would be contextualised and nuanced by images of the city. A list of twelve possible participants (all men) from the art world, literature, academia, as well as the local authorities and ordinary workers, is tentatively proposed (3). By page three, the flaws in the model are apparent, and Roos admits as much: a film destined for circulation abroad should not be based on talking heads, especially not if they are talking Danish. Roos suggests that this could be overcome by translating parts of the commentary into appropriate languages, while retaining enough of the original voices to communicate the speakers' personalities. This flies in the face of the established principle of avoiding dialogue in films for export (see Chapters 5 and 6). Nevertheless, the documentarist ambition of this first draft is clear. 'This is an experiment', admits Roos, but 'it will function as a direct and extremely personal advert for Copenhagen, and finally, it will be of significant cultural-historical value in the future' (4).

The second draft of the treatment, dated 15 December 1958, gives an update on progress with this 'experiment'. It has been horribly difficult, reports Roos (1958b: 1), to find the right mix of people who could articulate their relationship to the city. But six interviews have been recorded, and have formed the basis for a series of atmospheric vignettes, starting in a graveyard in January, and ending around mid-summer. Of historical interest here is the participation of Poul Henningsen, the lamp designer and cultural critic known as PH, whose cinematic national symphony *Danmark* (*Denmark*, 1935) was discussed in Chapter 4. PH's proposed monologue starts in the Tivoli Gardens, where his lamp designs have been installed, and brings us to his office high over Copenhagen. In Roos' description of this vignette, some of the most important ideas in the final film begin to emerge:

> It is the modern, final part of the city's history that [PH] narrates. About his struggle with it, and about town planning and cultural life, about satirical theatre and pubs and about what he thinks is the role of the city in people's lives, its real function. (Roos 1958b: 7)

PH then recites a poem listing the city's faults, with the refrain 'we love the city anyway'. As he finishes the last verse, the draft describes how the camera will look out over Rådhuspladsen, as the clock tower chimes the hour, while over the trees and rooftops the Tivoli fireworks blossom in the sky (7). Here we witness in draft form both the beginning and end of the finished film: the Tivoli fireworks that open it, and the final view over the Town Hall from a high vantage point. The theme of the modern, planned city is also in evidence. Intriguingly, given the concept behind this draft – that it is based on interviews already recorded – this leaves PH's (unacknowledged) fingerprints on the finished film.

Also included in the second draft is a role for Preben Hornung, an artist who steals the show in the final version of the film with his abstract canvases inspired by the harbour and its machinery. Already, Roos and Hornung have hit on the concept behind his appearance: 'a little art film within a film, which, as well as saying important things about the city, also gives an insight into modern, Danish painting' (Roos 1958b: 6). For this draft, though, Hornung's recorded conversation has inspired Roos to write a vignette centring on aesthetic continuities in Danish art from the Viking Age to the present day. These can be seen, comments Hornung, in ships, houses and even painting; and here the camera would trace this tradition to two examples of Arne Jacobsen's buildings, of which one is opposite Central Station (6) – that is, the SAS hotel which comes to loom over the finished film.

What is fascinating about these drafts is how they crystallise the ideas developed in conversation between Roos, his assistant the journalist Tørk Haxthausen, who recorded the interviews on tape, and the subjects. This quasi-ethnographic method has the effect of incorporating a range of perspectives on the past, present and future of the city into the evolving script. In fact, the third draft, submitted on 17 April 1959, explicitly adopts the notion of 'perspectives' to replace 'personalities' as the basis for the film's kaleidoscopic portrait of the city:

> Rather than being tied to personalities we achieve far greater freedom in terms of content and aesthetics when we can freely play with various interesting concepts. In other words the personalities are being replaced with concepts! In this way we can better stimulate the viewer, who is free to seek out his own area of interest and have his eyes opened to new ideas. And therefore this will not be a film with fixed opinions linked to personalities, but an exciting story in which perspectives are up for debate. (Roos 1959: 1–2)

In earlier versions, a kind of contrapuntal tension between voiceover reminiscences and images of the city had been proposed, in order to produce this sense of perspectival heterogeneity. Roos now envisages a film which will enact this principle via a range of filmic strategies: 'All the way through the film we explore a series of perspectives, which often contrast in terms of form: they are allowed to play off against each other in terms of content, colour, image and sound' (2). As we know from the reviews after the premiere, Roos was particularly lauded for his skill as an editor, and this draft also anticipates the important role that his cutting will play in constructing the celluloid city: 'a film like this one will not attain its final form at a writing desk – but on the streets of the city, amidst its pulsating life, and at the editing table' (2). Roos has thus come full circle to countenance, but re-work, the rhythmic montage and thematic taxonomies typical of the classic city symphony.

Sigvald Kristensen was sent this draft by Werner Pedersen at Dansk Kulturfilm, who asked him to look at it before it was sent on to the City Council for scrutiny (Pedersen 1959a). Kristensen's report on the text is typed and scribbled on so erratically as to suggest that he undertook the review in his own time and in a rush. But it offers a strikingly lucid and imaginative set of comments about the film's focus and structure, and its influence on the final film is palpable. Kristensen (1959) sees the potential for a 'brilliant' film in the draft, 'a rare chance to create a little work of art'. He thus encourages the development of the original aspects of the film, those that deviate from, or renew, the city symphony. He urges inclusion of a wider range of 'distinctive, curious, relatively unknown' aspects of city life. He wants to see a more distinctive 'leitmotiv' or conceptual source of coherence, citing Ruttmann's use of time as a connecting conceit and Sucksdorff's focus on love in the 'stony city'. For Roos' film, he suggests the pairings new-old, peace-noise, oasis-technology and life-art as possible frameworks. The tension between life and art, thinks Kristensen, is already there implicitly in the draft and is 'very original'.

Of all the films examined in this book, this is the best-documented instance of direct intervention in the aesthetics of a film by a representative of the Danish state that I have encountered, and it speaks volumes about the commitment in that milieu to the power of informational film as an art form – not merely a medium for communication.

'MUNICIPAL CHAMBERPOTS': MAKING FUN OF THE FUNDERS

It is, however, undeniable that *A City Called Copenhagen* was also shaped by the more prosaic needs of its funders. We have encountered a number of films in this book which were shaped by the filmmakers' creative solutions to the (sometimes competing) demands of the commission, but in this particular case, the issue of financial sponsorship is tackled head-on. During the development process, representatives of the Harbour Administration repeatedly pressed for more visibility for the Port of Copenhagen in the film, 'which it should be entitled to, given its position in the life of the city' (fn 1958b). At a review meeting in December 1958, it was suggested that including a harbour worker amongst the interviewees could contribute to satisfying the Harbour Administration's anxieties (fn 1958c). But Roos eventually adopted quite a different solution to this problem, a solution that emerges as one of the defining features of *A City Called Copenhagen*.

One of the distinctively droll features of the film is that it makes gentle sport with its own funders. While informational films tend to credit their backers in the opening or closing credits – and Roos' film also does the latter – the respective financial contributions of the Copenhagen City Council and the Harbour Administration are wittily integrated into the main body of the film. In the first instance, just under two minutes in, our first glimpse of the city after the opening slideshow of tourist postcards features a portly fisherman clad in a green checked coat and wellington boots, dangling his feet over a graffitied harbour wall and reeling in his line. 'There are not many fish in the harbour', comments the voiceover, 'but you have the right to look for yourself because Copenhagen' – here the voice assumes a tone of faux grandeur – 'is the capital of a democracy!' The scene switches to the assembly room of the Town Hall,

Figure 9.2   Jørgen Roos' *A City Called Copenhagen* refers knowingly to the necessity of crediting the film's sponsors.

with text superimposed to read 'This film is sponsored by the CITY COUNCIL of Copenhagen' and accompanied by a trumpet fanfare (see Figure 9.2). The amusing bathos of the right to fish in the harbour as the ultimate expression of democracy is striking enough to hammer home the connection between the ordinary citizen (the fisherman) to the collective structures of governance (the City Council).

This inaugurates a two-stage sequence in which the City Council's wide-ranging services are inventoried and visualised. The first stage revolves around money as the material expression of the symbiosis between 'the fifty-five members of the City Council' and the ordinary citizens. The sum of 1.5 billion kroner a year, we learn, pays for a myriad of everyday things which we now see on the screen before us: schools, dentistry, swimming pools, modern education, new school buildings, hospitals, fire stations, power stations, public parks, libraries, markets and street cars. The voiceover speeds up as the list progresses, as does the aural punctuation: after each item, a 'ching!' sound evokes a cash register at first, then the bell of a street car. As we career towards a stop sign, the narrator rounds off the list of amenities by saying 'and that's not all! But it's enough. Anyway, it's boring.' An exaggerated yawn is heard, the source of which is revealed to be a jowly but friendly looking dog. Having acknowledged the possible boredom of some viewers, the film earns some leeway to resume the list of City Council services, this time organised around the verbal motif of 'municipal'. Echoing the bathos inherent in the opening idea that the fisherman's futile wait for a catch is the ultimate expression of democracy, this new list applies the term 'municipal' to a range of activities that visually connect the private with the public. As small children toddle across the screen and dancers' multicoloured skirts swish, the narrator seems just as surprised as we are to witness not only 'municipal low-rental housing' but also 'municipal chamber pots in all the municipal kindergartens', and that 'there are even municipal dances in the parks'.

A final audiovisual flourish firmly reiterates the partnership of City Council and citizen: a resigned-looking man is shown paying his taxes at a counter. The narrator comments mischievously that 'the people of this city simply LOOOVE paying taxes!', and as the grinning teller demonstratively slides the proffered banknotes across to his side of the desk and begins to count them, the now recognisable trumpet fanfare provides an aural link back to the City Council. Nimble editing transforms the teller's hands as they count the bank-notes into the hands of a fishmonger ripping fish apart.

This is one of a number of witticisms in the film based on visual and aural juxtaposition. Others include a policeman's wolf whistle to a pretty young woman, preceded by a tracking shot upwards to a sweep thrusting his brush suggestively into a chimney pot; a segue from the clanging of fishing boat masts on the waterfront to the concluding vignette in a packed jazz club; and a sequence of cross-cuts between a child staring in horrified fascination at a laughing grotesque dummy at Bakken amusement park. At his editing table, Roos sees, and renders visible, connections everywhere across the city and on multiple scales. The film is true to Kristensen's intervention – emphasise the tension between art and life – and also to its original remit, to illustrate the connections between the individual citizens and the democracy they constitute together. In doing so, the film skirts dangerously close to Stein's diagnosis of how the city symphony erases 'the socioeconomic order's alienating, exploita-tive qualities' by rendering legible 'the usually overwhelming onslaught of technology, industry, and spectacle' (Stein 2013: 3–4). Roos is, after all, in the employ of that 'socioeconomic order' which is funding the film. If, as an artist, he cannot resist the temptation to make the city legible in all its pattern and relationality, he can nonetheless continue to employ humour and irony to make visible and audible the movement of money and services – or the munici-pal chamberpots.

The joke about the film's funders is all the more effective for being repeated much later, six minutes before the film's end. At this point, we have been intro-duced to painter Preben Hornung, whose artistic inspiration derives from the machinery of the harbour. With another trumpet fanfare, the film breaks off from following Hornung along the wharf on his bicycle to present an aerial shot of ships entering and leaving the port, with a similar caption superimposed: 'This film is also sponsored by THE HARBOUR ADMINISTRATION of Copenhagen'.

As in the case of the City Council, by poking gentle fun at the Harbour Administration's officiousness, Roos gains the necessary leeway to shoehorn a series of dry statistics about the port into the voiceover. Echoing the earlier admission (underlined by the yawning dog) that statistics are 'boring' and tell us little about what a city really is, here too the data is served up with a generous helping of irony. In between the lists of facts and figures about the harbour, the narrator, assisted by Hornung's expressive gestures, keeps up a meta-commentary of short asides. For example, the opening gambit, that Copenhagen Harbour is the largest in all of Scandinavia, is followed by a 'hmmm'. A statement that the port boasts 133,000 feet of wharfs is followed up with an almost inaudible aside, again from the same voice: 'That's a whole lotta wharfs!' A list of numbers and types of cranes – 130 for general cargo, sixty-eight for bulk cargo, two floating cranes that can lift forty tonnes each – is cross-cut with shots of Hornung pointing and making a cheeky popping noise. Crucially, this narrative strategy never tips over into derision for the data. The facts and figures are there in the film for the interested viewer, but the attention of those of a less technical bent is maintained via the wry and lively approach. The interests of the funders are acknowledged, but not allowed to dominate the film, nor the life of the city.

This is not the first time we have encountered this 'double-voiced' approach to delivering information; in Chapter 4, for example, we saw the 'useful idiot' voiceover strategy adopted by Theodor Christensen in his public information films for occupation-era theatrical distribution. Incorporating a ridiculously dim-witted and sceptical character into the voiceover as interlocutor liberates the audience to learn without losing face. Similarly, the ironic asides in *A City Called Copenhagen* generate sympathy with a range of viewers: those who are less technically minded as well as those who consider themselves too sophisticated for informational films are included in the web of addressees the film spins for itself, thanks to the narrator's (or rather, Hornung's) knowing wink. However, the wry and ironic tone of *A City Called Copenhagen* is not just for persuasive effect, but also integral to the film's branding of Denmark as a sophisticated, modern nation. Hornung's function in this regard is not just to make sarcastic comments. His abstract artworks inspired by the docklands are also a crucial tool in Roos' strategy of painting the modern city in colour – and it is to this palette that we now turn.

The first frames of *A City Called Copenhagen* explode into colour before our eyes – literally, since our first meeting with the city is heralded by the summer fireworks above the Tivoli amusement park. In a nod to the closing frames of Ruttmann's *Berlin*, above the illuminated Nimh Palace and against the night sky, golden, pink and greenish Catherine wheels, rockets and chrysanthemums whirl and boom to the 'ooohs' of the crowd gathered below. 'All movies about wonderful Copenhagen', announces the voiceover, 'have to end with the fireworks over the famous Tivoli Gardens'. After this false ending – 'So that was The End' teases the narrator, as THE END appears on screen – C O P E N H A G E N is spelled out letter by letter in monochrome, accompanied by a series of popping, clicking and giggling sounds. Colour then returns to centre-stage, with a slide show of postcard-style scenes gliding horizontally across the screen. These images are a litany of the contents of the tourist film to which *A City Called Copenhagen*, the viewer is realising, refuses to be reduced. The Little Mermaid glides into view, followed by the Royal Guard, then a variety of *smørrebrød* (open sandwiches), a smiling postman, the deer park and the Gefion Fountain. As well as playfully flagging the film as a moving picture, these images are all designed to establish its status as a colour film: the red of the postman's uniform, the green grass of the grazing land, the blue and white of the Royal Copenhagen porcelain plate on which rests Hans Christian Andersen's favourite *smørrebrød*, topped with browny-pink bacon. 'Oh very nice', intones the voiceover, 'but the city is more than that'. Cut to the harbour, where a lone fisherman sits centre-stage, clad in a strikingly green-checked donkey jacket.

Jørgen Roos broached the subject of filming *A City Called Copenhagen* on Eastman Color in mid-1958, at the screening of city symphony films which took place at Gutenberghus (Nielsen 1958c). Sigvald Kristensen was open to the idea, pointing out that if the extra funding could be found, a 35mm film could be shown in cinemas and at film festivals, though the Foreign Ministry would be using 16mm versions in its general distribution abroad. He also mused that the length of the film should be suitable for television. Helene Nielsen, administrator for Dansk Kulturfilm (and by extension MFU), was ready with an estimate of the additional costs associated with use of Eastman Color (20–25,000 kroner more). It was agreed that the matter would be discussed again when Roos had submitted a synopsis.

In fact, a note in the production files indicates that Nielsen had been discussing possible film formats with Roos in advance. In her letter advising Roos of the screening meeting, she adds:

> my plan to show a 16 mm print-down from Eastmancolor and a contact print from a 16 mm Kodachrome original did not win any support, as the

thinking is that it has already been decided to use 16 mm Kodachrome. You can always see what way the wind is blowing at the meeting and decide if you want to broach the subject. (Nielsen 1958b)

In other words, Nielsen had intended to demonstrate the relative quality of 16mm prints struck from two different colour originals: one from a 35mm Eastman Color film versus another copied from a 16mm Kodachrome reversal film original. In the event, 35mm Eastman Color was adopted as the shooting format. This would have repercussions not only for the film's distribution, as Kristensen foresaw, but also for its longer-term preservation and eventual restoration.

What was at stake in the choice between Kodachrome and Eastman Color? Roos' and Nielsen's reasoning is not recorded, but the first and most obvious reason for preferring Eastman Color is the possibility of theatrical distribution. A precedent had been set five years previously by the first major Danish film to be shot in colour, Bjarne Henning-Jensen's *Hvor bjergene sejler* (*Where Mountains Float*). A *kulturfilm*, albeit almost of feature film length, and shot on Eastman Color, it had been nominated for an Academy Award and for the Grand Prix at the Venice Film Festival. Secondly, Roos' and Nielsen's plan to screen samples of copies struck from the two formats also suggests that the relative image quality was an issue. Kodachrome's high level of contrast tended to intensify when copies were printed, resulting in dark shadows (Ivester n.d.). This would be of particular concern to makers of informational shorts destined to circulate in multiple copies on the non-theatrical circuit.

Ironically, had *A City Called Copenhagen* been shot on 16mm Kodachrome as originally planned, the film would not have suffered the fate that befell all Eastman Color films made before the mid-1980s: colour balance shift. The cyan and yellow dyes fade faster than the magenta, resulting in a bright pink image or, as Laura U. Marks (1997: 95) more poetically describes this effect, 'once-differentiated hues now a uniformly muddy pinkish brown'. This problem began to reveal itself in the mid-1970s, as some films started to fade after little more than a decade of life. It is now recognised that all negatives and prints made using the Eastman Color process prior to 1983 will have undergone colour balance shift. In comparison, even the earliest films made using Technicolor's more stable dye transfer process have retained their saturated look (Haines 2013: xvi), while Kodachrome film of all kinds is renowned for the endurance of its colour.

A City Called Copenhagen was restored by the Danish Film Institute as part of a broader programme of work on documentary and short films from the early 2000s onwards. While the original colour balance of the negative cannot be restored, the development of digital scanning has made it possible to reconstruct – at least approximately – the look of Eastman Color films through digital processing. What digital restoration cannot restore to us, however, is the original artefact. Colour, as conceived and captured by Roos, is the *sine qua non* of *A City Called Copenhagen*. This was a film planned and made at a time when shooting on colour was far from the norm in documentary film-making; its director fought for permission to film on Eastman Color, served as his own cinematographer, and made colour as concept and practice central to the film by incorporating the painter's point of view.

INTERNATIONAL DISTRIBUTION AND PRIZES

On 8 April 1961, Jørgen Roos returned to the now-complete SAS hotel complex, this time not to film, but to check in at the air terminal. He was on his way to Los Angeles via New York for the thirty-third Academy Awards; *A City Called Copenhagen* had been nominated in the category Short Subject Documentary (SFC 1961b). Roos' film did not win the Oscar, but he was amply compensated by a haul of international awards so extensive that a unique sub-folder in the production files was warranted: a prize-giving ceremony at the Town Hall in October 1961. Newspapers of the time show Jørgen Roos with his wife and daughter behind a table laden with medals and certificates. 'Everything on the table is yours!' declared Mayor Munk with an expansive sweep of his hand, reported the newspaper *Politiken*. The list of prizes was from well-known and more obscure film festivals, including Cannes, Buenos Aires, Mar del Plata, Bilbao, Rapallo and Montevideo as well as 'Hollywood' (Politiken 1961). Other honours for the film included screening at the Opening Gala of the 1960 Edinburgh Film Festival (EIFF 1960). Also, in February 1961, the seventh annual Oberhausen Film Festival (or Westdeutsche Kurzfilmtage) had honoured Roos in its own way, indicating the international renown he was starting to accrue. Not only did Oberhausen request that *A City Called Copenhagen* should be screened together with *Danish Design*, another of Roos' films, it also made him a member of the jury – a body chaired by none other than John Grierson, who was about to step down in favour of Bert Haanstra. And Denmark was made the focal nation of the festival, following in the footsteps of France and Britain (SFC 1961a).

From as far afield as the National film Library of New Zealand, praise was heaped upon Roos:

> [It] continues to be admired by everyone. Our national Film Unit was preparing a film on Wellington, but once they had seen your film on Copenhagen they decided to change their treatment completely. It is probably the best film we have ever seen on a city. (quoted in Benzon 1961)

Worldwide interest in the film flared up on and off through the 1960s. Four language versions had been planned originally: French, German, Spanish and British English, with the possibility of an American-English version (Berg 1957). As the hype around the film simmered, further discussions about the choice of language versions reveals a few interesting trends and tensions in multi-language film distribution. While the Danish Tourist Board was on record as wanting Norwegian and Swedish versions for distribution in those countries, the Foreign Ministry vetoed this on the grounds that 'it [was] a point of principle that Danish propaganda in Norway and Sweden should circulate in Danish' (Berg 1957). On the other hand, the Finnish version went so far as to re-edit the opening C O P E N H A G E N visual sequence into Finnish. The Esperanto Society of Denmark requested a version in the international language, but was turned down due to lack of funds (Esperantistforeningen 1959). Incongruously, Moscow had to make do with the American English version (Hauerslev 1960). As late as 1969, *A City Called Copenhagen* was one of a batch of nine Danish *kulturfilm* which were shipped to Tokyo and dubbed into Japanese in order to support the Danish Embassy's presence at the Osaka World Fair of 1970; Roos travelled to oversee the voiceover recordings (Johansen 1968).

The success of *A City Called Copenhagen* garnered invitations from a reported eight countries worldwide to give their capital cities 'the Roos Touch' (Rif 1962). Roos chose to follow up his Danish city symphony with films about Hamburg and Oslo. In response to these new projects, and in a somewhat back-handed compliment, the author and cultural commentator Klaus Rifbjerg commented that Roos was becoming typecast in the role of short city-film director, and wondered what had happened to this artist's encounter with his subject par excellence:

> I don't know if we ought to expect this work to renew documentary film. I only know that one ought to expect something essentially new from Jørgen Roos, who is one of our best, most artistically convincing documentarists and equipped with the best eye. We're still waiting. (Rif 1962)

'THE FUTURE'S ALREADY HERE': DANSK KULTURFILM'S HIGH-WATER MARK

As reported in Chapter 2, interviewed just before the premiere of *A City Called Copenhagen*, Jørgen Roos had the confidence in himself and in his chosen art form to assert that short films were not a 'springboard' to feature filmmaking, at least not for him. 'The short film', he insisted, 'ought to be held in the same high esteem as short stories and poems, which no-one would claim were less meaningful than novels' (Vest 1959).

In his many and varied contributions to the work of Dansk Kulturfilm and other agencies, as cameraman, editor and director, Roos himself had played a crucial role in consolidating the short non-fiction film as a respected artform in Denmark and beyond. But the future, as the voiceover of *A City Called Copenhagen* comments, was 'already here'; by the early 1960s, television was superseding narrow-gauge film as the medium of communication between state and citizens. And in its transition towards the status of respected cinema art, the Danish short film required a different kind of commissioning model for the new decade, as outlined in Chapter 8. The film's conviction that 'the future's already here' points us forward, too, to the present day. *A City Called Copenhagen* is only available to us today in a legible colour palette by dint of digital colour adjustment techniques. As the film closes with the energetic din of screaming schoolchildren running past the camera, we are catapulted into the film's digital afterlife and back into the online archive's interface – a condition of possibility for our engagement with the films in this book, which we now turn to consider more closely.

CONCLUSION

The 'making of' any enterprise – films, skyscrapers, facts, political meetings, initiation rituals, haute couture, cooking – offers a view that is sufficiently different from the official one. Not only does it lead you backstage and introduce you to the skills and knacks of practitioners, it also provides a rare glimpse of what it is for a thing to emerge out of inexistence.

(Latour 2005: 89)

This book has examined the 'making of' two of the enterprises on this list of Latour's: films and facts. As he suggests, digging into the processes from which such apparently self-evident entities emerge illuminates the contributions of practitioners and actants of various kinds. With the ANT principles outlined in Chapter 3 in mind, the film case studies have tried to trace how human and non-human interventions shaped each film from commissioning to screening. The facts which the films exist to promulgate emerge as such from the coalescence of material and social factors imbricated in their planning, production and distribution. And while the informational film itself exists to make objects and practices loquacious (Latour 2005: 79) by rendering them unfamiliar anew, our case studies have used production files and other sources to make the films 'talk'.

If a film is a 'condensed bit of a network' of 'hetereogenous relationships' (Gershon 2010: 164), the cases studied have tried to show how that condensing occurs, how the network crystallises. However, in theory, the network that results in and from an informational film is infinite; it could be explored further and in different directions. In closing, I want to suggest three further sets of artefacts in the network of Danish informational films that could be made to 'talk', *pace* the vagaries and constraints of research funding, requisite expertise and publishers' word limits.

MULTIPLE LANGUAGE VERSIONS

From Arthur Elton's time at MFU onwards, an important aspect of filmic strategy was to use voiceover and avoid dialogue in films earmarked for export. This was to simplify the translation process, obviating the need for dubbing, cuts or subtitles. While not all foreign-language versions and soundtracks of films have been preserved in the DFI's film archive, most production files include any translations of voiceover and some publicity materials. My own language competence is limited to English, French and the Scandinavian languages; while I was able to check a selection of translations for obvious textual alterations and found no dramatic revisions, the possibility remains that some foreign-language versions of films contain non-trivial mistranslations, additions, cultural equivalences or omission of linguistic content to synergise with on-screen content. Comparison across language versions and/or between manuscripts and surviving cuts would entail painstaking work by language and translation specialists; it might well reveal that such interventions could result in a substantive impact on the 'facts' produced by the film in specific cultural and historical contexts.

THE DIGITAL *DISPOSITIF*

Uppermost in many of the production files for Dansk Kulturfilm and MFU projects is a pro-forma withdrawing the film from circulation. Often, these date from the 1970s or 1980s, indicating that the films remained available for hire from Statens Filmcentral decades after the dissolution of Dansk Kulturfilm. By the 1980s, the items being withdrawn are often on VHS format, testifying to the enduring appeal of films which outlived the 16mm-based distribution system for which they were originally designed. Concomitantly, given the need to continue distributing the back catalogue of informational film, Statens Filmcentral also outlived its sibling institutions, to the extent that most film-specific production files were absorbed into its archival holdings, regardless of whether the films in question were originally commissioned or produced by Dansk Kulturfilm or MFU.

The name of Statens Filmcentral lives on in that of a new-generation documentary and short film exhibition service launched in 2014, Filmcentralen (www.filmcentralen.dk). In line with its predecessor, the contemporary Filmcentralen is primarily for registered users in educational contexts, but some films are available to stream freely. That the purpose of film preservation is to exhibit the films, and vice versa, was a mantra of Henri Langlois, the founder of the Cinémathèque française. Inspired by Langlois, *Preserve then Show* is the title of an anthology of essays published by the Danish Film Institute in 2002 (Nissen *et al.* 2002), at a time when the Institute had just carried out a comprehensive condition survey of its film archive and was helping to pioneer new digital preservation and restoration techniques such as that used to restore *A City Called Copenhagen*. Since that time, the DFI has continued to innovate, not least as regards the 'show' part of the equation. Its rich online resource *Carl Th. Dreyer: The Man and his Work* (carlthdreyer.dk, 2010) and the more recent participatory film geo-tagging project *Danmark på film* (www.danmarkpaafilm.dk, 2016) both exploit film streaming technology to make, respectively, Dreyer's informational films and orphan and amateur film available to anyone with internet access. The back catalogue of short and *novellefilm* produced under the auspices of New Danish Screen is freely available at <http://www.dfi-film.dk/nds-frontpage>.

All these sites make the kinds of films discussed in this book available in a new *dispositif*, a new technologically mediated encounter with the viewer (Fossati 2011: 127–8) that extends their circulation far beyond the 'withdrawn from circulation' message in the production files. If the end of cinema (Mulvey 2006; Usai 2001) is the critical foundation for an exploration of 'useful' films, another condition of possibility of such work is digital storage, restoration and exhibition. As Fossati insists, we find ourselves caught in a moment of hybridity and translation from analogue to digital, but 'with no real sense of the destination, we have a unique (and uniquely limited) point of view' (Fossati 2011: 14). Over the next few years, the state of the art in the digital mediation of Danish mid-twentieth-century informational film will be a revealing gauge of the possibilities and limitations of this moment.

The Impact of Informational Films

For a British scholar schooled in the necessity of tracking and evaluating the academic and non-academic impact of research, a surprising aspect of Dansk Kulturfilm's work was the absence of any substantial or consistent efforts to evaluate the social, economic or cultural effects of its film productions. To be sure, some production files include film review clippings, letters from happy customers passed on via the Foreign Ministry's Press Bureau and other diplomatic networks, and other anecdotal and incidental feedback. Statens Filmcentral's annual reports detail number of hires per film broken down into categories of organisation, with an estimated average number of viewers per hire. In the same reports, box office figures for the feature films with which *forfilm* were paired estimate audience numbers, but without taking into account any likely discrepancy between attendance during or attention to the *forfilm* versus the feature. What such figures cannot begin to tell us is what kind of impression the films made at an individual level, or on a statistically significant scale. For example, how many teenagers did Theodor Christensen's *Hvad skal jeg være?* (see Chapter 7) persuade to approach their careers advisor? Did *People's Holiday* (see Chapter 5) substantively influence the development of holiday pay legislation in Britain? We know, for example, that sales of Scandinavian furniture increased exponentially in the USA in the wake of the touring exhibition at which *Shaped by Danish Hands* was screened (see Chapter 8), but how could the impact of the film itself ever be teased out of such data – and does it make sense to do so? Developing meaningful quantitative and qualitative approaches to the socio-economic and other impacts of informational film would sharpen our understanding not just of the reception of this kind of media, but also of ways to argue for the cultural value of the Arts and Humanities more generally. That such analysis never explicitly crystallised as part of the remit of Dansk Kulturfilm, MFU or Statens Filmcentral speaks to the implicit and intrinsic value accorded to *kulturfilm* in its heyday in Denmark. In the burgeoning social-democratic welfare state, culture was its own end.

REFERENCES

Explanatory notes:
1. *This book draws on many primary materials archived by the Danish Film Institute, Copenhagen. The location of archival materials is indicated as follows: Author, document description/title, date, sub-folder(s) (where applicable), case file, archive collection, location (usually DFI).*
2. *The list is alphabetised according to the Danish alphabet, i.e. 'æ', 'ø' and 'å' come after 'z'.*

Achton Schmidt, I. (1968), [letter to Bent Barfod], 2.12.1968, Distribution, Noget om Norden, Filmsager, SFC, DFI.
Aften- og Ungdomskolen (1960), 'Idrætten under debat', *Aften- og Ungdomskolen*, 5.11.1960, p. 290, Enden på legen, Filmsager, SFC, DFI.
Alsted, C. (1979), *Ministeriernes Filmudvalg 1941–1946*, Speciale (Magisterkonferens), Institut for Filmvidenskab, Københavns Universitet.
Andersen, K. P. (2010), 'Toftegaard Bio, København', Biografmuseet, <http://www.biografmuseet.dk/news/2011/baaring/index.htm> (accessed 1 June 2013).
Anderson, B. (1991), *Imagined Communities: Reflections on the Origin and Spread of Nationalism*, rev. edn, London: Verso.
Andersson, J., and M. Hilson (2009), 'Images of Sweden and the Nordic Countries', *Scandinavian Journal of History*, 34:3, pp. 219–28, doi:10.1080/03468750903134681.
'Angligården' (n.d.), Heart Museum, <http://www.heartmus.dk/om-heart/omradet-omkring-heart/angligaarden.html> (accessed 25 December 2016).
Anonymous [probably A. Elton] (n.d.), 'Diverse materiale ... socialfilm', Filmsager, SFC, DFI.
Anonymous [possibly Mogens Skot-Hansen] (1946), [letter to Ole Palsbo], 13.6.1946, Korrespondance og noter vedr. forløbet, Health for Denmark, Filmsager, SFC, DFI.
Anonymous (1948a), 'Kunstfilm fra seks lande', *BT*, 8.6.1948, Kunstfilm kasse, Udklipsarkivet, DFI.

Anonymous (1948b), 'To film om kunst', *Nationaltidende*, 14.11.1948, Kunstfilm kasse, Udklipsarkivet, DFI.

Anonymous (1949), 'En store Farvefilm om de nordiske Lande', *Kristeligt Dagblad*, 10.8.1949, Noget om Norden MFU 1956/57, Filmsager, SFC, DFI.

Anonymous (195?), 'Film og Museer', *Berlingske Aftenavis*, 2.11.195?, Kunstfilm kasse, Udklipsarkivet, DFI.

Anonymous (1951), [article on Børge Høst article in SFC newsletter], 8.10.1951, *Østsjællands Folkeblad*, Kunstfilm kasse, Udklipsarkivet, DFI.

Anonymous (1952), 'Så kommer kunstfilmene igen', *Social-Demokraten*, 8.10.52(?), Kunstfilm kasse, Udklipsarkivet, DFI.

Anthony, S. (2011), 'The Future's in the Air: Imperial Airways and the British Documentary Film Movement', *Journal of British Cinema and Television*, 8: 3, pp. 301–21, doi:10.3366/jbctv.2011.0041.

Arbejdsministeriet (1946), [Letter to Søren Melson], 27.12.1946, Korrespondance og noter vedr. forløbet, Socialfilm (engelsk version), Filmsager, SFC, DFI.

Arbejds- og Socialministeriet (1945), [memorandum to MFU], 14.8.1945, Diverse materiale v/ korrespondance, økonomi, materiale og forevisning af alle fem social-film, Socialfilmene, Filmsager, SFC, DFI.

Art (1963), 'Erstatningskrav mod staten efter kortfilm i fjernsynet', *Ekstrabladet*, n.d., Enden på legen, Filmsager, SFC, DFI.

'Avanceret jazzteater på Alléscenen søndag' (1966), *Berlingske Tidende*, 20.1.1966, Præsentation, Herning 65, Filmsager, SFC, DFI.

Bang Carlsen, J. (2014), 'Togene ruller i alle retninger bort fra Fredericia', *Kosmorama*, 254, <http://www.kosmorama.org/Artikler/Togene-ruller.aspx>.

Barfod, B. (1954), 'Norden: En tegnefilm om Samarbejde og Fællesskab', Manuskripter og materiale, Noget om Norden MFU 1956/57, Filmsager, SFC, DFI.

Barker, J. (2009), *The Tactile Eye: Touch and the Cinematic Experience*, Berkeley: University of California Press.

Baudry, J.-L. (1986), 'Ideological effects of the basic cinematographic apparatus', trans Alan Williams, in P. Rosen (ed.), *Narrative, Apparatus, Ideology*, New York: Columbia University Press, pp. 286–98.

Beddington, J. (1945), [letter to Mogens Skot-Hansen], 10.8.1945, Diverse materiale v/ korrespondance, økonomi, materiale og forevisning af alle fem socialfilm, Socialfilmene, Filmsager, SFC, DFI.

Benjamin, W. (1999), 'Theses on the Philosophy of History', in Walter Benjamin, *Illuminations*, ed. H. Arendt, trans. H. Zorn, London: Verso.

Benoit-Lévy, J. (1949), [letter to Ib Koch-Olsen], 24.6.1949, Distribution og FN sponsorship, They Guide You Across/Sikkerhed i Luften, Filmsager, SFC, DFI.

Benzon, J. (1961), [Udenrigsministeriet, letter to DKF], 20.3.1961, Korrespondance og notater, A City Called Copenhagen, Filmsager, SFC, DFI.

Berg, O. (1957), [minutes of a meeting at Københavns Rådhus], 30.10.57, Korrespondance og notater, A City Called Copenhagen, Filmsager, SFC, DFI.

Berggreen, O. (1950), [letter to Agnar Hølaas], 26.10.1950?, Korrespondance og notater vedr. forløbene, Socialfilm (danske versioner) ('The Seventh Age og Health for Danmark'), SFC, DFI.

Bhabha, H. K. (1994), *The Location of Culture*, London: Routledge.

Billig, M. (1995), *Banal Nationalism*, London: Sage

Bjørn, C. (2000), 'Modern Denmark: a synthesis of converging developments', *Scandinavian Journal of History*, 25: 1–2, pp. 119–30.

Boisen, I. (n.d.), [introductory remarks for film screening], Ingolf Boisen særsamling, Det Danske Filminstitut.

Boisen, I. (1949), [handwritten letter to Ib Koch-Olsen], 14.5.1949, Distribution og FN sponsorship, They Guide You Across/Sikkerhed i Luften, Filmsager, SFC, DFI.

Boisen, I. (1950), [letter to Ib Koch-Olsen], 6.5.1950, Distribution og FN sponsorship, They Guide You Across/Sikkerhed i Luften, Filmsager, SFC, DFI.

Boisen, I. (1977), *Klip fra en filmmands liv*, Copenhagen: Nyt Nordisk Forlag.

Bondebjerg, I. (2012), *Virkelighedsbilleder: den moderne danske dokumentarfilm*, København: Samfundslitteratur.

Borish, S. M. (2004), *The Land of the Living: The Danish Folk High Schools and Denmark's Non-Violent Path to Modernization*, Miami: Blue Dolphin Press.

Brandt, M. (1961), 'Festlig Berlinale', *Biograf-Bladet*, 1961/8, pp. 208, 216–17, Enden på legen, Filmsager, SFC, DFI.

Breen, M. P. (1978), 'The rhetoric of the short film', *Journal of the University Film Association*, 30: 3, pp. 3–13, <http://www.jstor.org/stable/20687433>.

Browning, C. (2015), 'Small-state identities: promotions past and present', in L. Clerc, N. Glover and P. Jordan (eds), *Histories of Public Diplomacy and Nation-Branding in the Nordic and Baltic Countries: Representing the Periphery*, Leiden: Brill, pp. 281–300.

Brunetta, G. (2009), *The History of Italian Cinema: A Guide to Italian Film from its Origins to the Twenty-First Century*, trans Jeremy Parzen, Princeton: Princeton University Press.

B.T. (1961), 'Dansk chok, tyske gisp', *B.T.*, [no date/issue number], Enden på legen, Filmsager, SFC, DFI.

Bü (1968), [note re. distribution], 18.11.1968, Økonomi, Noget om Norden, Filmsager, SFC, DFI.

Burgess, C. (2010), 'Sixty years of Shell film sponsorship, 1934–94', *Journal of British Cinema and Television*, 7: 2, pp. 213–31.

Canjels, R. (2009), 'Films from beyond the well: a historical overview of Shell films', in V. Hediger and P. Vonderau (eds), *Films That Work: Industrial Film and the Productivity of Media*, Amsterdam: Amsterdam University Press, pp. 243–55.

Chow, P. (2016), 'A symptom of something real: the Øresund Region on film and television, 1999–2014', PhD Dissertation, University College London.

Christensen, T. (1942), [letter to M. Skot-Hansen], 25.4.1942, Gammelt Metal – Nye Varer, Filmsager, SFC, DFI.

Christensen, T. (1947a), [letter to Ib Koch-Olsen], 3.11.1947, Optagelser i Hamburg, Her er Banerne, Filmsager, SFC, DFI.

Christensen, T. (1947b), 'Vedr. Optagelserne til Her er banerne', Korrespondance, Her er Banerne, Filmsager, SFC, DFI.

Christensen, T. (1947c), [letter to Ib Koch-Olsen], 25.3.1947, Diverse Korrespondance, Her er Banerne, Filmsager, SFC, DFI.

Christensen, T. (1947d), 'HER ER BANERNE eller VI ER BANERNE', 4.6.1947, Diverse Korrespondance, Her er Banerne, Filmsager, SFC, DFI.

Christensen, T. (1948), 'RESPONSUM vedr. *Thorvaldsen*', 5 January, Manuskripter, Thorvaldsen, Filmsager, Statens Filmcentral særsamling, DFI.

Christensen, T. (1950), '"Mermaids and Horsepowers" (Working Title)', Marshall, 1956, Opgivne film – 1957 m.m., 1592 Dansk Kulturfilm, emneordnede sager, Rigsarkivet.

Christensen, T. (1954), 'Hvad skal jeg være? En kortfilm om erhvervsvalget. Drejebog sept.–okt. 1954', Manuskripter og materiale, Hvad skal jeg være?, Filmsager, SFC, DFI.

Christensen, T. (1958), 'Hvad skal der ske med Dansk Kulturfilm?', *Kosmorama*, 32, pp. 107–8, <http://video.dfi.dk/Kosmorama/magasiner/TheodorChristensen/Kosmorama32-p107-108-ocr.pdf> (accessed 15 January 2017).

Christensen, T., and K. Roos (1936), *FILM*, København: Levin & Munksgaard.

Christenson, L. (2002), 'Marshall Plan Films at National Archives', Marshall Foundation, <http://marshallfoundation.org/library/wp-content/uploads/sites/16/2014/07/Marshall-Plan-Films-Listing.pdf> (accessed 7 January 2017).

Clerc, L., and N. Glover (2015), 'Representing the small states of Northern Europe: between imagined and imaged communities', in L. Clerc, N. Glover and P. Jordan (eds), *Histories of Public Diplomacy and Nation-Branding in the Nordic and Baltic Countries: Representing the Periphery*, Leiden: Brill, pp. 3–22.

C.o.p. (1948), [meeting report], 11.12.1948, Korrespondance og notater angående forløbet, Biblioteket er åbent, Filmsager, SFC, DFI.

Couldry, N. (2008), 'Actor network theory and media: do they connect and on what terms?', in A. Hepp, F. Krotz, S. Moores and C. Winter (eds), *Connectivity, Networks and Flows: Conceptualizing Contemporary Communications*, Cresskill: Hampton Press, Inc., pp. 93–110.

Craig, C. (1996), *Out of History. Narrative Paradigms in Scottish and British Culture*, Edinburgh: Polygon.

Culler, J. (1999), 'Anderson and the novel', *Diacritics*, 29: 4 'Grounds of comparison. Around the work of Benedict Anderson', pp. 20–39.

Dam, B. (n.d.a), 'Statens Filmcentral (1938–1997)', *Filminstitutionernes historie*, Danish Film Institute, <http://www.dfi.dk/FaktaOmFilm/Filminstitutionernes-historie/Institutionerne/Statens-Filmcentral.aspx> (accessed 22 June 2013).

Dam, B. (n.d.b), 'Filmfonden (1964–1972)', *Filminstitutionernes historie*, Filmdatabasen, Det Danske Filminstitut, <http://www.dfi.dk/FaktaOmFilm/Filminstitutionernes-historie/Institutionerne/Filmfonden.aspx> (accessed 25 December 2016).

Danmarks Statistik (2000), *Befolkningen i 150 år*, Copenhagen: Danmarks Statistik.

Danske Erhvervs Jern- og Metalindsamling (1942), Møderefererat, 12.3.1942, Gammelt Metal – Nye Varer, Filmsager, SFC, DFI.

Dansk Folkeoplysnings Samråd (1955), [letter to Dansk Kulturfilm], 1.4.1955, Korrespondance vedr. produktion, Enden på legen, Filmsager, SFC, DFI.

Dansk Kulturfilm (n.d.), 'Súngorniásaungauna?', Manuskripter og materiale, Hvad skal jeg være?, Filmsager, SFC, DFI.

Dansk Kulturfilm (1933), *Love for Dansk Kulturfilm*, Copenhagen.

Dansk Kulturfilm (1949a), 'Pressemeddelelse: Filmen om atlanterhavsflyvningens sikkerhedstjeneste får urpremiere i Edinburgh', 2.9.1949, Økonomi, They Guide You Across/Sikkerhed i Luften, Filmsager, SFC, DFI.

Dansk Kulturfilm (1949b), *Dansk Kulturfilm og Ministeriernes Filmudvalg. Beretning for finansårene 1947–48 og 1948–49*, Copenhagen.

Dansk Kulturfilm (1952), *Dansk Kulturfilm og Ministeriernes Filmudvalg. Beretning for finansåret 1951–52*, Copenhagen.

Dansk Kulturfilm (1953), *Dansk Kulturfilm og Ministeriernes Filmudvalg. Beretning for finansåret 1952–53*, Copenhagen.

Dansk Kulturfilm (1955), 'Pressemeddelelse: Film om erhvervsvejledning', 16.9.1955, Korrespondance og notater vedr. forløbet, Hvad skal jeg være?, Filmsager, SFC, DFI.

Dansk Kulturfilm (1959), [uddrag af bestyrelsesreferat], 12.1.1959, Korrespondance vedr. produktion, Enden på legen, Filmsager, SFC, DFI.

Dansk Kulturfilm (1966), *Dansk Kulturfilm, Ministeriernes Filmudvalg, Statens Filmcentral: Kortfilmproduktionen 1965–66*, Copenhagen.

Dansk Kulturfilm og Ministeriernes Filmudvalg (1949), *Beretning for finansårene 1947–48 og 1948–49*, Copenhagen.

Dansk Kulturfilm og Ministeriernes Filmudvalg (1952), *Beretning for finansåret 1951–52*. Copenhagen.

D.D.S.G. & I. (De Danske Skytte-, Gymnastik- og Idrætsforeninger) (1960), '370.000 medlemmer ved 100 års-dagen', *Dansk Idræt*, 1960/10, p. 3, Enden på legen, Filmsager, SFC, DFI.

Derrida, J. (1996), *Archive Fever: A Freudian Impression*, trans. Eric Prenowitz, Chicago: University of Chicago Press.

Det Danske Luftfartsselskab (1948), [letter to Ib Koch-Olsen], 11.2.1948, Distribution og FN sponsorship, They Guide You Across/Sikkerhed i Luften, Filmsager, SFC, DFI.

Dreyer, Carl Th. (1945), [letter to Mogens Skot-Hansen], Korrespondance og notater vedr. Forløbet, The Seventh Age, Socialfilm (engelsk version), SFC, DFI.

Dreyer, Carl Th. (1947a), 'Thorvaldsen's Kunst', Manuscripter, Thorvaldsen, Filmsager, SFC, DFI.

Dreyer, Carl Th. (1947b) [letter to Ib Koch-Olsen], 12 November 1947, Manuskripter, Thorvaldsen, Filmsager, SFC, DFI.

Dreyer, Carl Th. (1947c), 'Storstrømsbroen. Synopsis', <http://www.carlthdreyer.dk/Filmene/Storstroemsbroen/Indspilningen.aspx> (accessed 8 July 2013).

Dreyer, Carl Th. (1951a), [letter to Ib Koch-Olsen], 7.10.1951, Korrespondance og notater vedr. forløbet, Noget om Norden MFU 1956/57, Filmsager, SFC, DFI.

Dreyer, Carl Th. (1951b), 'En Film om nordisk Samarbejde', Manuskripter og materiale, Noget om Norden – MFU 1956/57, Filmsager, SFC, DFI.

Drouzy, M. (1982), *Kildemateriale til en biografi om Carl Th. Dreyer*, Copenhagen: Københavns Universitet, Institut for Filmviddenskab.

Druick, Z. (2011), 'UNESCO, film and education: mediating postwar paradigms of communication', in Charles R. Acland and Haidee Wasson (eds), *Useful Cinema*, Durham: Duke University Press, pp. 81–102.

Drum, J., and D. Drum (2000), *My Only Great Passion: The Life and Films of Carl Th. Dreyer*, Lanham: Scarecrow Press.

Dupin, C. (2006), 'The postwar transformation of the British Film Institute and its impact on the development of a national film culture in Britain', *Screen*, 47: 4, pp. 443–51.

Durrance, T. (1949), [letter to Paul Geleff, Udenrigsministeriet], 25.11.1949, 'De første forhandlinger med IKO hhv Hølaas i efteråret og vinteren 1949–50', Emneordnede sager, 1592 Dansk Kulturfilm, Rigsarkivet.

Dymling, C. (1957), [letter to SFC], 21.2.1957, Distribution, Noget om Norden, Filmsager, SFC, DFI.

Ebbesen, S. (1948), [letter to Karl Bure, Udenrigsministeriets Pressebureau], 27.7.1948, Korrespondance og notater vedr. Forløbet, The Seventh Age, Socialfilm (engelsk version), SFC, DFI.

Educational Film Library Association, Inc. (n.d.), 'Comments on SOMETHING ABOUT THE NORTH from the Jurors of the American Film Festival', Versioner – Skandinavien, Noget om Norden – Versioner, Filmsager, SFC, DFI.

EIFF (Edinburgh International Film Festival) (1950), 'Festival Press Digest', Edinburgh Film Guild Archive.

EIFF (1960), 'Opening Gala Performance', Edinburgh Film Guild Archive.

Ekstrabladet (1953), 'Ny dansk film om kunsthåndværk?', 8.12.1953, Udvikling, Shaped by Danish Hands, Filmsager, SFC, DFI.

Elsaesser, T. (2005), *European Cinema: Face to Face with Hollywood*, Amsterdam: Amsterdam University Press.

Elsaesser, T. (2009), 'Archives and archaeologies: the place of non-fiction film in contemporary media', in V. Hediger and P. Vonderau (eds), *Films That Work: Industrial Film and the Productivity of Media*, Amsterdam, Amsterdam University Press, pp. 19–34.

Elton, A. (n.d.), 'Notes and terms of reference for the film on the Danish holiday system', People's Holiday, Socialfilmene, Filmsager, SFC, DFI.

Elton, A. (1945a), [letter to Terkel Terkelsen], 30.7.1945, Diverse materiale v/ korrespondance, økonomi, materiale og forevisning af alle fem socialfilm, Socialfilmene, Filmsager, SFC, DFI.

Elton, A. (1945b), 'The production of a film or films on the social institutions of Denmark', Diverse materiale v/ korrespondance, økonomi, materiale og forevisning af alle fem socialfilm, Socialfilmene, Filmsager, SFC, DFI.

Elton, A. (1945c), [letter to Mogens Skot-Hansen], 10.8.1945, Diverse materiale v/ korrespondance, økonomi, materiale og forevisning af alle fem socialfilm, Socialfilmene, Filmsager, SFC, DFI.

Elton, A. (1945d), [letter to Mogens Skot-Hansen], 3.10.1945, Diverse materiale v/ korrespondance, økonomi, materiale og forevisning af alle fem socialfilm, Socialfilmene, Filmsager, SFC, DFI.

Elton, A. (1946a), [memo on Dreyer's manuscript for *The Seventh Age*], Korrespondance og notater vedr. Forløbet, The Seventh Age, Socialfilm (engelsk version), SFC, DFI.

Elton, A. (1947), [letter to Ib Koch-Olsen], 13.12.1947, Optagelser i Hamburg, Her er Banerne, Filmsager, SFC, DFI.

Elton, A. (1948), 'Introduction', in Ebbe Neergaard (ed.), *Documentary in Denmark: One Hundred Films of Facts in War, Occupation, Liberation, Peace. 1940–1948.* Copenhagen: Statens Filmcentral, pp. 5–11.

Elton, A., and P. Brinson (1950), *The Film Industry in Six European Countries. A detailed study of the film industry in Denmark as compared with that in Norway, Sweden, Italy, France and the United Kingdom, etc.* Press Film and Radio in the World today. Paris: UNESCO.

Elvius, M. (1966), [letter to Minerva Film and Angli A/S], Løse papirer, Herning 65, Filmsager, SFC, DFI.

'En film om en fabrik' (1966), *Silkeborg Avis*, 22.1.1966, Løse papirer, Herning 65, Filmsager, SFC, DFI.

Esperantistforeningen for Danmark (1959), [letter to Overborgsmesterens Kontor], 13.1.1959, 'Japansk version', A City Called Copenhagen, Filmsager, SFC, DFI.

Fabjancic, M., and C. Nørrested (eds) (1984), *Statens kortfilm. Register over danske statslige kortfilm indtil 1980*, København, CA Reitzels forlag.

Filmdatabasen (Dansk Filminstitut) (n.d.), 'Gunnar Wangel 1912–1954', <http://www.dfi.dk/faktaomfilm/person/da/128768.aspx?id=128768> (accessed 31 January 2017).

Filmrådet (1965), [letter confirming funding for Herning 65], 19.2.1965, Økonomi, Herning 65, Filmsager, SFC, DFI.

Films of the Nations (1954), *Catalogue 1954*, New York: Films of the Nations Distributors, Inc., Shaped by Danish Hands, Filmsager, SFC, DFI.

fn (1958a), [memo from 'fn' dated 19.11.1958], Korrespondance og notater, A City Called Copenhagen, Filmsager, SFC, DFI.

fn (1958b), [note from 'fn' dated 27.11.1958], Korrespondance og notater, A City Called Copenhagen, Filmsager, SFC, DFI.

fn (1958c), [note from 'fn' dated 15.12.1958 minuting SFC meeting with Jørgen Roos], Korrespondance og notater, A City Called Copenhagen, Filmsager, SFC, DFI.

Foreningen Norden (2016), 'Om Foreningen', <http://www.norden.no/om-foreningen/> (accessed 19 January 2017).

Fossat, S. B. (2010), 'Karoline-ko undfanget i propagandafilm', Videnskab.dk, <http://videnskab.dk/kultur-samfund/karoline-ko-blev-undfanget-i-propagandafilm> (accessed 7 January 2017).

Fossati, G. (2011) [2009], *From Grain to Pixel: The Archival Life of Film in Transition*, Amsterdam: Amsterdam University Press.

Friis, H. (1947), [letter to Koch-Olsen], 10.5.1947, Diverse materiale, Socialfilmene, Filmsager, SFC, DFI.

Friis, H. (1958), [letter to SFC], 5.2.1958, Diverse korrespondance og notater vedr. de forskellige film, Diverse materiale ... socialfilm, Filmsager, SFC, DFI.

GCMF (The George C. Marshall Foundation) (n.d.), 'Marshall Plan Films', <http://marshallfoundation.org/library/collection/marshall-plan-films/#!/collection=635> (accessed 8 January 2017).

Gellner, E. (1983), Nations and Nationalism, New York: Cornell University Press.

Gershon, I. (2010), 'Bruno Latour, 1947–', in J. Simons (ed.), From Agamben to Zizek: Contemporary Critical Theory, Edinburgh: Edinburgh University Press, pp. 161–76.

Gershon, I., and J. Malitsky (2010), 'Actor-network theory and documentary studies', Studies in Documentary Film, 4: 1, pp. 65–78, doi:10.1386/sdf.4.1.65_1.

Greenblatt, S. (2010), 'A mobility studies manifesto', in S. Greenblatt (ed.), Cultural Mobility, Cambridge: Cambridge University Press, pp. 250–3.

Gress, E. (1959), [letter to Werner Pedersen], 11.2.1959, Versioner – Skandinavien, Noget om Norden – Versioner, Filmsager, SFC, DFI.

Grierson, J. (1966a) [1947], 'First principles of documentary', in F. Hardy (ed.), John Grierson on Documentary, Berkeley and Los Angeles: University of California Press, pp. 145–56.

Grierson, J. (1966b) [1947], 'The course of realism', in F. Hardy (ed.), John Grierson on Documentary, Berkeley and Los Angeles: University of California Press, pp. 199–211.

Grierson, J. (1979a), 'The E.M.B. Film Unit', in F. Hardy (ed.), Grierson on Documentary, London: Faber & Faber, pp. 47–51.

Grierson, J. (1979b), 'Documentary: A world perspective', in F. Hardy (ed.), Grierson on Documentary, London: Faber & Faber, pp. 203–24.

Guldberg, J. (2011), '"Scandinavian Design" as discourse: the exhibition Design in Scandinavia, 1954–57', Design Issues, 27: 2, pp. 41–58.

Haastrup, L. (2003), 'Grethe Philip (1916–2016)', Kvinfo, <http://www.kvinfo.dk/side/170/bio/1749/> (accessed 14 January 2017).

Haines, R. (2013), Technicolor Movies: The History of Dye Transfer Printing, Jefferson: McFarland & Co.

Harding, M., and E. Hiort (n.d.), 'Viggo Sten Møller', Dansk Biografisk Leksikon, 3. udg., Gyldendal 1979–84, <http://denstoredanske.dk/index.php?sideId=294759> (accessed 28 December 2016).

Hardy, F. (ca. 1947a), 'Denmark has thriving film movement today', Weekly Scotsman, D I, A: Vredens Dag, 145, Dreyer Archive, DFI.

Hardy, F. (1947b), 'Arts review', transcript of broadcast Wed. 29 January 1947, Scottish Home Service, D I, A: Vredens Dag, 145, Dreyer Archive, DFI.

Hardy, F. (1948), 'Denmark', Documentary 48, Edinburgh International Film Festival, pp. 16–18.

Hardy, F. (1949), 'Danish documentary', Documentary 49, Edinburgh International Film Festival, p. 18.

Hardy, F. (1966), 'Introduction', in F. Hardy (ed.), John Grierson on Documentary, Berkeley and Los Angeles: University of California Press, pp. 13–39.

Hardy, F. (1979a), 'Introduction', in F. Hardy (ed.), Grierson on Documentary, London: Faber & Faber, pp. 11–17.

Hardy, F. (ed.) (1979b), John Grierson: A Documentary Biography, London and Boston: Faber & Faber.

Hardy, F. (ed.) (1979c), John Grierson's Scotland, Edinburgh: The Ramsay Head Press.

Harvard, J., and P. Stadius (2016), 'A communicative perspective on the formation of the North: contexts, channels and concepts', in J. Harvard and P. Stadius (eds),

Communicating the North: Media Structures and Images in the Making of the Nordic Region, London: Routledge. (E-book)

Hasselbalch, H. (1947a), 'Stof tager Form', Shaped by Danish hands, Filmsager, SFC, DFI.

Hasselbalch, H. (1947b), 'Filmen om dansk Kunstindustri', Shaped by Danish hands, Filmsager, SFC, DFI.

Hauerslev, E. (1960), [letter to Kirsten Rode, Udenrigsministeriets Pressebureau], 27.6.1960, 'Korrespondance og notater', A City Called Copenhagen, Filmsager, SFC, DFI.

Hebo, T. (1960), [letter to Werner Pedersen], 25.4.1960, Korrespondance og noter vedr. produktion, Enden på legen, Filmsager, SFC, DFI.

Hediger, V., and P. Vonderau (2009), 'Introduction', in V. Hediger and P. Vonderau (eds), *Films That Work: Industrial Film and the Productivity of Media*, Amsterdam, Amsterdam University Press, pp. 9–16.

Hedling, E. (2015), 'The Battle of Dybbøl Revisited: the Danish Press reception of the TV-series *1864*', *Kosmorama*, 261, <http://www.kosmorama.org/ServiceMenu/05-English/Articles/1864.aspx>.

Helleskov Kleiner, A., and T. Heisz (2010), 'I dag er et trist jubilæum for dansk fodbold', *Politiken*, 16.7.2010, <http://politiken.dk/kultur/art4969588/I-dag-er-et-trist-jubil%C3%A6um-for-dansk-fodbold> (accessed 18 January 2017).

Hemsing, A. (1994), 'The Marshall Plan's European film unit, 1948–1955: a memoir and filmography', *Historical Journal of Film, Radio and Television*, 14, pp. 269–97.

Henningsen, P. (1968) [1933], *Hvad med Kulturen?*, København: Thaning & Appel.

Hertel, H. (1997), 'Da København blev moderne. Byens nye rum, kulturlivet og litteraturen 1917–60', in F. Lundgreen-Nielsen (ed.), *København læst og påskrevet. Hovedstaden som litterær kulturby*, Copenhagen: Museum Tusculanum, pp. 147–220.

Hertel, H. (2012), *PH – en biografi*, København: Gyldendal.

Higson, A. (1989), 'The concept of National Cinema', *Screen*, 30: 4, pp. 36–47, <https://doi-org.libproxy.ucl.ac.uk/10.1093/screen/30.4.36>.

'Historien om Heart' (n.d.), Heart Kunstmuseum, <http://www.heartmus.dk/om-heart/om-heart-1/historien-om-heart.html> (accessed 25 December 2016).

Hjort, M. (2000), 'Themes of Nation', in M. Hjort and S. MacKenzie (eds), *Cinema and Nation*, London: Routledge, pp. 103–18.

Hjort, M. (2005), *Small Nation, Global Cinema: The New Danish Cinema*, Minneapolis: University of Minnesota Press.

Hjort, M. (2006), 'Gifts, games and cheek. Counter-globalisation in a privileged small-nation context. The case of *The Five Obstructions*', in C. Thomson (ed.), *Northern Constellations: New Readings in Nordic Cinema*, Norwich: Norvik Press, pp. 111–29.

Hjort, M. (ed.) (2013), *The Education of the Filmmaker in Africa, the Middle East, and the Americas*, New York: Palgrave Macmillan.

Hjort, M., and U. Lindqvist (eds) (2016), *A Companion to Nordic Cinema*, London and New York: Wiley-Blackwell.

Hjort, M., and S. MacKenzie (2000), 'Introduction', in M. Hjort and S. MacKenzie (eds), *Cinema and Nation*, London: Routledge, pp. 1–16.

Hjort, M., and D. Petrie (2007), 'Introduction', in M. Hjort and D. Petrie (eds), *The Cinema of Small Nations*, Edinburgh: Edinburgh University Press, pp. 1–22.

Hjort Eriksen, S. (1948), [letter to Ib Koch-Olsen], 30.10.1948, Korrespondance og notater angående forløbet, Biblioteket er åbent, Filmsager, SFC, DFI.

Hjorth Nielsen, U. (n.d.), 'Bent Barfod', *Den Store Danske*, Copenhagen: Gyldendal, <http://denstoredanske.dk/index.php?sideId=44108> (accessed 18 January 2017).

Hoffmann, L. (2017), 'OBS: Historie', DR, <http://www.dr.dk/DR1/OBS/historie.htm> (accessed 30 April 2017).

H. St. (1973), 'Dansk Films Gode Ven', *Politiken*, 26.2.1973, Socialfilm, SFC, DFI.

Hvass, F. (1956), [letter to Udenrigsministeriet], 15.12.1956, Versioner – Skandinavien, Noget om Norden – Versioner, Filmsager, SFC, DFI.

Hvidberg-Hansen, G., and G. Oelsner (eds) (2011), *The Spirit of Vitalism: Health, Beauty and Strength in Danish Art, 1890–1940*, Copenhagen: Museum Tusculanum Press.

Hølaas, A. (1950), [letter to MFU], 29.11.1950, Korrespondance og notater vedr. forløbene, Socialfilm (danske versioner) ('The Seventh Age og Health for Danmark'), SFC, DFI.

Hølaas, A. (1951), [letter to A/S Johan Ankerstjerne], 10.3.1951, Diverse korrespondance, Thorvaldsen, Filmsager, SFC særsamling, DFI.

Hølaas, A. (1953), [letter to Grethe Philip], 16.12.1953, Korrespondance og notater vedr. forløbet, Hvad skal jeg være?, Filmsager, SFC, DFI.

Hølaas, A. (1954a), [letter to Dansk Kulturfilms Bestyrelse], 13.10.1954, Korrespondance og notater vedr. forløbet, Hvad skal jeg være?, Filmsager, SFC, DFI.

Hølaas, A. (1954b), [letter to Dansk Kulturfilms Bestyrelse], 6.11.1954, Korrespondance og notater vedr. forløbet, Hvad skal jeg være?, Filmsager, SFC, DFI.

Hølaas, A. (1954c), [letter to Mogens Lind], 14.7.1954, Korrespondance og notater vedr. forløbet, Noget om Norden MFU 1956/57, Filmsager, SFC, DFI.

Hølaas, A. (1955), [letter to SFC], 12.11.1955, Tysk version, They Guide You Across/ Sikkerhed i Luften, Filmsager, SFC, DFI.

Ivester, P. (n.d.), 'Guide to identifying color movie film stocks', *Paul's 16 mm Film Collecting Pages*, <http://www.paulivester.com/films/filmstock/guide.htm> (accessed 1 August 2015).

Jacobs, S. (2011), *Framing Pictures: Film and the Visual Arts*, Edinburgh: Edinburgh University Press.

Jakobsen, J. (2009), *Guld-Harald: Topscorer, idol, rebel*, Copenhagen: Gyldendal.

Jensen, Johannes V. (1944) [1917], 'Paa Motorcykel', *Nimbus Nyt*, 15–16, pp. 9–12, (Danish Film Institute, Dreyer Archive, D I, C: De nåede færgen, 1).

Jepsen, A. (1960), [letter to P. A. Tvede, Magistratens 1. Afdeling, Rådhuset], 22.1.1960, 'Præsentation af filmen om København', A City Called Copenhagen, Filmsager, SFC, DFI.

Jespersen, L. (2008a), 'Indledning', in E. Hansen and L. Jespersen (eds), *Samfundsplanlægning i 1950'erne: Tradition eller tilløb?* Administrationshistoriske studier 17, Copenhagen: Museum Tusculanums Forlag, pp. 9–26.

Jespersen, L. (2008b), 'Arbejdsmarkedsspørgsmål', in E. Hansen and L. Jespersen (eds), *Samfundsplanlægning i 1950'erne: Tradition eller tilløb?* Administrationshistoriske studier 17, Copenhagen: Museum Tusculanums Forlag, pp. 445–53.

J.L. (1966), 'Moseholms bekendtskaber', *Politiken*, 24.1.1966, Præsentation, Herning 65, Filmsager, DFC, DFI.

Johansen, K. (1953), [copy of letter from Danish Information Office], 3.3.1953, Diverse korrespondance, Thorvaldsen, Filmsager, SFC særsamling, DFI.

Johansen, K. (1968), [letter to SFC, 18.12.1968 re Japanese versions], 'Japansk version', A City Called Copenhagen, Filmsager, SFC, DFI.

Jones, M., and K. Olwig (eds) (2008), *Nordic Landscapes: Region and Belonging on the Northern Edge of Europe*, Minneapolis: University of Minnesota Press.

J.R. (1948), [report possibly by Jørgen Roos], 'Carl Th. Dreyer: "THORVALDSENS KUNST"', 6.3.1948, Manuscripter, Thorvaldsen, Filmsager, SFC, DFI.

Juul Andersen, I. (1946), [letter to Ib Koch-Olsen], December 1946, Indledning, Peter må vente, Filmsager, SFC, DFI.

'Kaptajn Jespersen laver dansk Film om Thorvaldsen' (1938), *Nyborg Social-Demokraten*, 25.8.1938, 'Aktuelt 1938–39–40', Palladium særsamling, DFI.

Kessler, F. (2006), 'The Cinema of Attractions as Dispositif', in W. Strauven (ed.), *The Cinema of Attractions Reloaded*, Amsterdam: Amsterdam University Press, pp. 57–69.

Kimergård, L. (n.d.a), 'Mødrehjælpen. Baggrund', *Carl Th. Dreyer – Liv og Værk*, Danish Film Institute, <http://www.carlthdreyer.dk/Filmene/Moedrehjaelpen/Baggrund.aspx> (accessed 8 July 2013).

Kimergård, L. (n.d.b), '*Thorvaldsen*: Background', *Carl Th. Dreyer: The Man and his Work*. Danish Film Institute, <http://english.carlthdreyer.dk/Films/Thorvaldsen/Background.aspx> (accessed 25 July 2014).

Kimergård, L. (1992), 'Carl Th. Dreyers kortfilmengagement i perioden 1942–1952', Cand. Phil. dissertation, University of Copenhagen.

Knuth, E. (1956), [letter to Udenrigsministeriet], 31.8.1956, Distribution, Noget om Norden, Filmsager, SFC, DFI.

Kobberrød Rasmussen, M. (2013), 'The Marshall films and the red short film gang', trans. Glen Garner, *Kosmorama*, 250, <http://www.kosmorama.org/ServiceMenu/05-English/Articles/The-Marshall-Films-and-the-Red-Short-Film-Gang.aspx>.

Koch-Olsen, I. (1947a), [memo on 'Kunstindustrifilmen'], 14.1.1947, Shaped by Danish Hands, Filmsager, SFC, DFI.

Koch-Olsen, I. (1947b), [letter to Viggo Sten Møller], 23.9.1947, Shaped by Danish Hands, Filmsager, SFC, DFI.

Koch-Olsen, I. (1947c), [letter to Viggo Sten Møller], 22.10.1947, Shaped by Danish Hands, Filmsager, SFC, DFI.

Koch-Olsen, I. (1947d), [letter to Generaldirektoratet for Statsbanerne], 11.6.1947, Økonomi, Her er Banerne, Filmsager, SFC, DFI.

Koch-Olsen, I. (1947e), [letter to Astrid Henning-Jensen], 8.10.1947, Indledning, Peter må vente, Filmsager, SFC, DFI.

Koch-Olsen, I. (1948a), [letter to Minerva film], 27.2.1948, Udvikling, Shaped by Danish Hands, Filmsager, SFC, DFI.

Koch-Olsen, I. (1948b), [letter to Hagen Hasselbalch], 19.5.1948, Udvikling, Shaped by Danish Hands, Filmsager, DFC, DFI.

Koch-Olsen, I. (1948c), [letter and telegram to Jean Benoit-Lévy, UNFB], 3.6.1948, Distribution og FN sponsorship, They Guide You Across/Sikkerhed i luften, Filmsager, SFC, DFI.

Koch-Olsen, I. (1948d), [letter to E. Hindahl], 3.4.1948, Diverse korrespondance, Her er Banerne, Filmsager, SFC, DFI.

Koch-Olsen, I. (1948e), [letter to Bodil M. Begtrup], 26.1.1948, Manuskripter, Peter må vente, Filmsager, SFC, DFI.

Koch-Olsen, I. (1949a), [letter to Paul Geleff, Udenrigsministeriet], 14.11.1949, 'De første forhandlinger med IKO hhv Hølaas i efteråret og vinteren 1949–50', Emneordnede sager, 1592 Dansk Kulturfilm, Rigsarkivet.

Koch-Olsen, I. (1949b), [letter to R. Lassen], 25.4.1949, Korrespondance og notater angående forløbet, Biblioteket er åbent, Filmsager, SFC, DFI.

Koch-Olsen, I. (1950), [letter to Minerva], 1.6.1950, Distribution og FN sponsorship, They Guide You Across/Sikkerhed i luften, Filmsager, SFC, DFI.

Koch-Olsen, I. (1951a), [note], 22.1.1951, Korrespondance og notater vedr. forløbene, Socialfilm (danske versioner) ('The Seventh Age og Health for Danmark'), SFC, DFI.

Koch-Olsen, I. (1951b), [note], 26.7.1951, Distribution og FNs Sponsorship, They Guide You Across/Sikkerhed i Luften, Filmsager, SFC, DFI.

Koch-Olsen, I. (1952a), [letter to Foreningen Norden i Danmark], 22.4.1952, Korrespondance og notater vedr. forløbet, Noget om Norden MFU 1956/57, Filmsager, SFC, DFI.

Koch-Olsen, I. (1952b), [letter to F. W. Wendt], 22.4.1952, Korrespondance og notater vedr. forløbet, Noget om Norden MFU 1956/57, Filmsager, SFC, DFI.

Koch-Olsen, I. (1953), [letter to Henrik Urne, chair of MFU], 30.12.1953, Korrespondance og notater, A City Called Copenhagen, Filmsager, SFC, DFI.

Koch-Olsen, I. (1954), [letter to H. P. Sørensen, Københavns Overborgmester], 18.2.1954, Korrespondance og notater, A City Called Copenhagen, Filmsager, SFC, DFI.

Koch-Olsen, I. (1955a), [letter to F. W. Wendt], 1.9.1955, Korrespondance og notater vedr. forløbet, Noget om Norden MFU 1956/57, Filmsager, SFC, DFI.

Koch-Olsen, I. (1955b), [note to Agnar Hølaas], 22.9.1955, Korrespondance og notater vedr. forløbet, Noget om Norden MFU 1956/57, Filmsager, SFC, DFI.

Koch-Olsen, I. (1956a), [letter to Mogens Lind], 13.3.1956, Korrespondance og notater vedr. forløbet, Noget om Norden MFU 1956/57, Filmsager, SFC, DFI.

Koch-Olsen, I. (1956b), [letter to Ebbe Neergaard], 24.9.1956, Versioner–Skandinavien, Noget om Norden – Versioner, Filmsager, SFC, DFI.

Koch-Olsen, I. (1957a), [note to Agnar Hølaas], 27.3.1957, Foretagne ændringer af filmen, (English), Denmark Grows Up, Filmsager, SFC, DFI.

Koch-Olsen, I. (1957b), [letter to Ebbe Neergaard], 5.4.1957, Distribution, Noget om Norden, Filmsager, SFC, DFI.

Koch-Olsen, I. (1957c), 'Dokumentarfilm i Danmark', *Dansk Kulturfilm 25 År*, Copenhagen, pp. 5–20.

Kongelig dansk Æroklub (1950), [invitation and programme], 3.2.1950, They Guide You Across/Sikkerhed i luften, Filmsager, SFC, DFI.

Kracauer, S. (1947), *From Caligari to Hitler: A Psychological History of the German Film*, Princeton: Princeton University Press.

Kristensen, S. (1950), [letter to Agnar Hølaas], 1.12.1950, Korrespondance og notater vedr. forløbene, Socialfilm (danske versioner) ('The Seventh Age og Health for Danmark'), SFC, DFI.

Kristensen, S. (1954), [letter to Københavns Overborgmester], 5.11.1954, Korrespondance og notater, A City Called Copenhagen, Filmsager, SFC, DFI.

Kristensen, S. (1955), [letter about US viewing figures], 17.3.1955, Shaped by Danish Hands, Filmsager, SFC, DFI.

Kristensen, S. (1957a), [letter to Københavns Overborgmester], 24.6.1957, Korrespondance og notater, A City Called Copenhagen, Filmsager, SFC, DFI.

Kristensen, S. (1957b), [letter to MFU], 6.11.1957, Versioner – Skandinavien, Noget om Norden – Versioner, Filmsager, SFC, DFI.

Kristensen, S. (1959), [comments on Roos' draft; signed SK], 'Udkast og manuskripter', A City Called Copenhagen, Filmsager, SFC, DFI.

Langlois, S. (2016), 'And Action! UN and UNESCO Coordinating Information Films, 1945–51', in P. Duedahl (ed.), *A History of UNESCO: Global Actions and Impacts*, Basingstoke: Palgrave Macmillan, pp. 73–96.

Larsen, L. R. (n.d.), 'Kortfilmrådet 1965–1972', *Filminstitutionernes historie*, Filmdatabasen, Det Danske Filminstitut <http://www.dfi.dk/FaktaOmFilm/Filminstitutionernes-historie/Institutionerne/Kortfilmraadet.aspx> (accessed 25 December 2016).

Lassen, R. (1946), [letter to Dansk Kulturfilm], 23.12.1946, Korrespondance og notater angående forløbet, Biblioteket er åbent, Filmsager, SFC, DFI.

Latour, B. (2005), *Reassembling the Social. An Introduction to Actor-Network-Theory*, Oxford: Oxford University Press.

Law, J. (2004), *After Method: Mess in Social Science Research*, London: Routledge.

Lind, M. (1954a), 'Kommentarer og nye notater til lystryksskitse 1–15', Manuskripter og materiale, Noget om Norden MFU 1956/57, Filmsager, SFC, DFI.

Lind, M. (1954b), [letter to Bent Barfod], 2.8.1954, Korrespondance vedr. produktion, Noget om Norden MFU 1956/57, Filmsager, SFC, DFI.

Linde-Laursen, A. (1999), 'Taking the national family to the movies: changing frameworks for the formation of Danish identity, 1930–1990', *Anthropological Quarterly*, 72: 1, pp. 18–33.

Lundberg, K. (1951), *Idræt på godt og ondt*, Copenhagen: Fremad.

Lundberg, K. (1959), [letter to Werner Pedersen], 7.6.1969, Korrespondance vedr. produktion, Enden på legen, Filmsager, SFC, DFI.

Lynch, K. (1960), *The Image of the City*, Cambridge: MIT Press.

MacDonald, R. (2013), 'Evasive enlightenment: *World Without End* and the internationalism of postwar documentary', *Journal of British Cinema and Television*, 10: 3, pp. 452–74, doi:10.3366/jbctv.2013.0150.

MacDonald, S. (1997), 'The city as the country: the New York City Symphony from Rudy Burckhardt to Spike Lee', *Film Quarterly*, 51: 2, pp. 2–20.

Marcus, L. (2010), '"A Hymn to Movement": The "City Symphony" of the 1920s and 1930s', *Modernist Cultures*, 5: 1, pp. 30–46, doi:10.3366/E2041102210000055.

Marklund, C., and K. Petersen (2013), 'Return to sender – American Images of the Nordic Welfare States and Nordic Welfare State Branding', *European Journal of Social Studies*, 43: 2, pp. 245–57, doi:10.1515/ejss-2013-0016.

Marks, L. (1997), 'Loving a disappearing image', *Cinemas: Revue d'Études Cinematographiques (Journal of Film Studies)*, 8: 1/2, pp. 93–111.

Marks, L. (2000), *The Skin of the Film: Intercultural Cinema, Embodiment and the Senses*, Durham: Duke University Press.

Marks, L. (2002), *Touch: Sensuous Theory and Multisensory Media*, Minneapolis: University of Minnesota Press.

Marshall, C. (1950), [letter to Eyvind Bartels, Danish Foreign Ministry Marshall Committee], 23.2.1950, Marshall, 1956 Opgivne film – 1957 m.m., 1592 Dansk Kulturfilm, emneordnede sager, Rigsarkivet.

Maruni, N., J.-J. Thorsen and J. Jacobsen (1965), [proposal for film Herning 65], Økononi, Herning 65, Filmsager, SFC, DFI.

McFarlane, L. (2011), 'A treat to touch. The material surface in three short films by Carl Th. Dreyer', *Opticon1826*, 10, pp. 1–7 <http://www.ucl.ac.uk/opticon1826/archive/issue10/articles/McFarlane.pdf>.

Mehring, F. (2012), 'The promises of "Young Europe": cultural diplomacy, cosmopolitanism, and youth culture in the films of the Marshall Plan', *European Journal of American Studies*, 7: 2, pp. 1–28.

Melson, S. (n.d.), [letter to Ib Koch-Olsen re censorship of People's Holiday], Diverse materiale, Socialfilm, Filmsager, SFC, DFI.

Melson, S. (1948), 'VESTKYSTEN (Biblioteksfilmen). Rapport: 3 die ekspedition til Jylland', Korrespondance og notater angående forløbet, Biblioteket er åbent, Filmsager, SFC, DFI.

Melson, S. (1949), [letter to Ib Koch-Olsen], 1.10.1949, Korrespondance og notater angående forløbet, Biblioteket er åbent, Filmsager, SFC, DFI.

MFU (Ministeriernes Filmudvalg) (1941–), *Mødereferater 1941–*. Ministeriernes filmudvalg særsamling, DFI.

MFU (1946), [notat], 29.5.1946, Korrespondance og notater vedr. forløbet, Socialfilm (engelsk version), Filmsager, SFC, DFI.

MFU (1947), Pressemeddelelse, 4.12.1947, Korrespondance og notater vedr. Forløbet, The Seventh Age, Socialfilm (engelsk version), SFC, DFI.

MFU (1950a), 'Grundlag for produktion af MFUs "Marshall-Film"', Marshall, 1956 Opgivne film – 1957 m.m., 1592 Dansk Kulturfilm, emneordnede sager, Rigsarkivet.

MFU (1950b), 'Plan til en Serie Kortfilm produceret af MFU for ECA Organisationen', Marshall, 1956 Opgivne film – 1957 m.m., 1592 Dansk Kulturfilm, emneordnede sager, Rigsarkivet.

MFU (1953), Mødereferat 8/1953 (9.12.1953), Økonomi, Hvad skal jeg være?, Filmsager, SFC, DFI.

MFU (1957), Mødereferat 2/1957, Distribution, Noget om Norden, Filmsager, SFC, DFI.

MFU (1958a), Mødereferat 1/1958 (7.1.1958), Korrespondance og notater, A City Called Copenhagen, Filmsager, SFC, DFI.

MFU (1958b), Mødereferat 2/1958 (6.2.1958), Korrespondance og notater, A City Called Copenhagen, Filmsager, SFC, DFI.

MFU (1958c), Mødereferat [udklip], 17.5.1958, Korrespondance og notater vedr. forløbet, Noget om Norden, Filmsager, SFC, DFI.

Miller, A. (1961) [1949], *Death of a Salesman: Certain Private Conversations in Two Acts and a Requiem*, Harmondsworth: Penguin.

Minerva Film (1949), [letter to Udvalget til Støtte af Danske Filmproduktion], 19.9.1949, Økonomi, They Guide You Across/Sikkerhed i Luften, Filmsager, SFC, DFI.

Minerva Film (1953), [quotation for production of US version], 16.12.1953, Shaped by Danish Hands, Filmsager, SFC, DFI.

Mirams, G. (1950), 'Art and the Cinema', *Design Review*, 3: 2, p. 19. <http://nzetc.victoria.ac.nz/tm/scholarly/tei-Arc03_02DesR-t1-body-d5.html> (accessed 12 June 2014).

Mlvr (2011), 'Carl Thomsen', Den store danske, Copenhagen: Gyldendal, <http://denstoredanske . dk / Dansk _ Biografisk _ Leksikon / Medier / Stadsbibliotekar / Carl _ Thomsen> (accessed 30 April 2017).

Mordhorst, M. (2015), 'Public diplomacy vs nation-branding: the case of Denmark after the Cartoon Crisis', in L. Clerc, N. Glover and P. Jordan (eds), *Histories of Public Diplomacy and Nation-Branding in the Nordic and Baltic Countries: Representing the Periphery*, Leiden: Brill, pp. 237–55.

Morrisett, A. (1961), 'Sweden: paradise and paradox', *Film Quarterly*, 15: 1, pp. 22–9 <http://www.jstor.org/stable/1210562> (accessed 3 August 2015).

Morten (1952), 'Haardt Brug for Film om dansk Kunst', *B.T.*, 20 November, Kunstfilm udklipssamling, DFI.

'Moseholms Jazzteater' (1966), *Aktuelt*, 24.1.1966, Præsentation, Herning 65, Filmsager, DFC, DFI.

Mulvey, L. (2006), *Death 24x a Second: Stillness and the Moving Image*, London: Reaktion.

Musiał, K. (2002), *Roots of the Nordic Model: Images of Progress in the Era of Modernisation*, Baden-Baden: Nomos Verlagsgesellschaft.

Musik og ungdom (1966), 'PROGRAM for Jazzkoncerten, søndag, den 23. januar på Alléscenen', Præsentation, Herning 65, Filmsager, SFC, DFI.

Mygdal-Meyer, T. (n.d.), 'The Aviator', *Carl Th. Dreyer – The Man and his Work*, Danish Film Institute, <http://english.carlthdreyer.dk/AboutDreyer/Biography/The-Aviator.aspx> (accessed 3 January 2017).

Møller, V. (1947a), [letter to Ib Koch-Olsen], 30.1.1947, Shaped by Danish Hands, Filmsager, SFC, DFI.

Møller, V. (1947b), [letter to Ib Koch-Olsen], 19.9.1947, Shaped by Danish Hands, Filmsager, SFC, DFI.

Møller, V. (1947c), [letter to Ib Koch-Olsen], 14.10.1947, Shaped by Danish Hands, Filmsager, SFC, DFI.

Neergaard, E. (1949), [letter to Minerva], 7.10.1949, Økonomi, They Guide You Across/Sikkerhed i Luften, Filmsager, SFC, DFI.

Nielsen, H. ['hn'] (1947), [note re screening], 9.1.1947, Korrespondance og notater angående forløbet, Biblioteket er åbent, Filmsager, SFC, DFI.

Nielsen, H. (1949), [letter to Ingefred Juul Andersen ML., formand for Foreningen af danske Husholdningslærerinder], 20.4.1949, Diverse, Peter må vente, Filmsager, SFC, DFI.

Nielsen, H. (1951), [note re phonecall with Ingolf Boisen], 29.8.1951, Distribution og FNs Sponsorship, They Guide You Across/Sikkerhed i Luften, Filmsager, SFC, DFI.

Nielsen, H. (1957), [letter to Udenrigsministeriets Pressebureau], 4.11.1957, Foretagne ændringer af filmen (English), Denmark Grows Up, Filmsager, SFC, DFI.

Nielsen, H. (1958a), [notat], 5.3.1958, 'Korrespondance og notater', A City Called Copenhagen, Filmsager, SFC, DFI.

Nielsen, H. (1958b), [letter to Jørgen Roos], 14.4.1958, Korrespondance og notater, A City Called Copenhagen, Filmsager, SFC, DFI.

Nielsen, H. (1958c), [notat dated 19.4.1958], Korrespondance og notater, A City Called Copenhagen, Filmsager, SFC, DFI.

Nielsen, M. (1960), 'Enden på legen', *Ungdom og Idræt*, 41, 16.10.1960, pp. 486–7, Enden på legen, Filmsager, SFC, DFI.

Nissen, D., L. R. Larsen, T. C. Christensen, J. S. Johnsen (eds) (2002), *Preserve then Show*, Copenhagen: DFI.

Nordea-Fonden (n.d.), 'Heerings gård', <https://www.nordeafonden.dk/heerings-gaard> (accessed 9 May 2015).

Nordic Cooperation (n.d.), 'The History of the Nordic Council: 1953–1971', <https://www.norden.org/en/nordic-council/bag-om-nordisk-raad/the-nordic-council/the-history-of-the-nordic-council/1953-1971> (accessed 18 January 2017).

Nordens Tidning (1956), 'En nordisk saga for vuxna', *Nordens Tidning*, 14: 4, pp. 2–3.

Nørrested, C., and C. Alsted (eds) (1987), *Kortfilmen og staten*, København, Eventus.

Olsen, P. L. (2003), 'Bodil Begtrup, 1903–1987', *Kvinfo*, <http://www.kvinfo.dk/side/171/bio/32/> (accessed 30 April 2017).

Orgeron, D., M. Orgeron and D. Streible (2012), 'Introduction', in D. Orgeron, M. Orgeron and D. Streible (eds), *Learning with the Lights Off: Educational Film in the United States*, New York: Oxford University Press, pp. 1–14.

Palsbo, S. (1948a), [letter to Ib Koch-Olsen], 15.7.1948, Manuskripter, Peter må vente, Filmsager, SFC, DFI.

Palsbo, S. (1948b), 'PETER MAA VENTE – !', Manuskripter, Peter må vente, Filmsager, SFC, DFI.

'Paul Gadegaard' (n.d.), Heart Museum, <http://www.heartmus.dk/om-heart/samlin gen/paul-gadegaard.html> (accessed 25 December 2016).

Pedersen, W. (1959a), [letter to Sigvald Kristensen], 20.4.1959, Korrespondance og notater, A City Called Copenhagen, Filmsager, SFC, DFI.

Pedersen, W. (1959b) (ed.), *Kunstfilm i Danmark*, Copenhagen: Dansk Komité for Kunstfilm.

Pedersen, W. (1959c), [note on meeting], 23.3.1959, Korrespondance vedr. produktion, Enden på legen, Filmsager, SFC, DFI.

Pedersen, W. (1965), [letter to Jens Jørgen Thorsen], Økonomi, Herning 65, Filmsager, SFC, DFI.

Persson, H. T. R. (2013), 'Scandinavia', in I. O'Boyle and T. Bradbury (eds), *Sport Governance: International Case Studies*, London and New York: Routledge, pp. 167–83.

Petersen, C. O. (1949), [letter to SFC], 8.6.1949, Afslutning, Biblioteket er åbent, Filmsager, SFC, DFI.
Pierre (1950), 'Staten har ansvar for Danmarks fiasco', *Aftenbladet*, 11.3.1950, Kunstfilm kasse, Udklipsarkivet, DFI.
Politiken [anonymous reviewer] (1960), 'En by ved navn København', *Politiken*, 12.1.1960, Løse papirer, A City Called Copenhagen, Filmsager, SFC, DFI.
Politiken (1961), 'Hele bordet er Deres', *Politiken*, 22.10.1961, 'Præmieoverrækkelse', A City Called Copenhagen, Filmsager, SFC, DFI.
Porsby, P. (1967), 'Herning 1965', *Kirke og film* 7, 10.8.1967, Løse papirer, Herning 65, Filmsager, SFC, DFI.
Rask, E. (n.d.), 'Allé-Scenen', *Den Store Danske*, Copenhagen: Gyldendal, <http://denstoredanske.dk/index.php?sideId=36109> (accessed 25 December 2016).
Raskin, R. (n.d.), 'Story design in the Short Fiction Film', Raindance Film Festival lecture, <http://www.raindance.co.uk/site/picture/upload/raskins_article.pdf> (accessed 20 January 2017).
Raskin, R. (2002), *The Art of the Short Fiction Film: A Shot by Shot Study of Nine Modern Classics*, Jefferson: McFarland.
Ren, C., and S. Gyimóthy (2013), 'Transforming and contesting nation branding strategies: Denmark at the Expo 2010', *Place Branding and Public Diplomacy*, 9: 1, pp. 17–29.
Rif. [Klaus Rifbjerg] (1962), 'Noget om Hamburg. For en indbudt kreds vistes i går JRs nye dokumentarfilm', *Politiken*, 19.12.1962, Avisudklip, Mappe II: Versioner, A City Called Copenhagen, Filmsager, SFC, DFI.
Rifbjerg, K. (1960), *Konfrontation. Digte*, København: Det Schønbergske Forlag.
Riis, J. (1998), 'Toward a poetics of the short film', *p.o.v. – A Danish Journal of Film Studies* 5, pp. 133–50, <http://imv.au.dk/publikationer/pov/Issue_05/section_4/artc1A.html> (accessed 16 January 2017).
Rode, K. (1963), [letter], 15.3.1963, Diverse korrespondance og notater vedr. de forskellige film, Diverse materialer, Socialfilmene, Filmsager, SFC, DFI.
Roos, J. (n.d.), 'Jørgen Roos about Dreyer', *Carl Th. Dreyer – The Man and his Work*, Danish Film Institute, <http://english.carlthdreyer.dk/AboutDreyer/Working-method/Joergen-Roos-about-Dreyer.aspx> (accessed 2 June 2013).
Roos, J. (1950), '*Den strømlinjede gris*, Speakerudkast', Marshall Filmene, Dansk Kulturfilm, Rigsarkivet.
Roos, J. (1958a), 'Forslag til en film om "København"', Korrespondance og notater, A City Called Copenhagen, Filmsager, SFC, DFI.
Roos, J. (1958b), '"KØBENHAVN", Foreløbig disposition', Korrespondance og notater, A City Called Copenhagen, Filmsager, SFC, DFI.
Roos, J. (1959), 'Filmen om København', Korrespondance og notater, A City Called Copenhagen, Filmsager, SFC, DFI.
Roos, J. (1968), 'Theodor, set af Jørgen Roos', *Kosmorama*, 84, pp. 150–1, <http://video.dfi.dk/Kosmorama/magasiner/TheodorChristensen/Kosmorama84-p150-151-ocr.pdf> (accessed 16 January 2017).
Rudfeld, K. (1950), [letter from Arbejds- og Socialministeriernes Statsvidenskabelige konsulent], 1.4.1950, Korrespondance og notater vedr. forløbene, Socialfilm (danske versioner) ('The Seventh Age og Health for Danmark'), Filmsager, SFC, DFI.
Russell, P. (2013), 'Dust and Shadows ... A Progress Report', *Journal of British Cinema and Television*, 10: 3, pp. 415–29, doi:10.3366/jbctv.2013.0148.
SAS (Scandinavian Airline Systems) (2009), 'SAS timeline: more than 60 years in the sky', <https://www.flysas.com/upload/International/SKI/Media-center/Mediakit/Oct09/SAS%20timeline.pdf> (accessed 1 January 2017).

Sayers, J. (2011), 'How text lost its source: magnetic recording cultures', PhD dissertation, University of Washington.

Schepelern, P. (n.d.), 'Novellefilm', *Den Store Danske*, Copenhagen: Gyldendal, <http://denstoredanske.dk/index.php?sideId=133214> (accessed 21 January 2017).

Schepelern, P. (2006), 'Danmarksfilmen – 2 – Debat', *PH dengang og nu*: Video podcasts, 11.10.2006, 13:30, Københavns Universitet, <http://purl.ku.dk/podcast/PH_051006_2.mp4> (accessed 10 January 2017).

Schultz, S. (1947), [letter to Ib Koch-Olsen], 17.11.1947, Manuskripter, Thorvaldsen, Filmsager, SFC, DFI.

Schultz, S. (1948), [letter to Ib Koch-Olsen], 24.9.1948, Forløb, Thorvaldsen, Filmsager, SFC, DFI.

Schultz, S. (1949), [letter to Ib Koch-Olsen], 28.1.1949, Diverse korrespondance, Thorvaldsen, Filmsager, SFC, DFI.

Schultz, S. (1962), 'Kunstfilm i Thorvaldsens Museum', *Meddelelser fra Thorvaldsens Museum 1962*, pp. 79–83, <http://arkivet.thorvaldsensmuseum.dk/artikler/kunstfilm-i-thorvaldsens-museum> (accessed 4 August 2014).

The Scotsman (1948), 'The Cinema', [extract reproduced and sent to Udenrigsministeriets Pressebureau from the Danish Embassy in London], 11.5.1948, Korrespondance og notater vedr. Forløbet, The Seventh Age, Socialfilm (engelsk version), Filmsager, SFC, DFI.

Scottish Screen Archive (n.d.), 'Full Record for *Waverley Steps*', <http://movingimage.nls.uk/film/0114> (accessed 31 January 2017).

Sculpting the Past (n.d.), 'Hvor bjergene sejler', Det Danske Filminstitut, <http://www.sculptingthepast.dk/Film-oversigt/Kunst-og-videnskab/Hvor-bjergene-sejler.aspx> (accessed 20 January 2017).

Sedgwick, E. (2003), *Touching Feeling: Affect, Pedagogy, Performativity*, Durham: Duke University Press.

Sevel, O. (2006), *Nordisk Film: Set indefra*, Viborg: Aschehoug.

SFC (Statens Filmcentral) (1944), 'Kartofler', Dansk Kulturfilm, Rigsarkivet.

SFC (1948a), *Documentary in Denmark: 100 Films of Facts in War, Occupation, Liberation, Peace*, Copenhagen: Statens Filmcentral.

SFC (1948b), *Beretning angaaende Finansaaret 1947–48*, Statens Filmcentral særsamling, DFI.

SFC (1949), *Beretning angaaende Finansaaret 1948–49*, Statens Filmcentral særsamling, DFI.

SFC (1950), [pressemeddelelse], 6.5.1950, Marshall, 1956 Opgivne film – 1957 m.m., 1592 Dansk Kulturfilm, emneordnede sager, Rigsarkivet.

SFC (1951), *Beretning angaaende Finansaaret 1950–51*, Statens Filmcentral særsamling, DFI.

SFC (1952), *Beretning angaaende Finansaaret 1951–52*, Statens Filmcentral særsamling, DFI.

SFC (1953), *Beretning angaaende Finansaaret 1952–53*, Statens Filmcentral særsamling, DFI.

SFC (1954), *Beretning angaaende Finansaaret 1953–54*, Statens Filmcentral særsamling, DFI.

SFC (1956), *Beretning angaaende Finansaaret 1955–56*, Statens Filmcentral særsamling, DFI.

SFC (1960a), *Beretning angaaende Finansaaret 1959–60*, Statens Filmcentral særsamling, DFI.

SFC (1960b), 'Pressemeddelelse', [re *A City Called Copenhagen*], Præsentation af filmen om København, A City Called Copenhagen, Filmsager, SFC, DFI.

SFC (1960c), *117 Short Films from Denmark*, Copenhagen: Statens Filmcentral, SFC særsamling, DFI.

SFC (1961a), 'Pressemeddelelse', [re *A City Called Copenhagen*], Distribution, A City Called Copenhagen, Filmsager, SFC, DFI.

SFC (1961b), *Beretning angaaende Finansaaret 1960–61*, Statens Filmcentral særsamling, DFI.

SFC (1962), *Beretning angaaende Finansaaret 1961–62*, Statens Filmcentral særsamling, DFI.

Skot-Hansen, M. (1945a), [letter to Kontorchef Karl I. Eskelund, Udenrigsministeriet], 27.7.1945, Diverse materiale v/ korrespondance, økonomi, materiale og forevisning af alle fem socialfilm, Socialfilmene, Filmsager, SFC, DFI.

Skot-Hansen, M. (1945b), [letter to Terkel Terkelsen], 30.7.1945, Diverse materiale v/ korrespondance, økonomi, materiale og forevisning af alle fem socialfilm, Socialfilmene, Filmsager, SFC, DFI.

Skot-Hansen, M. (1945c), [report on UK and US versions of social film], n.d., Diverse materiale v/ korrespondance, økonomi, materiale og forevisning af alle fem socialfilm, Socialfilmene, Filmsager, SFC, DFI.

Skot-Hansen, M. (1946a), [letter to Tage Nielsen, director, Palladium Film], 24.10.1946, Korrespondance og noter vedr. forløbet, Health for Denmark, Filmsager, SFC, DFI.

Skot-Hansen, M. (1946b), [letter to PH = Poul Henningsen?], Korrespondance og notater vedr. Forløbet, Socialfilm (engelsk version), Filmsager, SFC, DFI.

Skot-Hansen, M. (1947), [letter to Søren Melson], 9.4.1947, Diverse materialer, socialfilm, Filmsager, SFC, DFI.

Sobchack, V. (2000), 'What my fingers knew: the cinesthetic subject, or vision in the flesh', *Senses of Cinema*, 5, <http://sensesofcinema.com/2000/conference-special-effects-special-affects/fingers/> (accessed 26 January 2017).

Socialdemokratisk Forbund (2017) [1945], '"Fremtidens Danmark": Socialdemokratiets Valgprogram 1945', Danmarkshistorien.dk, <http://danmarkshistorien.dk/leksikon-og-kilder/vis/materiale/fremtidens-danmark-socialdemokratiets-valgprogram-1945/> (accessed 12 January 2017).

'The Social Film' (1946), [draft screenplay], 13.7.1946, Afslutning, English, Denmark Grows Up, Filmsager, SFC, DFI.

Spöhrer, M. (2016), 'Preface', in M. Spöhrer and B. Ochsner (eds), *Applying the Actor-Network Theory in Media Studies*, Hershey: IGI Global, pp. xiv–ix.

Steedman, C. (2001), 'Something She Called a Fever: Michelet, Derrida, and Dust', *American Historical Review*, 106: 4, pp. 1159–80, <http://www.jstor.org/stable/2692943>.

Stein, E. (2013), 'Abstract space, microcosmic narrative, and the disavowal of modernity in *Berlin: Symphony of a Great City*', *Journal of Film and Video*, 65: 4, pp. 3–16.

Steinthal, H. (1960a), 'Dét er København', *Politiken*, 3.2.1960, Avisudklip, Mappe II: Versioner, A City Called Copenhagen, Filmsager, SFC, DFI.

Steinthal, H. (1960b), 'Kunsten i dag bliver skabt – PAA TRODS!', *Politiken*, 14.2.1960, Avisudklip, Mappe II: Versioner, A City Called Copenhagen, Filmsager, SFC, DFI.

Stg. (1960), 'København i ny glimt', *Berlingske Tidende*, 3.2.1960, Avisudklip, Mappe II: Versioner, A City Called Copenhagen, Filmsager, SFC, DFI.

Strick, P., and P. Houston (1972), 'Interview with Stanley Kubrick regarding *A Clockwork Orange*', *Sight & Sound*, Spring 1972, <http://www.visual-memory.co.uk/amk/doc/0070.html> (accessed 1 January 2017).

Struckmann, E. (1947), [letter to Ib Koch-Olsen], 24.10.1947, Manuskripter, Thorvaldsen, Filmsager, SFC, DFI.

Struckmann, E. (1948), [letter to Ib Koch-Olsen], 10.7.1948, Diverse korrespondance, Thorvaldsen, Filmsager, SFC, DFI.

Sørensen, J. (2006), 'Danmarksfilmen – 2 – Debat', *PH dengang og nu*: Video podcasts, 11.10.2006, 13:30, Københavns Universitet, <http://purl.ku.dk/podcast/PH_051006_2.mp4> (accessed 10 January 2017).

Sørensen, L. (2013), 'En svækket stat forstærker sin propaganda', Besættelsen: Før, Under og Efter, Sculpting the Past, Danish Film Institute, <http://www.sculptingthepast.dk> (accessed 30 January 2017).

Sørensen, L. (2014), *Dansk film under Nazismen*, København: Lindhardt & Ringhof.

Sørenssen, B. (2001), 'Reviewed work: *Exotic Europe: Journeys into Early Cinema* (2000)', *The Moving Image: The Journal of the Association of Moving Image Archivists*, 1: 2, pp. 182–4, <http://www.jstor.org/stable/41167074>.

Tarp, S. (1949), 'Film og Musik, 1', *Dansk Musiktidsskrift*, 24, pp. 5–12, D I, C: Thorvaldsen, 4, Dreyer arkiv, DFI.

Team Denmark (2005), *Eliteidrættens kanon*, Copenhagen: Kulturministeriet, <http://kum.dk/uploads/tx_templavoila/Eliteidraettens_kanon_2005.pdf> (accessed 15 January 2017).

Terkelsen, T. (1945), [letter to Mogens Skot-Hansen], 13.8.1945, Diverse materiale v/ korrespondance, økonomi, materiale og forevisning af alle fem socialfilm, Socialfilmene, Filmsager, SFC, DFI.

Thomsen, C. (1947), [letter to Ib Koch-Olsen], 21.5.1947, Korrespondance og notater angående forløbet, Biblioteket er åbent, Filmsager, SFC, DFI.

Thomson, C. (2010), 'The artist's touch: Dreyer, Thorvaldsen, Venus', *Carl Th. Dreyer – The Man and his Work*, Danish Film Institute, <http://english.carlthdreyer.dk/AboutDreyer/Visual-style/The-Artists-Touch-Dreyer-Thorvaldsen-Venus.aspx>.

Thomson, C. (2013a), 'Lamps, light and enlightenment. On PH's *Danmark* and Ole Roos' *PH lys*', *Kosmorama*, 249, <http://www.kosmorama.org/ServiceMenu/05-English/Articles/Lamps-Light-and-Enlightenment.aspx>.

Thomson, C. (2013b), *Thomas Vinterberg's FESTEN (The Celebration)*, Nordic Film Classics, Seattle: University of Washington Press.

Thomson, C. (2015a), 'History unmade: Carl Th. Dreyer's unrealised *Mary, Queen of Scots*', *Kosmorama*, 260, <http://www.kosmorama.org/ServiceMenu/05-English/Articles/History-unmade.aspx>.

Thomson, C. (2015b), '"The Slow Pulse of the Era": Carl Th. Dreyer's film style', in T. de Luca and N. Barradas Jorge (eds), *Slow Cinema*, Edinburgh: Edinburgh University Press, pp. 47–58.

Thomson, C. (2016a), '"Education, enlightenment, and general propaganda": Dansk Kulturfilm and Carl Th. Dreyer's short films', in M. Hjort and U. Lindqvist (eds), *A Companion to Nordic Cinema*, London: Wiley-Blackwell, pp. 78–97.

Thomson, C. (2016b), 'Body culture and film culture in Thorvaldsen's Museum 1932–63', in S. Ayres and E. Carbone (eds), *Sculpture and the Nordic Region*, London: Routledge, pp. 130–45.

Thomson, C., and M. Hilson (2014), 'Beauty in Bacon: *The Pattern of Co-operation* and the export of postwar Danish democracy', *Kosmorama*, 255, <http://www.kosmorama.org/Artikler/Beauty-in-Bacon.aspx>.

Tybjerg, C. (2013), 'Pissing into the well: Dreyer, film propaganda and cognitive theory', *Kosmorama*, 243, <http://www.kosmorama.org/ServiceMenu/05-English/Articles/Pissing-into-the-Well.aspx>.

Udenrigsministeriet (1951), [letter to Agnar Hølaas], 15.3.1951, Shaped by Danish Hands, Filmsager, SFC, DFI.

Udenrigsministeriet (1954), [letter to MFU], 16.7.1954, Shaped by Danish Hands, Filmsager, SFC, DFI.

Ulrichsen, E. (1949), 'Thorvaldsen bliver levende og en statsinstitution til grin. Nye Landvindinger for dansk Kortfilm', *Nationaltidende*, 27.1.1949, D I, C: Thorvaldsen, 3, Dreyer arkiv, DFI.

UNESCO (1950), 'UNESCO helps educational films over frontier barriers', *UNESCO Courier*, 3: 2, (1 March 1950), p. 2.

Uricchio, W. (1995), 'The past as prologue? The Kulturfilm before 1945', in H. Heller and P. Zimmermann (eds), *Blicke in die Welt: Reportagen und Magazine des nordwestdeutschen Fernsehens in den 50er und 60er Jahren*, Konstanz: Verlag Oelschlaeger, pp. 263–87.

Usai, P. C. (2001), *The Death of Cinema: History, Cultural Memory and the Digital Dark Age*, London: British Film Institute.

Vest (1959), 'Kbh anskuet fra utraditionelle vinkler', *Information*, 12.12.1959, Avisudklip, Mappe II: Versioner, A City Called Copenhagen, Filmsager, SFC, DFI.

Vinding, O. (1950), 'Dansk Dunderfiasko ved Filmkongressen', *Berlingske Aftenavis*, 24.2.1950, Kunstfilm udklipssamling, DFI.

V-r. (1960), 'Københavns-filmen spræller af humør', *Aktuelt*, 3.2.1960, Avisudklip, Mappe II: Versioner, A City Called Copenhagen, Filmsager, SFC, DFI.

Ward, R. (2003), 'Extra added attractions: the short subjects of MGM, Warner Brothers and Universal', *Media History*, 9: 3, pp. 221–44, doi:10.1080/136888003 2000145542.

Wasson, H., and C. Acland (2011), 'Introduction: Utility and Cinema', in C. Acland and H. Wasson (eds), *Useful Cinema*, Durham: Duke University Press, pp. 1–14.

Watkins, L. (2013), 'The materiality of film', in P. Graves-Brown and R. Harrison (eds), *The Oxford Handbook of the Archaeology of the Contemporary World* (Oxford Handbooks Online), Oxford: Oxford University Press, doi:10.1093/oxfordhb/9780199602001.013.044.

Wendt, F. (1959), [letter to SFC], 14.10.1959, Korrespondance og notater vedr. forløbet, Noget om Norden MFU 1956/57, Filmsager, SFC, DFI.

Witte, E. (1949), [letter and invoice to Dansk Kulturfilm], 19.5.1949, Indledning, Peter må vente, Filmsager, SFC, DFI.

Wright, B. (1947), 'Danish documentary', *Documentary 47* (Journal of the Edinburgh International Film Festival), p. 24.

Ørskov, F. (2016), 'Filmmaking and nation building: discourses of "Danishness" in the state-initiated production of short films in the immediate post-war era', in J. Rasson and Z. Reed (eds), *Annual of Medieval Studies at CEU*, 22, Budapest: Central European University, pp. 249–60.

Østergård, U. (1996), 'Peasants and Danes: the Danish national identity and political culture', in G. Eley and R. Suny (eds), *Becoming National. A Reader*, Oxford: Oxford University Press, pp. 179–222.

INDEX